Web 2.0
Concepts and Applications

Web 2.0
Concepts and Applications

Gary B. Shelly
Mark Frydenberg, Bentley University

Shelly Cashman Series®
A part of Course Technology, Cengage Learning

COURSE TECHNOLOGY
CENGAGE Learning

Australia • Brazil • Japan • Korea • Mexico • Singapore • Spain • United Kingdom • United States

COURSE TECHNOLOGY
CENGAGE Learning

Web 2.0: Concepts and Applications
Gary B. Shelly
Mark Frydenberg

Executive Editor: Kathleen McMahon
Associate Acquisitions Editor: Reed Curry
Associate Product Manager: Jon Farnham
Editorial Assistant: Lauren Brody
Director of Marketing: Cheryl Costantini
Marketing Manager: Tristen Kendall
Marketing Coordinator: Stacey Leasca
Print Buyer: Julio Esperas
Content Project Manager: Matthew Hutchinson
Development Editor: Karen Stevens
Proofreader: Foxxe Editorial Services
Indexer: Rich Carlson
Management Services: Pre-Press PMG
Art Director: Marissa Falco
Text Design: Joel Sadagursky
Cover Design: Curio Press
Cover Photos: Tom Kates Photography
Illustrator: Pre-Press PMG
Compositor: Pre-Press PMG
Printer: RRD Menasha

For product information and technology assistance, contact us at
Cengage Learning Customer & Sales Support, 1-800-354-9706

For permission to use material from this text or product,
submit all requests online at **cengage.com/permissions**
Further permissions questions can be emailed to
permissionrequest@cengage.com

Library of Congress Control Number: 2009943342

ISBN-13: 978-1-4390-4802-3

ISBN-10: 1-4390-4802-9

Course Technology
20 Channel Center Street
Boston, MA 02210
USA

Cengage Learning is a leading provider of customized learning solutions with office locations around the globe, including Singapore, the United Kingdom, Australia, Mexico, Brazil and Japan. Locate your local office at:
international.cengage.com/region

Cengage Learning products are represented in Canada by Nelson Education, Ltd.

For your lifelong learning solutions, visit **course.cengage.com**

Purchase any of our products at your local college store or at our preferred online store
www.CengageBrain.com

Printed in the United States of America
1 2 3 4 5 6 17 16 15 14 13 12 11

Contents

Chapter 5

Connecting People

Chapter 6

Linking Data

Preface

The Shelly Cashman Series® offers the finest textbooks in computer education. We are proud of the fact that our textbook series has been the most widely used series in educational instruction.

In this Shelly Cashman Series® Web 2.0: Concepts and Applications book, you will find an educationally sound and easy-to-follow pedagogy that artfully combines screen shots, drawings, and text with full color to produce a visually appealing and easy-to-understand presentation of Web 2.0. A conceptual framework combined with practical knowledge gives students the understanding they need to master quickly changing technology.

The book's six chapters emphasize key concepts and skills necessary for today's students to be Web 2.0 literate. Computer literacy has evolved over the years from learning to write simple computer programs to developing skills using desktop productivity applications. The recent shift of applications and data from the desktop to the Web has brought about another stage in the evolution of computer literacy education requiring today's students to be both computer literate as well as Web literate, and increasingly, Web 2.0 literate. This book provides a framework for developing Web 2.0 literacy while introducing introductory information technology concepts through the lens of Web 2.0 examples.

Objectives of This Textbook

Web 2.0: Concepts and Applications is intended for use in a one-unit introductory Web 2.0 course or in a course that teaches introductory computer concepts. It might be paired with a traditional concepts textbook, an applications textbook, or a Web/Internet textbook to provide an innovative approach to teaching a semester-long introductory course on computer, Web, or technology literacy.

The objectives of this book are to:

- Present Web 2.0 as an evolution of the Web by tracing technology and social developments that led to the development of Web 2.0.
- Introduce students to the latest Web 2.0 applications.
- Make complex Web technology concepts accessible to the beginning student.
- Use Web 2.0 examples to illustrate information technology concepts.
- Discuss social and business uses of Web 2.0 applications.
- Integrate the use of student blogs and class wikis throughout the text in end-of-chapter exercises.
- Supplement chapter content with relevant online video and questions for testing student understanding.
- Teach students how to master Web 2.0 tools with hands-on Tutorials.
- Provide experiential learning with end-of-chapter exercises that encourage students to explore Web 2.0 applications on their own.
- Encourage students to make Web 2.0 tools part of their daily lives.

Some familiarity with computers and the Web is assumed. Students should be able to accomplish the following tasks on their computers prior to using this book:

- Navigate to sites on the Web using a Web browser.
- Find information on the Web using a search engine.
- Create an account on a Web site and sign in to a Web site.
- Create basic documents with productivity applications, such as word processing, spreadsheet, and presentation programs.
- Send and receive e-mail messages.
- Manage the Windows desktop, folders, and files.
- Download and install software applications.

Organization of This Textbook

Web 2.0: Concepts and Applications provides an introduction to the concepts, technologies, and applications with which students interact every day on the Web. The material comprises six chapters and a glossary/index.

CHAPTER 1 – THE WEB BECOMES 2.0 Chapter 1 introduces students to how the Web has evolved, from a tool for linking documents to a platform for linking people, and also introduces some of the social and technological developments that contributed to this change.

Web 2.0 concepts include characteristics of Web 2.0 applications and understanding the Web as a platform for applications.

Technology concepts include the role of the client, server, and Internet in accessing and providing Web pages and an introduction to presentation technologies such as Flash, AJAX, and JavaScript for creating a rich user experience.

Students learn to identify features of Web 2.0 applications and interact with Gmail.

CHAPTER 2 – PUBLISHING ONLINE Chapter 2 introduces students to blogs and wikis as tools for publishing online content.

Web 2.0 concepts include the use of blogs and wikis for both personal and business use, Web traffic and context-sensitive Web advertising, and search engine optimization.

Technology concepts include the role of HTML and Cascading Style Sheets in presenting Web content, the function of a Web server in providing Web content, and elements of a three-tiered architecture found in many Web 2.0 applications.

Students learn to create and manage a Blogger blog.

CHAPTER 3 – SYNDICATING CONTENT Chapter 3 introduces students to RSS and Atom feeds for syndicating online content and making content available to other applications.

Web 2.0 concepts include subscribing to and creating Web feeds and podcasts.

Technology concepts include differentiating between client and Web applications, understanding XML as a language for describing information, and representing Web feed content.

Students learn to subscribe to, read, and manage Web feeds using Google Reader.

CHAPTER 4 – ORGANIZING INFORMATION Chapter 4 introduces students to tagging as a means of organizing digital information.

Web 2.0 concepts include how the Web promotes a grassroots classification scheme known as a folksonomy, the use of Creative Commons to license Web content for reuse, and how Web 2.0 companies make money.

Technology concepts include hierarchical vs. nonhierarchical organization, geotagging, and organizing, finding, and filtering data.

Students learn to upload and tag photos on Flickr and tag bookmarks on Delicious.

CHAPTER 5 – CONNECTING PEOPLE Chapter 5 introduces students to personal and business uses of social networking.

Web 2.0 concepts include common features of social networking applications, elements of Facebook, MySpace, and LinkedIn profiles, and special-purpose social networks.

Business concepts include the Long Tail and the use of data from social networks in Customer Relationship Management software. Social issues include managing privacy online and the impact of Twitter on popular culture.

Technology concepts include embedding content from one Web site on another and the role of metadata to provide additional information about content.

Students learn to create a presence on Twitter and configure the Google Friend Connect social network on their blogs.

CHAPTER 6 – LINKING DATA Chapter 6 introduces students to technologies for linking data and applications on the Web. The chapter introduces Cloud computing as an emerging technology that allows consumers and businesses to interact with both data and applications on the Web and presents the Semantic Web as the vision of a future Web 3.0.

Web 2.0 concepts include platform, infrastructure, and software as a service, mashups, collaboration with Google Docs, intelligent agents, and a prelude to Web 3.0.

Business examples include how Amazon implements virtualization and how Starbucks makes use of Platform as a Service.

Technology concepts include interacting with XML data and Web services, using application programming interfaces (APIs) to access XML-based Web content, the structure of distributed applications, and the Semantic Web.

Students learn to interact with XML data by creating mashup applications using Google Spreadsheets and to deploy their applications to their blogs.

Visual Walkthrough of the Book:
Web 2.0: Concepts and Applications

Web site creation tools. Using online blog, wiki, or Web-site creation tools, a Web designer will specify the HTML structure and CSS styles to be applied to a particular page. After the application requests the desired content from the database, the application will apply the HTML tags and CSS styles to generate the resulting Web page. The ability to apply different styles (CSS) and formatting (HTML) to content makes it possible to deliver that same content to many different devices, from laptop computers to mobile phones.

Web applications, which are used to create, edit, delete, and display content, are organized into functional components: the display of information, the processing of information, and the interactions with a database. The client application, such as a Web browser, displays the content and processes user interactions, including keystrokes and mouse clicks. The Web server receives and processes the user's instructions. The database server stores the actual content in an online database. These functional components and the interactions between them constitute the **architecture** of a Web application. Blogging and wiki applications, along with many Web applications, are designed by using what is known as a **three-tiered architecture**, in which each tier, or functional component, is responsible for one of these specific processing tasks. Figure 2-4 uses the process of interacting with a blog to illustrate the three-tiered architecture employed by many Web-based applications.

Three-Tiered Architecture

Presentation Tier

The user requests to see five most recent blog posts from the Web server.

The user's Web browser displays five most recent blog posts.

Middle Tier

The Web server hosting the blogging application requests blog data from its database server.

The Web server applies HTML and CSS styles to format the data for display.

Database Tier

The database server retrieves the requested data from the database.

The database server sends the requested data back to the Web server for processing.

Figure 2-4 Architecture of blogs, wikis, and other Web-based applications.

The **presentation tier** deals with the presentation of information in the browser and the experience of users working with that information. It handles all aspects of displaying the user interface and processing any keystrokes or mouse clicks. The presentation tier may handle content that includes HTML-formatted text, images, and hyperlinks; forms in which the user enters information that is then sent to the server for processing; or applications that make use of presentation technologies such as JavaScript, AJAX, or Flash to provide a rich user experience within the browser.

Explanatory figures clarify complex technology concepts.

Table 6-2 Platform as a Service Providers

Provider	Logo	Description
Windows Azure		A Cloud operating system for developing and managing Web applications hosted on servers at Microsoft data centers. Integrated with Microsoft's software development tools.
Amazon Elastic Compute Cloud (EC2)	amazon web services	Provides resources to increase or decrease memory and processing power as needed in order to run Web applications over Amazon's computing environment.
Google App Engine		Enables the development of automatically scaled Web applications running on the same systems used for Google applications. Integrated with Google services including maps, calendar, and documents.
Force.com	force.com	Provides tools for developing and deploying Web-based business applications that run on the Salesforce.com platform.

Each PaaS provider offers developers the storage, processing, and bandwidth necessary to deploy, manage, and host scalable Internet applications. The Cloud provides additional processing capacity on a remote server. Service agreements between PaaS providers and their customers describe the levels of service that each provider makes available to its customers, including system availability, system performance, storage capabilities, and the ability to recover data.

> **SIDEBAR** | Starbucks Uses Platform as a Service

Starbucks used Salesforce CRM when developing My Starbucks Idea, their customer feedback and social network discussed in Chapter 5. Salesforce also provides a development platform known as Force.com for software developers to create, deploy, and manage Web applications. Salesforce CRM powers Starbucks' Pledge5 Web site, shown in Figure 6-10, which encourages customers to take part in community service.

Because the Pledge5 site was going to be promoted on national television, it needed to be able to handle the hundreds of thousands of anticipated users who would visit after viewing the program. Force.com provided a scalable infrastructure, connectivity to Facebook, and Web site management tools necessary to rapidly build and deploy this application.

Starbucks uses Salesforce CRM to build, deploy, and manage their Pledge5 site

Figure 6-10 Starbucks' Pledge5 Web site is built using the Salesforce application platform.

The Sidebar feature offers information on social, technical, or business issues related to the topics in each chapter to provide the student with additional context. The book's Sidebars include information about streaming video, multimedia formats, Web 2.0 business models, copyright and licensing of Web content, Twitter and popular culture, as well as how familiar companies apply Web 2.0 technologies.

Detailed step-by-step diagrams illustrate how Web 2.0 processes work.

To use Ping-O-Matic, you enter the title and URL of your blog and select the services that you wish to ping. Search engines access the Ping-O-Matic to determine which sites have new content. By limiting the scope of the search, blog search engines only have to index pages containing new content, as shown in Figure 2-43.

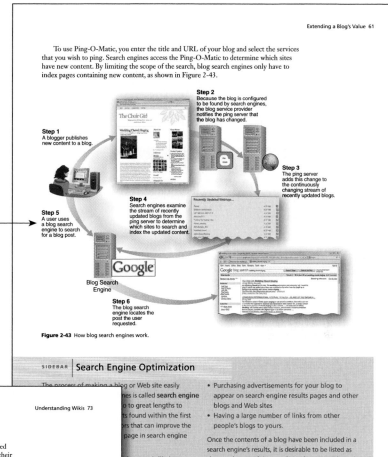

Step 1
A blogger publishes new content to a blog.

Step 2
Because the blog is configured to be found by search engines, the blog service provider notifies the ping server that the blog has changed.

Step 3
The ping server adds this change to the continuously changing stream of recently updated blogs.

Step 4
Search engines examine the stream of recently updated blogs from the ping server to determine which sites to search and index the updated content.

Step 5
A user uses a blog search engine to search for a blog post.

Step 6
The blog search engine locates the post the user requested.

Blog Search Engine

Figure 2-43 How blog search engines work.

SIDEBAR **Search Engine Optimization**

The process of making a blog or Web site easily ... nes is called **search engine** ... o to great lengths to ... ts found within the first ... rs that can improve the ... page in search engine ... ich a user is likely to ... codes for search engine ... words) in the header of a

- Purchasing advertisements for your blog to appear on search engine results pages and other blogs and Web sites
- Having a large number of links from other people's blogs to yours.

Once the contents of a blog have been included in a search engine's results, it is desirable to be listed as close to the top of the search results as possible so that people are more likely to find it. A higher placement within search results is more likely to drive traffic to a blog, since people are more likely to click links that appear on the first few pages of search results.

Wikipedia

All of the content found in Wikipedia, the successful online encyclopedia, is generated by its contributors. Wikipedia depends upon people coming together to contribute their expertise on a variety of topics. Over time, the Wikipedia community established policies to guide contributors who support the site by adding and reviewing its articles. Wikipedia has experienced exponential growth since it began and is still growing. In 2010, Wikipedia contained more than 3.1 million articles.

"Wikipedia is first and foremost an effort to create and distribute a free encyclopedia of the highest possible quality to every single person on the planet in their own language. Asking whether the community comes before or after this goal is really asking the wrong question: the entire purpose of the community is precisely this goal."

Jimmy Wales, cofounder of Wikipedia

Anyone who registers as a Wikipedia contributor can create or edit an article on Wikipedia. Every article must be approved before it can be published. Wikipedia, like many other online wikis, encourages beginners to become familiar with using the wiki editor to create or modify content by experimenting with text in the site's Sandbox page. The **Sandbox page**, shown in Figure 2-53, is a page that is dedicated to learning how to use the wiki application software and does not affect the content of actual pages.

link to edit the Sandbox page

a Wikipedia contributor experimented with entering mathematical formulas for an article in Wikipedia

Figure 2-53 Wikipedia's Sandbox page.

Quotes from Web 2.0 leaders are found throughout the chapters.

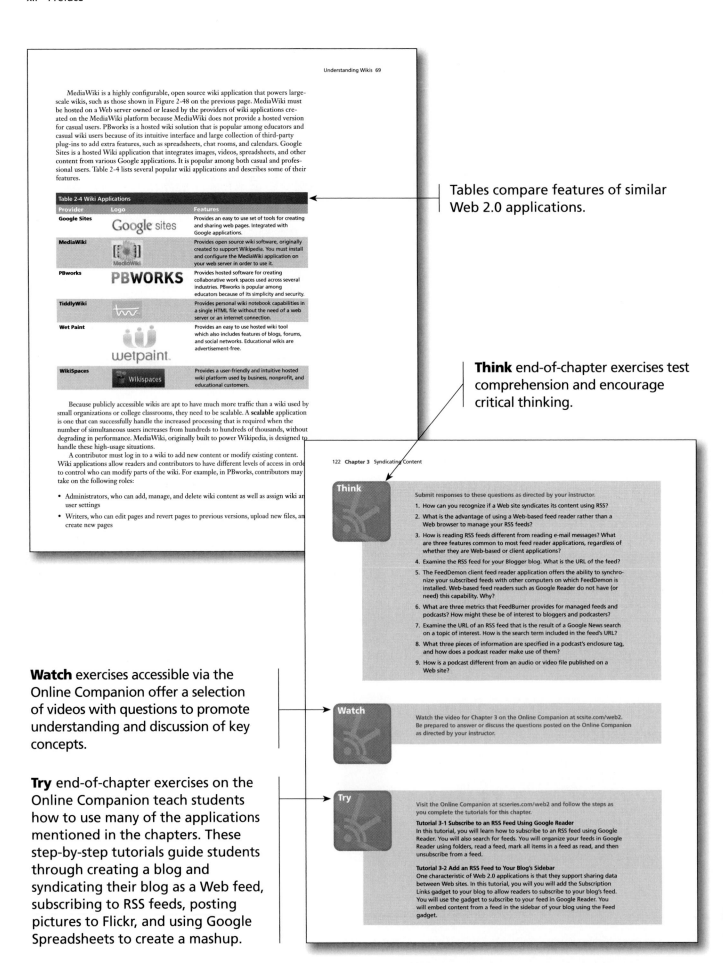

Understanding Wikis 69

MediaWiki is a highly configurable, open source wiki application that powers large-scale wikis, such as those shown in Figure 2-48 on the previous page. MediaWiki must be hosted on a Web server owned or leased by the providers of wiki applications created on the MediaWiki platform because MediaWiki does not provide a hosted version for casual users. PBworks is a hosted wiki solution that is popular among educators and casual wiki users because of its intuitive interface and large collection of third-party plug-ins to add extra features, such as spreadsheets, chat rooms, and calendars. Google Sites is a hosted Wiki application that integrates images, videos, spreadsheets, and other content from various Google applications. It is popular among both casual and professional users. Table 2-4 lists several popular wiki applications and describes some of their features.

Table 2-4 Wiki Applications

Provider	Logo	Features
Google Sites	Google sites	Provides an easy to use set of tools for creating and sharing web pages. Integrated with Google applications.
MediaWiki	MediaWiki	Provides open source wiki software, originally created to support Wikipedia. You must install and configure the MediaWiki application on your web server in order to use it.
PBworks	PBWORKS	Provides hosted software for creating collaborative work spaces used across several industries. PBworks is popular among educators because of its simplicity and security.
TiddlyWiki		Provides personal wiki notebook capabilities in a single HTML file without the need of a web server or an internet connection.
Wet Paint	wetpaint	Provides an easy to use hosted wiki tool which also includes features of blogs, forums, and social networks. Educational wikis are advertisement-free.
WikiSpaces	Wikispaces	Provides a user-friendly and intuitive hosted wiki platform used by business, nonprofit, and educational customers.

Because publicly accessible wikis are apt to have much more traffic than a wiki used by small organizations or college classrooms, they need to be scalable. A **scalable** application is one that can successfully handle the increased processing that is required when the number of simultaneous users increases from hundreds to hundreds of thousands, without degrading in performance. MediaWiki, originally built to power Wikipedia, is designed to handle these high-usage situations.

A contributor must log in to a wiki to add new content or modify existing content. Wiki applications allow readers and contributors to have different levels of access in order to control who can modify parts of the wiki. For example, in PBworks, contributors may take on the following roles:

- Administrators, who can add, manage, and delete wiki content as well as assign wiki and user settings
- Writers, who can edit pages and revert pages to previous versions, upload new files, and create new pages

Tables compare features of similar Web 2.0 applications.

Think end-of-chapter exercises test comprehension and encourage critical thinking.

122 **Chapter 3** Syndicating Content

Think

Submit responses to these questions as directed by your instructor.

1. How can you recognize if a Web site syndicates its content using RSS?
2. What is the advantage of using a Web-based feed reader rather than a Web browser to manage your RSS feeds?
3. How is reading RSS feeds different from reading e-mail messages? What are three features common to most feed reader applications, regardless of whether they are Web-based or client applications?
4. Examine the RSS feed for your Blogger blog. What is the URL of the feed?
5. The FeedDemon client feed reader application offers the ability to synchronize your subscribed feeds with other computers on which FeedDemon is installed. Web-based feed readers such as Google Reader do not have (or need) this capability. Why?
6. What are three metrics that FeedBurner provides for managed feeds and podcasts? How might these be of interest to bloggers and podcasters?
7. Examine the URL of an RSS feed that is the result of a Google News search on a topic of interest. How is the search term included in the feed's URL?
8. What three pieces of information are specified in a podcast's enclosure tag, and how does a podcast reader make use of them?
9. How is a podcast different from an audio or video file published on a Web site?

Watch exercises accessible via the Online Companion offer a selection of videos with questions to promote understanding and discussion of key concepts.

Watch

Watch the video for Chapter 3 on the Online Companion at scsite.com/web2. Be prepared to answer or discuss the questions posted on the Online Companion as directed by your instructor.

Try end-of-chapter exercises on the Online Companion teach students how to use many of the applications mentioned in the chapters. These step-by-step tutorials guide students through creating a blog and syndicating their blog as a Web feed, subscribing to RSS feeds, posting pictures to Flickr, and using Google Spreadsheets to create a mashup.

Try

Visit the Online Companion at scseries.com/web2 and follow the steps as you complete the tutorials for this chapter.

Tutorial 3-1 Subscribe to an RSS Feed Using Google Reader
In this tutorial, you will learn how to subscribe to an RSS feed using Google Reader. You will also search for feeds. You will organize your feeds in Google Reader using folders, read a feed, mark all items in a feed as read, and then unsubscribe from a feed.

Tutorial 3-2 Add an RSS Feed to Your Blog's Sidebar
One characteristic of Web 2.0 applications is that they support sharing data between Web sites. In this tutorial, you will you will add the Subscription Links gadget to your blog to allow readers to subscribe to your blog's feed. You will use the gadget to subscribe to your feed in Google Reader. You will embed content from a feed in the sidebar of your blog using the Feed gadget.

Blog exercises are designed to have students apply what they have learned in the chapter to their blog, from adding a gadget to the sidebar to embedding a YouTube video. Blog exercises also propose open-ended opinion questions for students to write about on their blogs.

Explore exercises encourage students in hands-on discovery of Web 2.0 applications in order to better understand the Web 2.0 concepts discussed in each chapter. Students apply what they have learned in the chapter as they interact with new features of Web 2.0 applications.

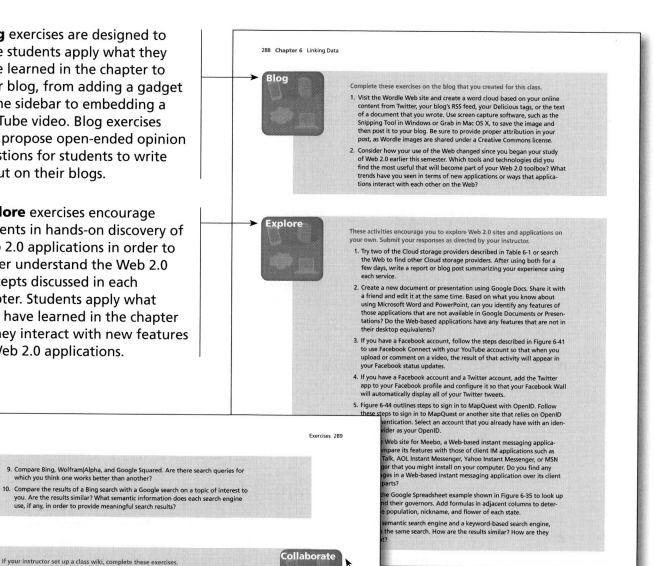

288   Chapter 6   Linking Data

Blog

Complete these exercises on the blog that you created for this class.

1. Visit the Wordle Web site and create a word cloud based on your online content from Twitter, your blog's RSS feed, your Delicious tags, or the text of a document that you wrote. Use screen capture software, such as the Snipping Tool in Windows or Grab in Mac OS X, to save the image and then post it to your blog. Be sure to provide proper attribution in your post, as Wordle images are shared under a Creative Commons license.

2. Consider how your use of the Web changed since you began your study of Web 2.0 earlier this semester. Which tools and technologies did you find the most useful that will become part of your Web 2.0 toolbox? What trends have you seen in terms of new applications or ways that applications interact with each other on the Web?

Explore

These activities encourage you to explore Web 2.0 sites and applications on your own. Submit your responses as directed by your instructor.

1. Try two of the Cloud storage providers described in Table 6-1 or search the Web to find other Cloud storage providers. After using both for a few days, write a report or blog post summarizing your experience using each service.

2. Create a new document or presentation using Google Docs. Share it with a friend and edit it at the same time. Based on what you know about using Microsoft Word and PowerPoint, can you identify any features of those applications that are not available in Google Documents or Presentations? Do the Web-based applications have any features that are not in their desktop equivalents?

3. If you have a Facebook account, follow the steps described in Figure 6-41 to use Facebook Connect with your YouTube account so that when you upload or comment on a video, the result of that activity will appear in your Facebook status updates.

4. If you have a Facebook account and a Twitter account, add the Twitter app to your Facebook profile and configure it so that your Facebook Wall will automatically display all of your Twitter tweets.

5. Figure 6-44 outlines steps to sign in to MapQuest with OpenID. Follow these steps to sign in to MapQuest or another site that relies on OpenID ... entication. Select an account that you already have with an iden- ... vider as your OpenID.

... Web site for Meebo, a Web-based instant messaging applica- ... mpare its features with those of client IM applications such as ... Talk, AOL Instant Messenger, Yahoo Instant Messenger, or MSN ... ger that you might install on your computer. Do you find any ... ges in a Web-based instant messaging application over its client ... parts?

... the Google Spreadsheet example shown in Figure 6-35 to look up ... d their governors. Add formulas in adjacent columns to deter- ... e population, nickname, and flower of each state.

... semantic search engine and a keyword-based search engine, ... the same search. How are the results similar? How are they ... ?

Exercises   289

9. Compare Bing, Wolfram|Alpha, and Google Squared. Are there search queries for which you think one works better than another?

10. Compare the results of a Bing search with a Google search on a topic of interest to you. Are the results similar? What semantic information does each search engine use, if any, in order to provide meaningful search results?

If your instructor set up a class wiki, complete these exercises.

1. Perform a search on ProgrammableWeb or Mashable for interesting mashups. Contribute links for interesting mashups to the class wiki.

2. Perform your own Twitter search for Web 3.0 or Semantic Web. Create a Wikipedia-style article about Web 3.0 based on resources that you find from your search.

Collaborate

Collaborate exercises are designed for classes whose instructors have set up a wiki for their students to use. These exercises promote collaboration among students using a wiki to share favorite Web resources, create collaborative study sheets, and write their own Wikipedia-style pages on Web 2.0 topics. Instructions on setting up a class wiki can be found in the Instructor Resources.

Online Companion

The *Web 2.0: Concepts and Applications* Online Companion allows students to further explore the content of this book. It contains a list of hyperlinks to all of the Web sites mentioned in each chapter, and online Tutorials and videos from the Watch exercises at the end of each chapter. The online Tutorials have step-by-step, screen-by-screen instructions to enable students to develop skills using Web 2.0 tools. Each Watch video is followed by questions that allow students to demonstrate understanding of video content.

Instructor Resources

The Instructor Resources include both teaching and testing aids.

INSTRUCTOR'S MANUAL Includes lecture notes summarizing the chapter sections and figures found in every chapter, teacher tips, classroom activities, lab activities, and quick quizzes in Microsoft Word files.

SYLLABUS Easily customizable sample syllabi that cover policies, assignments, exams, and other course information.

FIGURE FILES Illustrations for every figure in the textbook in electronic form.

POWERPOINT PRESENTATIONS A multimedia lecture presentation system that provides slides for each chapter. Presentations are based on chapter objectives.

SOLUTIONS TO EXERCISES Solutions or rubrics for all end-of-chapter exercises.

TEST BANK & TEST ENGINE Test banks include 112 questions for every chapter, featuring objective-based and critical thinking question types and including page number references and figure references, when appropriate. Also included is the test engine, ExamView, the ultimate tool for your objective-based testing needs.

SAM 2007: Assessment & Training and Project Grading Solutions

SAM (Skills Assessment Manager) is a robust assessment, training and project based system that enables students to be active participants in learning valuable Microsoft Office 2007 skills. A set of testbank questions ties directly to each applicable chapter in this book. Let SAM be an integral part of your students' learning experience!

Content for Online Learning

Course Technology has partnered with the leading distance learning solution providers and class-management platforms today. To access this material, instructors will visit our password-protected instructor resources available at www.cengage.com/coursetechnology. Instructor resources include the following: additional case projects, sample syllabi, PowerPoint presentations per chapter, and more. For additional information or for an instructor username and password, please contact your sales representative. For students to access this material, they must have purchased a WebTutor PIN-code specific to this title and your campus platform. The resources for students may include (based on instructor preferences), but not limited to: topic review, review questions, and practice tests.

CourseCasts Learning on the Go Always Available . . . Always Relevant.

Our fast-paced world is driven by technology. You know because you are an active participant—always on the go, always keeping up with technological trends, and always learning new ways to embrace technology to power your life. Let CourseCasts, hosted by Ken Baldauf of Florida State University, be your guide to weekly updates in this ever-changing space. These timely, relevant podcasts are produced weekly and are available for download at http://coursecasts.course.com or directly from iTunes (search by CourseCasts). CourseCasts are a perfect solution to getting students (and even instructors) to learn on the go!

CourseNotes

Course Technology's CourseNotes are six-panel quick reference cards that reinforce the most important concepts and features of a software application in a visual and user-friendly format. CourseNotes serve as a great reference tool during and after the student completes the course. CourseNotes are available for software applications, such as Microsoft Office 2007, Word 2007, PowerPoint 2007, Excel 2007, Access 2007, and Windows 7. There are also topic based CourseNotes available for Best Practices in Social Networking and Hot Topics in Technology. Visit www.cengage.com/ct/coursenotes to learn more!

About Our Covers

The Shelly Cashman Series is continually updating our approach and content to reflect the way today's students learn and experience new technology. This focus on student success is reflected on our covers, which feature real students from Bentley University using the Shelly Cashman Series in their courses and reflect the varied ages and backgrounds of the students learning with our books. When you use the Shelly Cashman Series, you can be assured that you are learning computer skills using the most effective courseware available.

Acknowledgements

Thanks to my colleagues at Cengage who encouraged me to write this book. Gary Shelly, Series Author, Cheryl Costantini, Marketing Director, and Kathleen McMahon, Executive Editor, appreciated the educational opportunities for Web 2.0 since our earliest discussions. Reed Curry, Associate Acquisitions Editor, and Karen Stevens, Development Editor, served as coach and guide throughout the process.

Thanks to J. Douglas Robertson, Chair of the Computer Information Systems Department at Bentley University, for his support in my taking on this project and to Bentley University for providing an environment that encourages my learning and teaching new technology. My students, Brandon Schug and David Lanphear, shared their Facebook and LinkedIn profiles; alumnus Eric Olson shared his band's MySpace page. Students in my Technology Intensive IT 101 course at Bentley from 2006-2008 saw this material and Web 2.0 unfold; students in my CS 299 Web 2.0 Technology, Strategy, and Community course reviewed the end-of-chapter exercises.

This book would not have been possible without many friends and followers on Twitter and Instant Messenger who responded to requests and inquiries. Special thanks to Daniel Buchoff, Corinne Hoisington, and Ryan Norris, who, through their ubiquitous online presence, offered immediate feedback, information, and encouragement.

1 | The Web Becomes 2.0

Overview

The World Wide Web has changed the way that people do business, communicate, and share information with each other. Since its inception in the early 1990s, the World Wide Web has evolved from a collection of Web sites containing pages of static or infrequently changing text, images, and hyperlinks to support interactive Web applications for performing business transactions, sharing and viewing photos and videos, chatting, and collaborating. Web 2.0 is a name given to these many new uses of the World Wide Web that have emerged since the beginning of its second decade.

Web 2.0 is characterized by interactive applications that allow users to participate in contributing, organizing, and creating their content. As a result, the overall quality of the site improves. Figure 1-1 shows several popular Web 2.0 sites, displayed in different Web browsers, including:

- Facebook, a popular social networking Web site originally created for college students to keep track of their current friends, has grown to become an online directory where people of all ages turn to find long-lost friends. It is effective because of the large number of visitors who regularly update their profiles or status messages to inform their friends of their latest happenings.

- Flickr, a Web site for uploading and storing digital photographs, provides a space for its users to share their photos. Users can take advantage of **tags**, or keywords, to identify and organize photos in personally meaningful ways.

- YouTube, an online community Web site for people to upload and watch videos, stores videos that also can be embedded in other Web sites.

- Wikipedia, a collaborative online encyclopedia, relies on its contributors to write, review, and update the millions of articles it contains.

- Gmail, a browser-based e-mail application, is similar to e-mail applications you might expect to see installed on a desktop or laptop computer. Gmail users also may communicate with each other using an integrated instant messaging application that runs within the browser.

In each of these cases, the more user-generated content (status updates, personal information, and contacts on Facebook and Gmail, photos on Flickr, videos on YouTube, and articles on Wikipedia) that people post, the more likely it is that they and others will return to these sites to see what is new. The creators of each of these sites provided a framework for their users to add the content that makes the sites interesting.

Figure 1-1 Web 2.0 applications allow users to gather and share information, video, or photographs; communicate; and collaborate online.

Web 2.0 sites rely upon the fact that many people will visit them and provide new content that keeps them fresh. More content leads to more users; an increase in the number of users increases the likelihood that many of them will participate by providing their own new content.

How the Web Has Changed

The fact that users of Web 2.0 sites can contribute to their content makes popular Web sites today very different from early Web sites. Initially, Web pages contained mostly text and small graphics that only the developers of a site could update. The earliest Web sites were often a collection of hyperlinks to other resources on the World Wide Web.

Founded in 1995, Yahoo! is an Internet portal and service provider and one of the earliest and most successful Internet start-up companies. Figure 1-2 shows the Yahoo! home page as it appeared in 1997. These images were obtained by using the Wayback Machine, an application hosted on The Internet Archive that has been taking regular snapshots of pages on the World Wide Web since the mid-1990s.

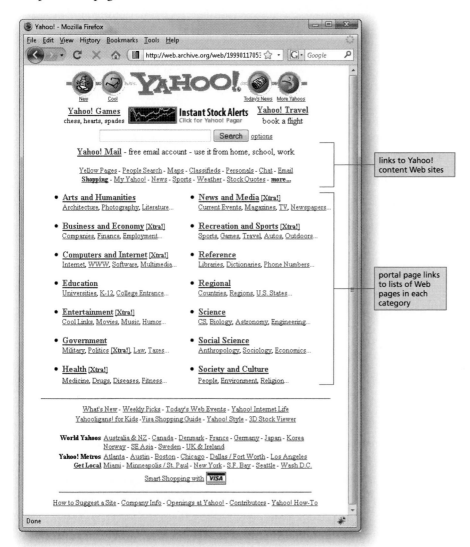

Figure 1-2 The Yahoo! Web site as it appeared in 1997.

The 1997 Yahoo! page is representative of how many Web pages looked at that time. Because connecting to the early Internet was slow by today's standards, Web designs were simple and the content was often static. Very few graphics appeared on a Web page, with the exception of a few small icons on the top of the page. Graphics were minimized in order to reduce the amount of time that a page took to load. The original Yahoo! Web site served as a portal page containing hyperlinks that formed a directory of resources on the Web (Figure 1-3 on the following page). To see the day's news, users had to click the News link on the home page to view a page with a list of hyperlinks to news by category. After selecting a category, it took a third click to get to a list of headlines. A fourth click was necessary to actually read a news story.

Step 1
To read the News, a user would click the News link from the Yahoo! home page.

Step 2
From the News page, a user would click the Headlines link to see Top Stories.

Step 3
From the Top Stories page, a user would click a headline link of interest in order to read the story.

Figure 1-3 Drilling down to read the news on the Yahoo! 1997 Web site.

In contrast, the 2009 Yahoo! Web site, shown in Figure 1-4 on the following page, is much more visually appealing than its 1997 predecessor. The site provides the user with a rich browsing experience with its modular, customizable layout and bold graphics.

Switching between tabs updates the news block with topical headlines. The news is more accessible; users do not have to drill down through a series of pages to find it. The list of portal topics has been replaced by a list of services that Yahoo! now provides to its users, from a list of all Yahoo! content sites to Yahoo! Yellow Pages, a business portal and directory. The site also displays advertising as a source of revenue. Users must sign in to Yahoo! in order to see their customized content and layout selections.

Yahoo! offers more than a search engine and directory. Other services include applications such as Yahoo! Messenger and Yahoo! Mail, Web-based chat and e-mail services. The My Yahoo! portal page allows users to customize the location and content of each region on the page. Supplying a zip code will cue the site to display local news and weather information. Because a Web browser is not the only device through which users will access Yahoo!, Yahoo! offers a mobile version for use on cell phones.

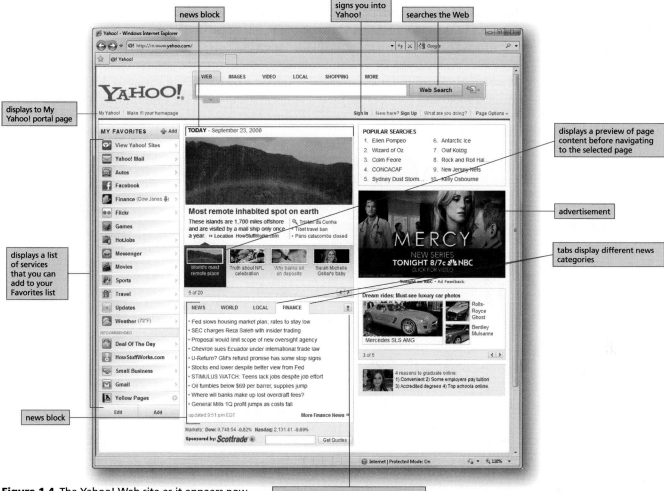

Figure 1-4 The Yahoo! Web site as it appears now.

Social and Technological Developments that Led to Web 2.0

Web 2.0 is the result of several evolutions that all occurred around the same time:

- The Internet advanced to the point where connectivity is available almost everywhere.
- The personal computer evolved into an appliance that is found in many homes, schools, and offices.
- Mobile phones emerged as devices capable of both making calls and accessing the World Wide Web.
- The Web browser became a widely available and easy-to-use tool for exploring the Web.
- Web-based applications were developed for use on many different devices.
- Web developers used the Web to deploy new versions of software applications.
- Society embraced these technological changes to the point where they are not only encouraged but expected.

As faster ways to connect to the Internet developed, the ways that people used the World Wide Web changed. Personal computers first connected to the Internet through dial-up, in which a home telephone line was connected to a modem, tying up the home phone while online. Dial-up was the most common way to access the Internet because it was easy to set up and the service was inexpensive.

Wider availability of digital subscriber lines (DSL), cable, satellite, and fiber-optic service providers enabled many home users to replace their dial-up services with high-speed broadband technologies. Broadband connectivity uses a cable modem or DSL to bring the Internet into the home either through copper or fiber-optic cables or home phone lines. Broadband connections are permanent—allowing your computer to be constantly connected to the Internet. Broadband connections also provide greater **bandwidth**, the speed at which information travels over the Internet, which makes it easier to download digital images, audio and video, large files, documents, and software applications (Figure 1-5).

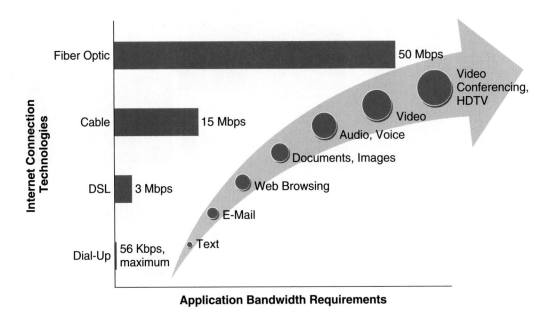

Figure 1-5 Bandwidth requirements increase with the complexity of Internet applications.

In the 1990s, many new companies took advantage of the global reach of the Internet and used the World Wide Web to conduct business. These companies conducted business almost exclusively on the Web and were called **dot-coms** because they established themselves by registering a domain name with a .com suffix. These companies included Internet service provider America Online, bookseller Amazon, and travel discounter Priceline. In addition, existing companies that traditionally conducted business in physical stores also created Web sites and began to sell their products and services online. This expansion in using the Internet for commerce required its infrastructure to support global communication. Many companies invested in laying fiber-optic cables across the ocean, resulting in a truly global Internet.

By 2001, the aftermath of September 11 and a changing economy caused many of the dot-coms to go out of business. The collapse of the dot-coms, or the bursting of the dot-com bubble, left in its shadow a transcontinental fiber-optic network infrastructure that was beginning to be used in new ways.

While infrastructure improvements were connecting servers around the world to the Internet, computers in homes, offices, and schools were connecting to the Internet using fast wireless and broadband access. The increase in bandwidth meant that more data could be downloaded in less time. Web sites took advantage, offering Web pages that contained many more graphics, animated graphics, audio files, and, occasionally, small videos than before. Larger data files demanded larger hard drive capacities on personal computers to store all of this information after downloading it. Faster transmission speeds and larger storage spaces at lower cost had a positive impact on the kinds of information that people could share. The commercialization of digital cameras and video equipment and their convergence with mobile phones, along with the growth in personal computer usage, allowed the average person to easily create and share multimedia with others.

A shift was taking place in how people were using the World Wide Web. It was no longer simply a tool for disseminating information and facilitating commerce, as in the past, but it was becoming a platform for social networking, collaboration, and communication. The Web browser had become the tool through which all of these applications were possible.

The Web Browser

The continued development of the Web browser was one of the key elements that contributed to the evolution of Web 2.0. A **Web browser** is a software application for accessing and viewing Web pages. The Mosaic Web browser (Figure 1-6), which was later marketed commercially as the Netscape Web browser, was the first graphical interface to the World Wide Web. Mosaic was developed for computers running the Unix operating system and later became available for personal computers running the Mac and Windows operating systems. It was one of the first software applications that looked and worked the same way on different operating systems. Mosaic was distributed for free to more than a million educational and noncommercial users in its first year, making the World Wide Web easily accessible

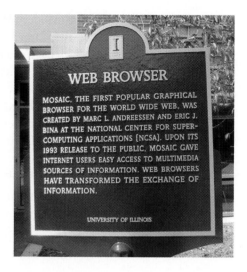

Figure 1-6 Plaque marking the development of the first Web browser.

The Internet Explorer browser became popular when Microsoft distributed it as part of Windows 95. Windows 95 was the first personal computer operating system to include built-in features for accessing the Internet. Internet Explorer's popularity is due, in part, to the fact that it has been included with every copy of the Windows operating system sold since Windows 95. Not everyone could use Internet Explorer, however, as development was discontinued for the Mac or Linux operating systems.

In order for Web sites to reach the maximum number of people, they have to be able to be displayed by as many different Web browsers as possible. Competition among Web browser developers plays a part in the continued development of the browser. New features are introduced in successive versions to keep up with or outpace the competition. Web browsers such as Internet Explorer 8, Safari 4, Firefox, and Google Chrome have implemented additional features to respond to developments in Web technologies; however, many user interface features in these popular browsers are the same as those found in the earliest versions of Mosaic. Figure 1-7 compares features of Mosaic running on a Macintosh computer in 1996 with the Firefox 3 browser.

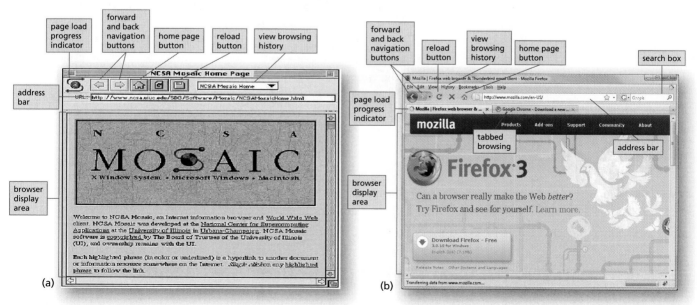

Figure 1-7 Comparing features of the Mosaic browser as it appeared on a Macintosh computer in 1996 (a) with Firefox 3 today (b).

Modern Web browsers have streamlined their appearance to increase usability and to leave a larger area for displaying a Web page. Because early browsers could display only one Web page at a time, users who wanted to view many Web pages at once opened many browser windows, which required more computer resources. To simplify the problem of having multiple browser windows open at the same time, tabbed browsing became a common interface element. **Tabbed browsing** allows users to open new Web pages in a single browser window and to navigate between multiple Web pages by switching between tabs at the top of the browser window. Browser developers have continued to innovate as shown in Figure 1-8:

- Chrome uses the address bar for entering either a URL or a search term.
- Chrome and Safari 4 both display thumbnail images of a user's most recently visited Web sites when creating a new tab page.
- Internet Explorer 8 uses the new tab page to introduce the user to new features of the browser.

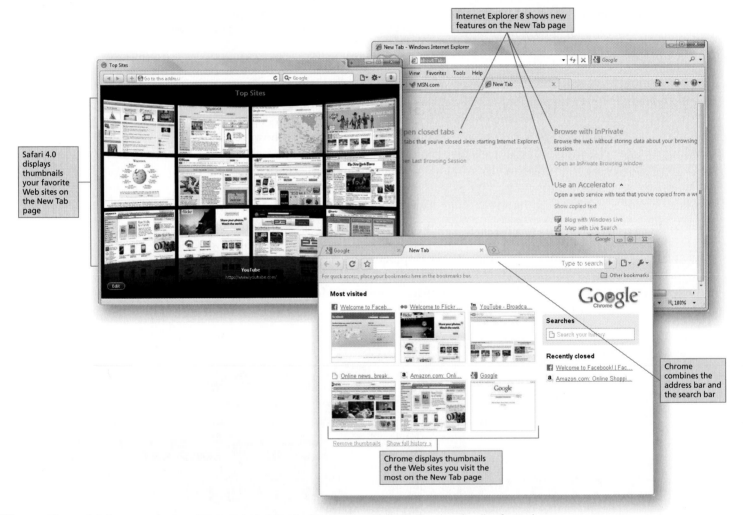

Figure 1-8 Features of newer browsers include tabbed browsing and displaying thumbnails of popular or recently visited Web sites.

Features of Web 2.0 Applications

Web 2.0 is a revolution resulting from both technology developments and a social shift in how people use the World Wide Web. Web 2.0 encourages a culture of participation by providing tools that facilitate the creation of online communities that link people as well as the

"Web 2.0 is the business revolution in the computer industry caused by the move to the Internet as platform, and an attempt to understand the rules for success on that new platform. Chief among those rules is this: Build applications that harness network effects to get better the more that people use them."

Tim O'Reilly (pictured) founder of O'Reilly Media, popularized the concept; the term Web 2.0 was coined by O'Reilly employee and Web pioneer Dale Dougherty in 2004.

information they share. Web 2.0 is characterized by fully featured applications that run within the browser and offer rich user experiences. With Web 2.0, data is stored separately from instructions for how the data should be displayed so that content can be accessible from a variety of Internet-enabled devices.

A Culture of Participation

Many Web 2.0 sites promote a culture of participation by inviting users to become part of an online conversation through reading and commenting on others' blogs or writing their own, editing articles on Wikipedia, sharing multimedia, or using collaboration tools. The resulting new and updated content, known as harnessing collective intelligence, encourages people to return to these Web sites. For example, the quality of an article on Wikipedia may improve as many different people add their own contributions to it or discuss what would make it better. YouTube and Flickr remain interesting because of the built-in ability for users to share their videos and photos online.

Digg is a Web site that allows its readers to submit interesting news stories that they find online and digg, or vote for, the news stories that others submitted. Digg displays the highest-ranked stories on its Web site, shown in Figure 1-9. This process democratizes the Web, as the community's collective input determines the content displayed on the site.

number of diggs indicates the number of people who voted for each story

Figure 1-9 Digg links both people and information that they share.

| ## Selecting a Username

Your username for personal or professional accounts might be your e-mail address or your first initial or first name followed by your last name. If you prefer a username that is more anonymous or more playful, you might select a nickname (such as Web-girl) or some part of your name with a meaningful number appended (such as rhonda2000). To make it easier to remember and also promote a common identity on the Web, many people try to register the same username across different applications.

In order for the conversation to take place, however, users of Web 2.0 sites need to create accounts on these sites. A **username**, or **login name**, is a unique code name that identifies you to a particular Web site.

Your **password** is a security code associated with your username. The password that you enter should be easy for you to remember but hard for others to guess. Many sites require a minimum password length and a mix of uppercase, lowercase, numeric characters, and other keyboard symbols to achieve greater **password strength**, a measure of how well a password resists being discovered.

During the **authentication** process, the browser sends your username and password to the application to check that the **credentials** that you entered, generally your username and password, match those on file in the application's user account database. If they match, you are able to access the site. Figure 1-10 shows the screen in which a user enters a desired login name, checks its availability, and chooses a password when creating a Gmail account.

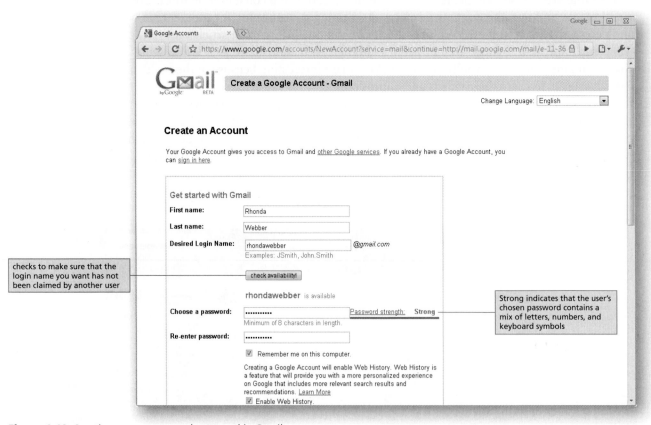

Figure 1-10 Creating a username and password in Gmail.

To minimize having to create a different account for each Web site a user may visit, a user may register a digital identity with OpenID. Many Web sites use this service to allow users access with a common digital identity. With OpenID, you only need to remember one username and one password.

Once you have an account on a Web site, you might be able to create a **profile page**, on which you provide additional information about yourself that may be of interest to other users of that site. Profile pages are popular on social networking applications, as they enable users to connect with each other based on similar interests or demographics.

The Web as a Platform for Running Applications

The World Wide Web is increasingly being used as a platform for supporting software programs hosted on remote Web servers. Users interact with these remote applications using a Web browser. Although many people use the terms World Wide Web and Internet interchangeably, there is a difference, shown in Figure 1-11. The Internet provides a hardware foundation for exchanging information over a computer network. It encompasses the worldwide network of computer networks, containing servers, routers, and switches needed to facilitate the transfer of data from one computer to another.

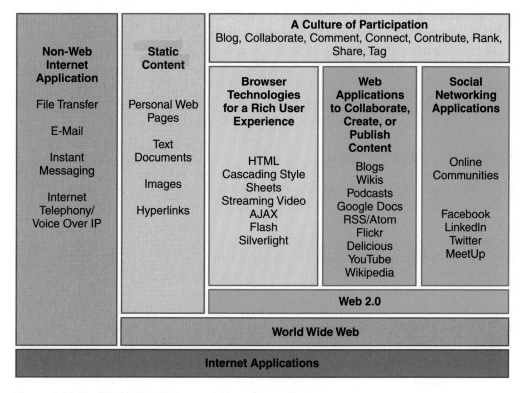

Figure 1-11 The World Wide Web as a platform for applications.

An environment that supports creating and running software applications is known as a computing **platform**. The Internet is a platform for running both Web and non-Web applications. The protocols for transferring files, sending e-mail messages, instant messaging, and Internet telephony (Voice Over IP) are all examples of applications that run on the Internet and operate independent of the World Wide Web. The World Wide Web is an Internet application that itself supports the creation of applications that run within a Web browser. Web 2.0 applications provide browser interfaces to collaborate, create or publish online content, or support social networking. Web 2.0 applications may also interact with non-Web Internet applications, enabling you to upload files, check e-mail messages, send instant messages, or make voice and video calls from applications running within a Web browser.

Web 2.0 makes use of several technologies to enhance the user's experience so that the experience of interacting with these online applications feels similar to interacting with applications that are installed on the desktop. A Web application is accessed via a Web browser over a network. Because the application and the data that it accesses actually reside on a Web server, Web applications are different than applications that are installed on your computer's hard drive. For example, your Web browser, productivity software such as Microsoft Word and Microsoft Excel, and Apple's iTunes are all software applications that are installed on your computer's hard drive, as are the data files that you might create or manage with them (the documents, spreadsheets, or songs, for example). By comparison, each time that you access Web-based applications such as Gmail to check your e-mail messages, you interact with the application in your Web browser. The application, hosted on a Web server, accesses your user data stored on a database server on the Internet. Your data is available from any computer connected to the Internet, as soon as you log on to the application and regardless of the operating system that you may be using on your own computer.

For application developers, the ability for applications to be deployed over the Internet and run within a Web browser represents an important shift in how companies can provide software to their customers. For example, the costs of deploying a Web application are significantly lower than printing, packaging, and distributing software on CDs and DVDs. The process of updating software is easier. In traditional software development, **beta** refers to a state of testing of software applications prior to their final release. Unlike software that you might purchase on CD at a store and install on your computer's hard drive, Web 2.0 applications tend to be in a state of **perpetual beta**, in which developers continually release incremental updates. With perpetual beta, each time that you log in to a Web application, you access the most current version of the application.

A Database-Backed Web

Web 2.0 is often referred to as a **read/write Web** or a **database-backed Web** because Web-based applications read from or write to a database when they access or update content. Unlike simple Web sites whose pages do not change unless someone manually writes the code for them, many complex Web sites, including Web 2.0 sites, rely on online databases, from which the applications access and process the data to display. A **Web server** processes requests for Web pages sent over the Internet from a Web **client,** such as a personal computer, and responds by sending back the Web pages that the client requested. This is known as the **client-server model**. Figure 1-12 illustrates the steps involved when a client computer requests a static Web page from a Web server. When you enter a URL of a Web site in your browser, your computer makes a request to a Web server to obtain

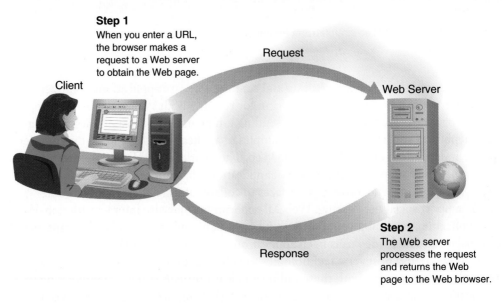

Step 1
When you enter a URL, the browser makes a request to a Web server to obtain the Web page.

Client

Request

Web Server

Response

Step 2
The Web server processes the request and returns the Web page to the Web browser.

Figure 1-12 Client-server model: Accessing static content.

that page. If the page contains static content, the Web server will locate the content and send it back as a response to the Web browser.

Web applications, hosted on a Web server, access data stored in a database server available on the World Wide Web. Figure 1-13 illustrates the steps involved when a client computer requests a Web page containing dynamic content. If the requested Web page contains dynamic content, such as a blog, the application on the Web server will connect to the database server to obtain that blog's posts. The blog application receives the data from the database server and assembles it into the blog's Web page. The Web server then returns the Web page to the browser to display.

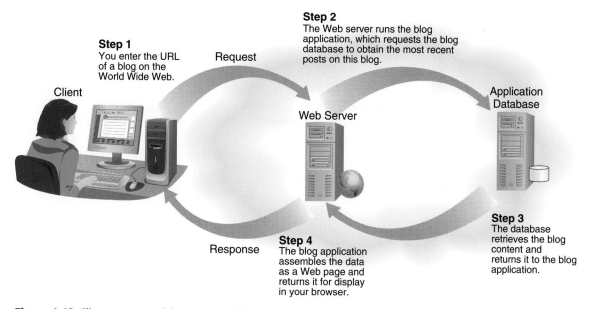

Step 1
You enter the URL of a blog on the World Wide Web.

Request

Step 2
The Web server runs the blog application, which requests the blog database to obtain the most recent posts on this blog.

Client

Web Server

Application Database

Response

Step 4
The blog application assembles the data as a Web page and returns it for display in your browser.

Step 3
The database retrieves the blog content and returns it to the blog application.

Figure 1-13 Client-server model: Accessing Web content from a database.

Software Accessible on Many Devices

You can browse Web content from almost anywhere on almost any electronic device that has a screen: an Internet-connected television set, a netbook, a laptop or desktop PC, a personal digital assistant (PDA), a gaming console, or a cell phone (Figure 1-14). Users have an expectation that software applications will operate equally well on all of these different devices and that their data will be available. User data must be stored and synchronized between many different devices. When information is stored on the Web, it is available where you are as long as you have an Internet-connected device with which to access it.

Figure 1-14 Smartphone, netbook, Xbox 360, and iPod touch are all Internet-connected devices.

In order for Web applications to run on different devices, it is important that they are designed in such a way that separates the process of accessing information from the process of displaying that information. Applications that distinguish between the data and how the data is displayed are easier to adapt to run on many different devices. For example, content stored on the Web, such as Google maps or blog posts, is the same regardless of the device on which it is accessed. Figure 1-15 shows Google maps on an iPhone and in a Web browser. Note that the maps are the same, but the platform (in this case, the device, its operating system, and the browser used) for displaying them differs.

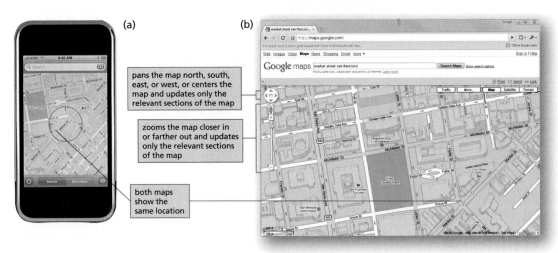

Figure 1-15 Google map on an iPhone (a) and in a browser (b).

Rich User Experience

Many Web 2.0 sites offer users a rich experience within the Web browser, comparable to the experience of interacting with desktop applications and operating systems. Elements of a rich user experience include pull-down menus, drag and drop, and integrated multimedia. These features were formerly found only in desktop applications; now, Web browsers can mimic and, in many cases, improve upon that experience.

A challenge in accomplishing dynamic display in Web applications lies in the way that a Web client and a Web server communicate. Every time that a client sends a request to the Web server, the server responds with the entire Web page. This often causes the content in the browser to appear to flicker as the browser renders the entire page. Web developers avoid this behavior by using technologies such as AJAX, Adobe Flash, and Microsoft Silverlight to create Web applications that feature consistent user interfaces across different browsers and that fully support integration of multimedia, including images, audio, video, and animation.

When a user interacts with an AJAX-enabled Web page, the browser sends each interaction to the Web server without waiting for previous updates from the server, which results in updating only those parts of the Web page that change as a result of each interaction, instead of requiring the user to wait for the entire Web page to refresh. AJAX is often used to facilitate user interactions, such as navigating maps within a browser or offering typing suggestions as a user enters data in text boxes on a form in a Web page.

Google Maps uses AJAX to allow the user to reposition a map or zoom in and out by dragging the map or maneuvering the scroll bar (Figure 1-16). When doing so, only the map portion of the window will be updated in the browser.

The map image is a composite display of several smaller rectangular images. Each time that the user repositions the map, Google Maps loads images from a mapping image server and displays only those images of the new parts of the map that appear as a result of the

Figure 1-16 Google Maps uses AJAX to dynamically update the display.

repositioning. Google Maps uses AJAX to make this smooth display possible. Prior to the development of AJAX, the Web page would have to refresh entirely for each incremental step until the desired location on the map appeared in the browser window.

Another use of AJAX employed by many Web sites is to limit the number of appropriate choices based on a user's input. **Predictive look-ahead**, or AutoComplete, provides suggestions of valid responses based on letters that a user enters in a text box. This technique is often implemented on search engines to help the user decide on a search term and on travel sites to locate airport codes of travel destinations. On the travel site Kayak, as the user types the letter N in the destination window, the application queries a database for all airports that begin with N. As the user enters the next letter, E, Kayak updates the drop-down list with only those airports that begin with NE. When the user enters a W, as shown in Figure 1-17, the drop-down list in the browser displays all of the destinations that begin with the letters NEW. Upon typing the next letter, A, Kayak finds that

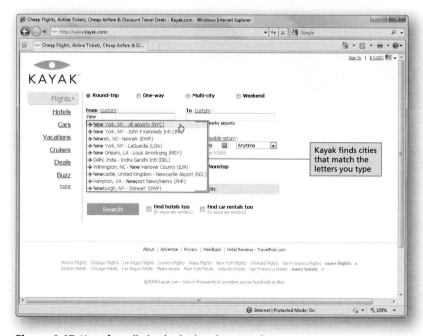

Figure 1-17 Use of predictive look-ahead on Kayak.

only Newark is a valid airport destination. At any time, the user may click on the desired choice, and its value will fill in the text box automatically without requiring the user to enter the remaining letters.

Whereas AJAX relies on standard Web technologies to provide an engaging user experience without having the user install any specialized software components, two other popular technologies, Flash and Silverlight, require the installation of browser plug-ins. A browser **plug-in** is a software component that enables dynamic, animated display and functionality within a Web browser. Flash and Silverlight plug-ins are available for many browsers and multiple operating systems. Using a browser plug-in ensures that a user's experience with the application will be consistent, regardless of the Web browser used to access the application.

Many rich Internet applications allow users to create, stream, or view video. To capture video from a Webcam connected to a user's computer, Web applications commonly use a Flash component. Figure 1-18 shows an example of the Flash component to capture video as implemented on Viddler, a Web application for creating and publishing videos within the browser.

Figure 1-18 Viddler uses a Flash plug-in to access a Webcam and microphone in order to broadcast or record video on the Web.

Summary

Web 2.0 is the name given to the shift in how people have come to use the World Wide Web, from a tool for sharing documents to a platform for linking people and running Web applications. Many Web 2.0 sites allow users to share their knowledge, opinions, images, or videos. Web 2.0 promotes a culture of participation, where users participate in creating content that improves the overall quality and value of Web applications. Users interact with Web 2.0 applications in a Web browser and from many different Internet-connected devices. Many Web applications make use of software technologies such as AJAX, Flash, and Silverlight to provide a dynamic, interactive experience.

Submit responses to these questions as directed by your instructor.

1. Name three important historical and technology developments that enabled the shift in how people use the Web, a shift that became known as Web 2.0.

2. One of the characteristics of Web 2.0 applications is that they use the Web as a platform. What does this phrase mean to you?

3. Given the many functions of modern Web browsers today (load and display Web pages, run applications, play multimedia), is "browser" still an appropriate name for this type of application? What might you name it instead?

4. What are some advantages to distributing software over the Web rather than through printed physical media such as CDs or DVDs?

5. How does AJAX improve a user's experience while visiting a Web site?

Watch the video for Chapter 1 on the Online Companion at **scsite.com/web2**. Be prepared to answer or discuss the questions posted on the Online Companion as directed by your instructor.

Visit the Online Companion at **scsite.com/web2** and follow the steps as you complete the tutorials for this chapter.

Tutorial 1-1 Install the Google Chrome Web Browser
Google Chrome is one of several Web browsers you can choose as an alternative to Internet Explorer. If Chrome is not installed on your computer already, complete this tutorial to install it and then try out some of its features. If Chrome is already installed on your computer, follow similar steps to install one of the other browsers mentioned in this chapter. If you are unable to install software in your computer lab, visit the Google Chrome Web site and review the features.

Tutorial 1-2 Create a Gmail Account
Gmail, Google's e-mail service, is an example of a software application that runs within a Web browser. In order to access it, you need a Google ID. While you can register any e-mail address as a Google ID, this book assumes that you have a Gmail address, and that you register it as your Google ID. Your Google ID allows you to access many of Google's online applications, including Gmail; Blogger, Google's blogging platform; and Google Docs, for collaboration. If you already have a Gmail address, you may use it, or you may create a different one for this class.

Explore

These activities encourage you to explore Web 2.0 sites and applications on your own. Submit your responses as directed by your instructor.

1. Use a search engine to find the Internet Archive Web site, which hosts the Wayback Machine Web application. Enter the URL of your hometown newspaper, your college or university, or another site of interest, and compare an early version of the site with the current version. When did the Wayback Machine first archive the site? What elements of the site have remained the same? What is different? Note that the Wayback machine may not archive all of the images on a Web site, so it is likely that some images will not appear.

2. Alexa is a Web site that tracks the most popular sites on the World Wide Web. Visit the Top Sites page of the Alexa Web site and review the first 10 sites on the top 500 list. Which are Web 2.0 sites? What factors do you think contribute to their popularity?

3. Use a search engine to find a list of popular Web 2.0 applications, and select a Web 2.0 application of interest to you. What Web 2.0 features does it incorporate?

4. Set up your Gmail account as shown in Tutorial 1-2, exchange Gmail addresses with a friend, and send each other an e-mail message. Identify two different ways that Gmail uses AJAX to provide a rich experience as you send, reply to, delete, or manage your e-mail messages.

5. If you have access to a Webcam, set up an account and create a video using Viddler. Name two ways that the site uses Flash as part of the user experience. Note: The application may prompt you to install the Flash plug-in if it is not already installed for the browser you are using.

2 | Publishing Online

Overview

Blogs and wikis are two Web 2.0 tools that allow users to publish content online. **Blogs** (short for Web logs) are Web sites that function as online journals, containing a collection of articles, or posts. One or more people may contribute posts to a blog, and readers can share comments on each post. **Wikis** (named after the Hawaiian word for quick) are collections of searchable, linked Web pages that users can create or edit collaboratively. Readers of a wiki may change the content of any of the pages that the wiki contains. Both blogs and wikis contribute to the Web 2.0 culture of participation because they enable people to easily share their ideas and knowledge on the World Wide Web.

Blogs often contain news, images, videos, or personal stories. Wikis collect and organize information into a collection of searchable, linked Web pages. Organizations and educators use wikis to promote collaboration and create a central location for managing shared information. Both blogs and wikis, shown in Figure 2-1 on the next page, involve their readers in the process of creating online content and, as a result, build online communities.

Figure 2-1 Examples of blogs and wikis include a personal blog (a); a class wiki in Google Sites (b); a news blog (c); and a page from Wikipedia (d).

Figure 2-1 shows examples of blogs and wikis. Figure 2-1(a) shows a personal blog that accounts the experiences of a choir participant. Figure 2-1(b) is a wiki created for a technology class using Google Sites, a web-based application for building collaborative Web sites. Figure 2-1(c) shows the AC360 blog, which provides details and background to accompany Anderson Cooper's news program on CNN. Figure 2-1(d) shows a page from Wikipedia, a popular online encyclopedia.

Users create the content of both blogs and wikis. The ease of creating this content is made possible, in part, by blogging and wiki applications, which provide a rich user interface and do not require extensive technical know-how. Users can focus on creating their content, while the applications take care of storing and displaying it.

A **Web site** is a collection of related Web pages that are usually hosted on the same server. Simple Web sites are often coded by hand, whereas complex Web sites with frequently updated content often make use of software applications to enter, modify, or delete content. Blogs and wikis are two different types of Web sites for which anyone can create content by using a Web-based blogging or wiki application. A blog typically serves as a forum for a single person or for members of an online community who want to share and comment on each other's experiences and opinions. A wiki, on the other hand, is a collective online effort in which contributors share knowledge, collaborate on projects, or document organizational procedures.

One way to get a sense of the popularity of blogs and wikis is to examine a graph illustrating the number of Google searches for these terms over time. Google Trends is an application that compares the number of Google searches for different terms during a period of time. Google Trends looks at the data in two ways. The Search Volume index indicates the percentage of searches on Google for the selected terms (in this case, blog and wiki), relative to the total number of searches on Google during the same period of time. The News reference volume indicates the number of times that each term appeared in Google News results. The chart in Figure 2-2 displays the number of searches for the terms blog and wiki between 2004 and 2009.

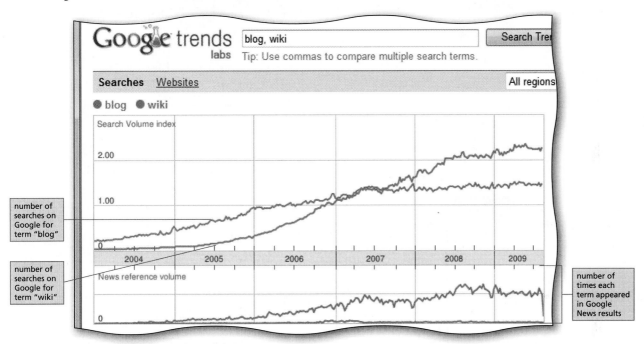

Figure 2-2 Growth in popularity of blogs and wikis.

As the chart in Figure 2-2 suggests, blogs were more popular than wikis prior to 2007, when the lines cross in the Search Volume index graph. Blogs first became popular in 1999, and the increasing number of free blogging tools has contributed to their steady growth since then. The popularity of the user-contributed encyclopedia Wikipedia has increased the awareness of wikis since it was introduced in 2001. The News reference volume chart at the bottom suggests that blogs have been in the news much more frequently than wikis.

The Structure of Web-based Applications

Blogs and wikis both offer users a simple way to publish content to the Web without the need to know **HTML** (Hypertext Markup Language). HTML uses a set of codes called **tags** to instruct a Web browser how to display the information contained on a Web page. HTML tags describe how to format text with headings, paragraphs, line breaks, and hyperlinks. Instructions for how to add images, embed multimedia, structure online forms, and navigate a Web site are also coded with HTML. A complementary technology called **Cascading Style Sheets** (CSS) contains specifications for the fonts, colors, layout, and placement of these HTML elements on a Web page.

Selecting the View Source or View Source Code option within your browser displays a Web page's underlying HTML code. Figure 2-3 displays a page from Bentley University's Web site and some of its corresponding HTML code.

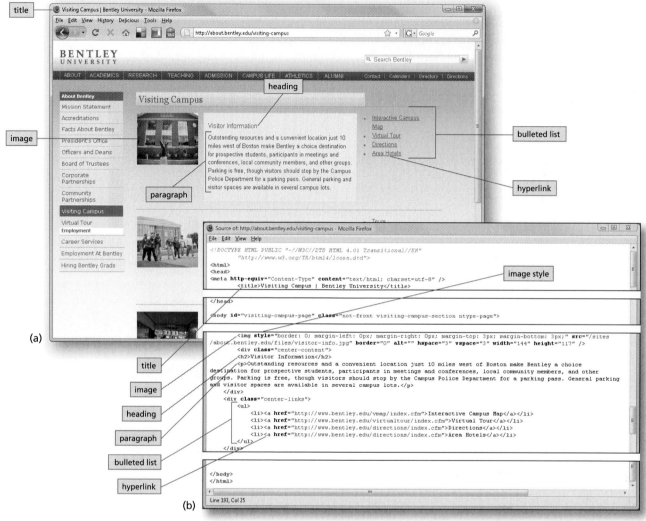

Figure 2-3 A Web page (a) and some of its corresponding HTML source code (b).

The source code for the Web page contains text marked up with HTML tags that describe how to display that content. The tags are enclosed with angle brackets (< >). The page begins with an <html> tag to indicate that the content is written using HTML. The header section includes HTML for the title of the page that appears in the browser's title bar. The body section contains the HTML code for the entire page content. The HTML markup for the Visitor Information section of the page, featured in Figure 2-3, contains markup for an image, a header, a paragraph, an unordered (bulleted) list, and several hyperlinks. The image uses CSS styles to describe its border and placement on the page.

When Web pages are created manually, HTML tags are applied to each piece of content that appears on a page. This process works for small Web sites that do not change very often, but as Web sites grow in size and the need to update them frequently increases, the process of coding every page by hand becomes overwhelming, if not impossible. This time-consuming process is almost eliminated when Web content is stored in a database and managed by Web-based applications, such as blogging or wiki applications, or by other

Web site creation tools. Using online blog, wiki, or Web-site creation tools, a Web designer will specify the HTML structure and CSS styles to be applied to a particular page. After the application requests the desired content from the database, the application will apply the HTML tags and CSS styles to generate the resulting Web page. The ability to apply different styles (CSS) and formatting (HTML) to content makes it possible to deliver that same content to many different devices, from laptop computers to mobile phones.

Web applications, which are used to create, edit, delete, and display content, are organized into functional components: the display of information, the processing of information, and the interactions with a database. The client application, such as a Web browser, displays the content and processes user interactions, including keystrokes and mouse clicks. The Web server receives and processes the user's instructions. The database server stores the actual content in an online database. These functional components and the interactions between them constitute the **architecture** of a Web application. Blogging and wiki applications, along with many Web applications, are designed by using what is known as a **three-tiered architecture**, in which each tier, or functional component, is responsible for one of these specific processing tasks. Figure 2-4 uses the process of interacting with a blog to illustrate the three-tiered architecture employed by many Web-based applications.

Three-Tiered Architecture

Presentation Tier

The user requests to see five most recent blog posts from the Web server.

The user's Web browser displays five most recent blog posts.

Middle Tier

The Web server hosting the blogging application requests blog data from its database server.

The Web server applies HTML and CSS styles to format the data for display.

Database Tier

The database server retrieves the requested data from the database.

The database server sends the requested data back to the Web server for processing.

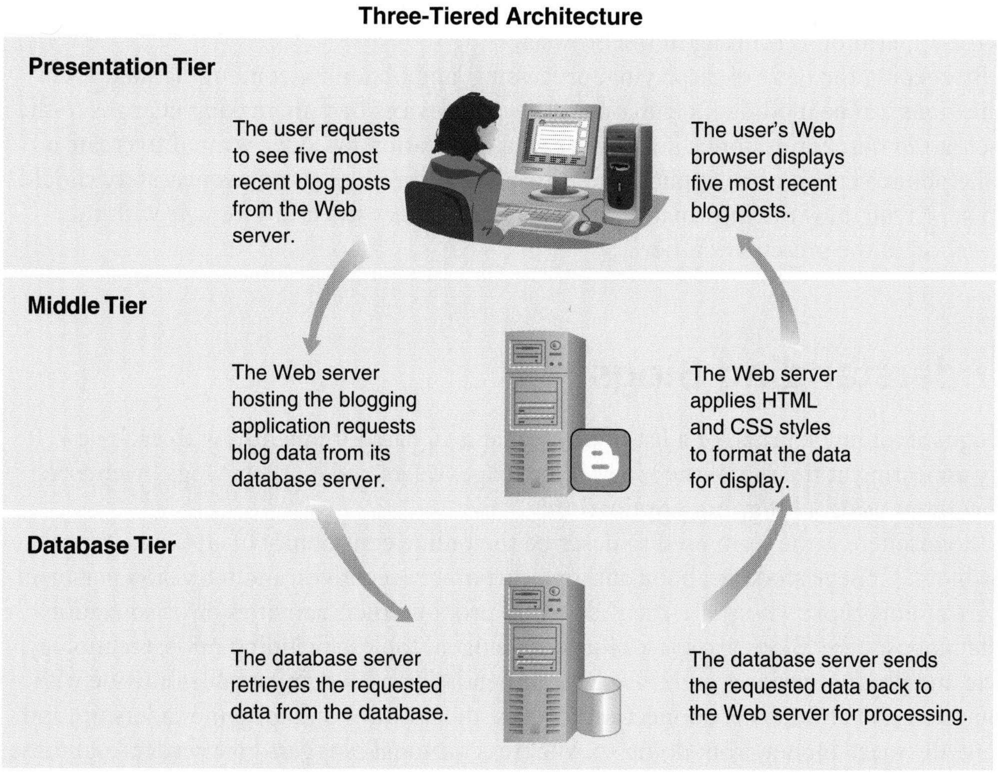

Figure 2-4 Architecture of blogs, wikis, and other Web-based applications.

The **presentation tier** deals with the presentation of information in the browser and the experience of users working with that information. It handles all aspects of displaying the user interface and processing any keystrokes or mouse clicks. The presentation tier may handle content that includes HTML-formatted text, images, and hyperlinks; forms in which the user enters information that is then sent to the server for processing; or applications that make use of presentation technologies such as JavaScript, AJAX, or Flash to provide a rich user experience within the browser.

This exchange of information between client and server enables the user to interact with Web applications by using a Web browser.

The **middle tier**, also known as the **business logic tier**, is responsible for processing user input from the presentation tier, interacting with information from the database tier, and delivering the formatted information to the user's browser. The middle tier stores applications that handle any decision making and analysis of information that is retrieved from or stored in a database. The software that provides a blog or wiki's behavior resides on this tier.

The **database tier** is responsible for retrieving the requested information from the database. The database tier makes these results available to the application running in the middle tier for processing.

Developers design Web applications so that the processing necessary for the actions required by each tier is independent of the processing necessary for actions required by the other tiers. The processing for each of these three areas often takes place on three separate computers, although it is possible that a database might reside on the same server that processes the application's business logic.

The user interacts with a blog, wiki, or other Web application through a Web browser. When the user saves or updates content, the browser sends the changes to the Web server, where the application saves the changes to a database. This continuous stream of interactions between the Web browser and the Web server makes it appear to the user as if the application is running in the browser.

By keeping the tasks of displaying, processing, and obtaining content distinct, Web applications can be modified to run on a variety of devices by only making changes to the presentation tier. For example, if a blog or wiki application provider wanted to create a mobile phone version of an application, the only software modifications necessary should be in specifying how the information is displayed and how the user interacts with the application in the presentation tier.

Understanding Blogs

A blog is an online journal, or a list of posts, that is updated frequently, with each new entry appearing at the top of the blog's home page. Users update their blogs by entering new content using a **blogging application**.

Blogosphere is the term used to describe the online community of all bloggers and their blogs. College students, book authors, corporate executives, and television personalities are among those who share their ideas and promote their activities or organizations in the blogosphere. Blogs are spaces for discussing all topics, including news, technology, movie and product reviews, and travel recommendations. Blogging enables anyone with a computer and an Internet connection to share their stories online, gain readership, and potentially make money from doing so. Whereas personal bloggers give readers a glimpse into their lives, professional bloggers use their blogs as outlets to publish their work or promote other aspects of their businesses. In fact, professional bloggers often rely on advertising to make money from their blogs.

The Google Student Blog, shown in Figure 2-5, shares news and information about Google's products and technologies that are of interest to students. Google staff members write the Google Student Blog using Blogger, a Google-owned blogging application.

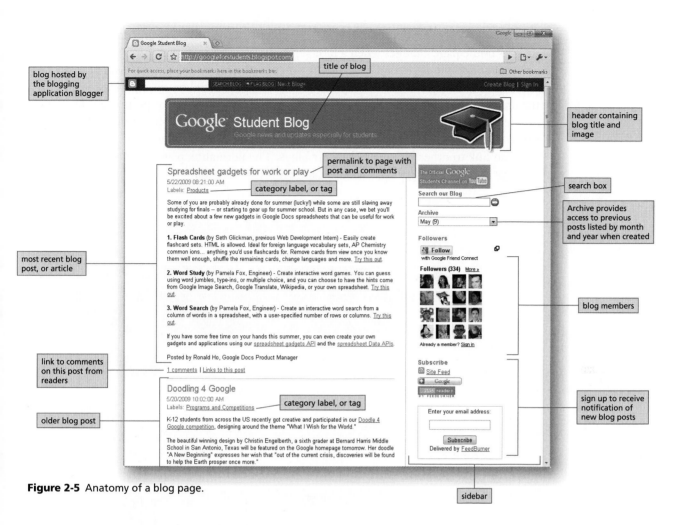

Figure 2-5 Anatomy of a blog page.

The home page of the Google Student Blog, like most blogs, contains the following elements:

- A header that displays the title of the blog and a branding image or logo

- Blog posts, or articles, containing text, pictures, audio, or video that appear in reverse chronological order

- Category labels, or tags, that group related posts

- Reader comments or links to reader comments

- A **sidebar** containing additional content, which may appear on either the left or right side of the blog posts or, occasionally, on both sides

- An **archive** section that provides access to previous blog posts listed by the month and year when they were created

People who post to their blogs are often referred to as **bloggers**. Many bloggers configure their blogs to allow readers to comment on posts in order to encourage a discussion within the blog itself. Reading a blog's comments offers a sense of the public opinion on the issue addressed in the post. Many bloggers include links to their own blogs when commenting on posts that appear on other blogs. A link from one blog to another is an effective way to continue the conversation and provide readers with more related information.

Because blogs display the most recent article first, the post that appears at the top of a blog's home page changes when a blogger updates his or her blog. When a blogger adds a new post to a blog, the blogging application places the new post at the top of the page and automatically generates a unique URL for this post based on the title of the post or the date on which it was posted. This URL is called a **permalink**, or permanent link, and can be used to link to a specific article on a blog. Most blogging applications will use the title of a blog post as a hyperlink to the post's permalink page. By using permalinks, bloggers can link to other blog posts in their blogs. The permalink page, shown in Figure 2-6, displays the entire blog post, including any reader comments.

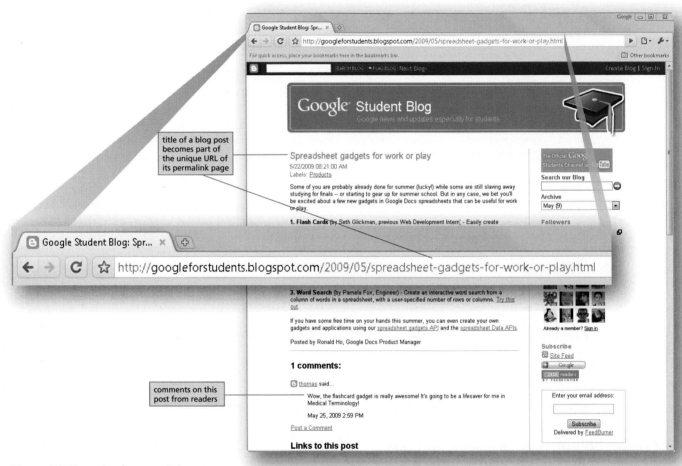

Figure 2-6 Example of a permalink page.

A blog often has a sidebar area that remains in place when new articles are posted. Sidebars often run the length of the blog's home page and typically contain specialized static and dynamic content chosen by the blogger. The sidebar shown in Figure 2-5 on the previous page includes:

- A search box, which allows readers to search the blog for posts containing specified search terms

- An archive, which offers a way to access older posts, either by month and year, or by selecting dates from a calendar

- A list of readers who follow the blog, known as **blog members**

- Links to methods by which readers can be notified when new posts are added to the blog

Other types of sidebar content can include hyperlinks to the blogger's favorite blogs or Web sites, also known as a **blog roll**, or contact information for the blog owner. Sidebars can also contain functionality offered by the blogging application, such as searching the blog or accessing its archives. Finally, a sidebar also can contain content that originates from other Web sites, such as status updates from Twitter, a social networking Web site, or images from Flickr, a photo-sharing Web site.

Exploring the Blogosphere

Blogs empower individuals to share their own stories; consumers to post reviews of products, movies, and restaurants; politicians to reach out to their voters; celebrities to talk to their fans; and corporate executives to write about their companies. Figure 2-7 shows several examples from the blogosphere.

Figure 2-7 From the blogosphere: a senator's blog (a), a corporate executive's blog (b), a technology blog (c), and a student's blog (d).

Many companies use both Web sites and **corporate blogs** to communicate with their customers. A corporate Web site contains pages of information about the company, its officers, and corporate locations, as well as jobs, products, and customer case studies. Much of the Web site content does not change frequently. A corporate blog, in contrast, allows a company to quickly respond to customer concerns or share insights into their business processes. A corporate blog also can provide a forum for customers to comment and provide immediate feedback. Blogs are seen as informal communications between a company or a company's executive and the company's customers, whereas corporate Web sites are often the company's more formal channel of communication.

Consider the Web site and blog for Whole Foods Market, a natural and organic supermarket chain, shown in Figure 2-8. The Web site contains product information, store locations, company news, and information about the company. The Whole Story blog contains more informal stories, offering recipes and healthy eating advice, as well as links to audio and video content. To promote the integration between their blog and their corporate Web site, Whole Foods offers links from the home page of their Web site to favorite posts on their blog, as well as links from their blog to the Web site.

Figure 2-8 Whole Foods corporate Web site (a) and blog (b).

Some bloggers have become **citizen journalists**, using their blogs as a space to share their thoughts about news and events as they happen. For example, a blogger on the scene of a flood or another national disaster might take pictures at the event with a cell phone and upload them to a blog as the event is taking place. Figure 2-9 shows CNN's iReport, a Web site that CNN hosts for capturing user-generated news content. This immediacy has changed how the news media operates.

Figure 2-9 CNN's iReport is a blog for breaking news with reports by citizen journalists.

It used to be that news was only available in newspapers and on television and radio. But because blogs can be updated in minutes, some bloggers report breaking news stories before the stories appear on television or radio broadcasts. Many people now get their news solely from online sources. In response, most traditional news outlets have expanded to include an online presence, and many traditional media journalists have added blogging to their reporting workload.

The Huffington Post, shown in Figure 2-10(a) on the next page, has become one of the more popular news and opinion blogs on the Web. Each day, guest bloggers contribute stories on politics, environmental issues, and other current events while also linking to traditional news media Web sites for additional information. For news and commentary about Internet culture, Rocketboom, shown in Figure 2-10(b), broadcasts daily video reports in a blog format.

Figure 2-10 News blogs: The Huffington Post (a) and Rocketboom (b) are popular online news sites.

Traditional media also use blogs as a way to expand their offerings from newspaper, radio, or television to the Web. Newspapers and television Web sites host blogs that often provide readers with additional information, images, audio, or video that could not be included in a newspaper or on the air due to space or time constraints. For example, The *New York Times* book blog, Paper Cuts, shown in Figure 2-11(a), often features video interviews with authors whose books are being reviewed. The Daily Nightly, an NBC blog about the network's evening newscast, shown in Figure 2-11(b), features contributions from several NBC news personalities.

(a)

offering audio or video in a
blog adds to the offerings of
a traditional newspaper

blog post

reader
comments
on post

(b)

Figure 2-11 Blogs that extend traditional media: Paper Cuts, a *New York Times* blog about books (a), and The Daily Nightly, a blog that shares insights into the *NBC Nightly News* (b).

Searching Frequently Updated Web Content

Web content is dynamic because people constantly interact with and add new information on the Web. The **World Live Web** is a term used to refer to the ever-changing nature of all types of information on the World Wide Web, such as news headlines, frequently updated blogs, updates on social networks, and popular terms on search engines. Figure 2-12 on the next page shows several Web sites that continuously display recent user-generated content so that other users can see what is popular right now.

Figure 2-12 The World Live Web is a term that reflects the continuously changing content across the World Wide Web.

The World Live Web changes with every new blog post or comment, every video added to YouTube, every bookmark shared on Delicious (a social bookmarking Web site), every article ranked on Digg, and every status message posted on Facebook and Twitter. Searching the Web for recently posted information becomes incredibly important on the World Live Web.

Search results from standard search engines, such as Google or Bing, may include posts from blogs along with content from other types of Web sites. Dedicated blog search engines, such as Technorati and Google Blog Search, limit their searching to blogs. Search results from dedicated blog search engines can include blog posts that were uploaded just minutes ago, as shown in Figure 2-13. Other constantly updated sites of the World Live Web, such as Delicious, Digg, and YouTube, provide their own search engines to enable users to find content on their sites that might be too new to be indexed by traditional search engines.

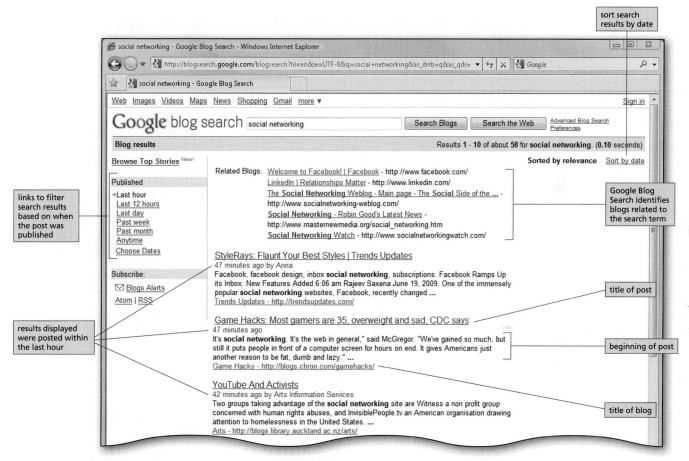

Figure 2-13 Search results using Google Blog Search include blog posts updated within the last hour.

A search for the phrase "social networking" on Google Blog Search displays articles that were posted less than an hour earlier. Search results include the title of the post, a selection of text from the beginning of the post itself, and the title of the blog. Links to the left of the results allow you to filter your search results based on when the post was published. Search results include a listing of suggested blogs whose titles are related to the search term. You also can choose to sort the search results by date in order to display the most recent blog post at the top of the list.

Technorati, another dedicated blog search engine, monitors the Web frequently for the latest information posted to blogs, as shown in Figure 2-14. By searching Technorati, you can find out what bloggers are saying about a particular topic, company, product, or issue.

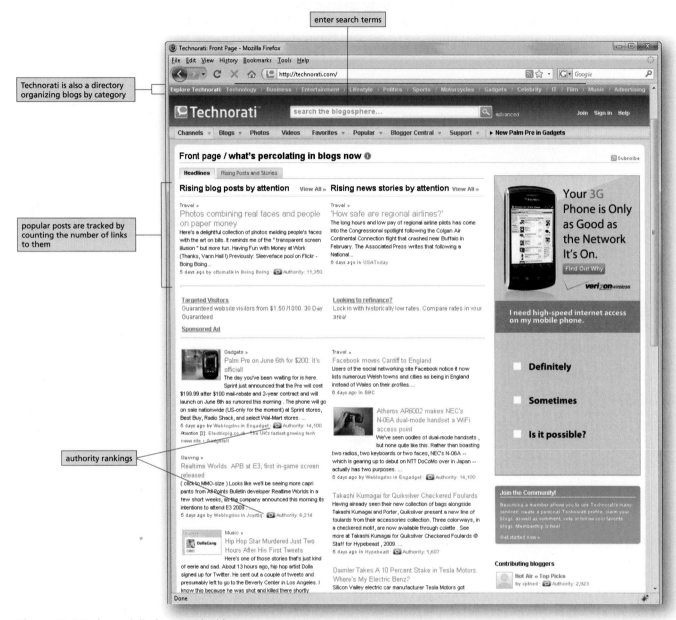

Figure 2-14 Technorati displays popular blog posts.

With Technorati, you can narrow down your search results based on language, an article's popularity, and whether the search terms appear within the article or are identified as keywords, as shown in Figure 2-15.

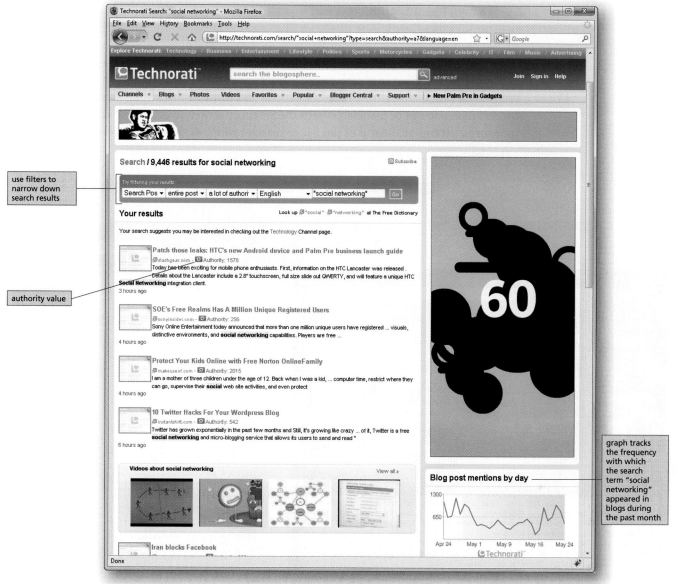

use filters to narrow down search results

authority value

graph tracks the frequency with which the search term "social networking" appeared in blogs during the past month

Figure 2-15 The Technorati search results page includes authority values and filters.

Technorati assigns each blog an **authority value** to describe how influential it is in the blogosphere. A blog's authority value is based on how current a blog is and the number of recent hyperlinks to it. A blog's authority value may change depending on what topics are currently being discussed on the blogosphere, and how often other blogs or Web sites reference its posts. The presence of hyperlinks to your blog from other blogs can act as an endorsement of your blog. Bloggers try to achieve high authority values in order to increase readership. Advertisers like blogs with a high readership because ads placed on those blogs are likely to be more profitable. The search results page includes a variety of filters for narrowing your search results, including whether Technorati should search sites or posts; whether the results should be of high, medium, or low authority value; and whether the results should be sorted by relevance or date. Technorati also tracks the frequency that a search term has appeared in various blogs during the past month.

Though blog search engines will find blog posts on specific topics, many bloggers register their blogs with blog directory Web sites, such as Technorati or BlogCatalog, so that readers can easily discover them. Some bloggers will pay a blog directory service to have their blogs associated with specific categories. Purchasing a sponsored listing ensures top placement in search results, which gives those blogs greater visibility. When you search BlogCatalog for a blog about food and drink, for example, those blogs whose owners paid a fee to be associated with the category food and drink will appear in the sponsored listings at the top of the list of search results, as shown in Figure 2-16.

Figure 2-16 Use BlogCatalog to search for blogs by category (a) and view category search results (b).

Web-Based Blogging Applications

Blogging applications allow bloggers to create, configure, and post new content to their blogs. Two of the most popular blogging applications are Blogger and WordPress. Blogger began as free blogging service provider and was purchased by Google in 2003. WordPress provides its blogging software for users to download for free and install on their own servers. Both Blogger and WordPress offer a blog-hosting service.

When using a blog-hosting service, the casual blogger need not be concerned with how to configure a Web server or how to set up the databases required to support a Web-based blogging application. The blogging application provider handles these technology details. A disadvantage of using a hosted blog application is that users are limited to the design templates and features that the hosting service supports. In addition, because the same server may host blogging applications for several different companies, the blog or wiki application may run slowly during times of peak demand.

Blogger, WordPress, and other blogging providers, shown in Table 2-1, offer basic functionality for free. Some may charge fees for access for advanced features. These advanced features may include customized site design templates, increased storage space on the server, or associating a domain name with a blog. Blogs created on Windows Live Spaces and Yahoo! 360 can be associated with a user's profile on the related social networking Web sites.

Table 2-1 Popular Blogging Applications

Provider	Logo	Features
Blogger	Blogger	Provides an easy to use blogging platform with many customizable themes. Integrated with Google applications.
Windows Live Spaces	Windows Live Spaces	Provides free blogging integrated with your MSN or Windows Live account.
WordPress	WORDPRESS.COM	Provides a customizable, open source blogging platform and content management tool with many plug-ins and themes. You can also host the software on your own ISP for full control.
Yahoo! 360	YAHOO! 360° BETA	Provides a blogging platform and photo-sharing to connect with other Yahoo! users.

Many people use Blogger for their first blog because of its intuitive user interface for adding content to a blog and customizing the blog's appearance. Blogger has many design templates to help achieve a look that reflects the purpose or theme of a blog. Blogger also provides ways to include a variety of third-party content within blog posts or in a blog's sidebar. Google has integrated Blogger with other Google services such as Picasa, Google's photo-sharing service; AdSense, Google's advertising service; and Friend Connect, a social networking application that lets readers discover each other. The tutorials at the end of this chapter will show you how to use Blogger to create, configure, and post to a Blogger blog.

WordPress's blogging software, available from www.wordpress.org, is popular among businesses, nonprofit organizations, and other high-volume bloggers. These advanced users install and manage WordPress on their own servers in order to have full control over creating accounts for their users and customizing their blogs' features and appearances. WordPress's blogging software runs many popular and highly visible blogs from variety of industries. The technology blog TechCrunch, as well as blogs maintained by the *New York Times*, CNN, Harvard University, Ford Motor Company, and NASA, are all powered by WordPress. Chef Emeril Lagasse's blog also is built using WordPress. Figure 2-17 on the next page displays some of the WordPress features that Emeril's blog uses.

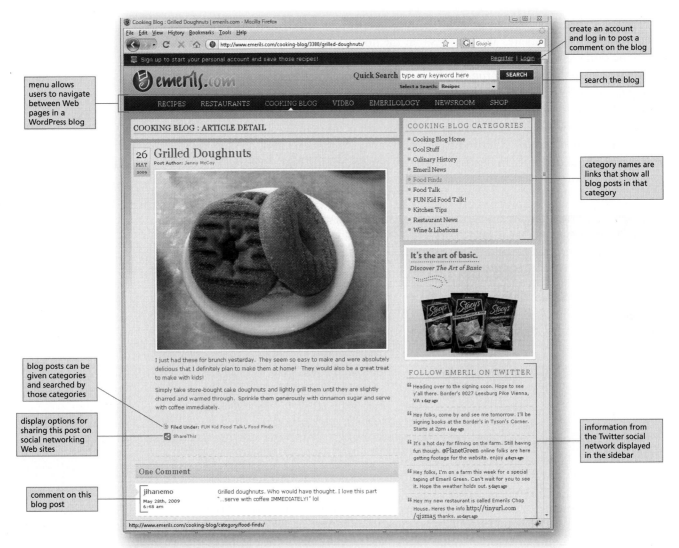

menu allows users to navigate between Web pages in a WordPress blog

create an account and log in to post a comment on the blog

search the blog

category names are links that show all blog posts in that category

blog posts can be given categories and searched by those categories

display options for sharing this post on social networking Web sites

comment on this blog post

information from the Twitter social network displayed in the sidebar

Figure 2-17 Features of Emeril's WordPress blog.

When selecting software solutions, businesses often choose between proprietary and **open source software**. Proprietary software, such as Microsoft's Windows operating system and Office suite of productivity applications, is created, maintained, supported, enhanced, and sold by a single company. In contrast to proprietary applications, **open source software**, along with its source code, is available to the public for free, with a license that permits users to install, run, and enhance the software. Open source software must follow specific design and development guidelines as agreed upon by a community of software developers. This community involvement and investment in the process of creating open source applications results in software applications that tend to be of high quality at low or no cost and provides users with an alternative to purchasing popular name-branded software applications from software vendors.

WordPress is an open source blogging application. Developers have access to its underlying source code and can create and share their own enhancements with other users. For example, WordPress developers have created additional modules, or **plug-ins**, to enhance WordPress functionality, including sidebar accessories such as photo galleries, guest books, and polls. Similarly, bugs often are quickly identified and fixed, resulting in high-quality software products.

WordPress allows users to create additional Web pages to accompany a blog page in order to create a robust Web site. In this way, it functions as a content management system. Content management systems (CMS) allow Web site developers and authors to design, create, configure, and publish content online. Drupal is an open source,

Web-based content management system for creating and publishing complex Web sites. Content management systems like Drupal are generally used by professional Web developers to create large-scale Web sites for companies and organizations, and typically require more specialized knowledge to use effectively. In contrast, simpler content management systems such as Blogger and WordPress make it possible for everyone to create an online presence regardless of their technical expertise.

Interacting with a Blogger Blog

The basic components of most blogging applications include the ability to create and edit blog posts, to configure the blog's settings, and to select a design template and customize its layout. This section introduces how to use blogging applications by using the example of Blogger. Most blogging applications offer similar features.

In order to use a blogging application, you first must create an account with that application. After creating an account in Blogger and specifying a name and URL for your blog, Blogger displays your Dashboard page, as shown Figure 2-18.

Figure 2-18 The Dashboard page is displayed when you log in to Blogger.

The Dashboard page is the point of entry for managing your blog. Blogger allows you to create multiple blogs using the same account and link all of your blogs to your profile information. From the Dashboard, you can create a new post in your blog, edit existing posts, change the settings for your blog, modify the layout, or update your profile information.

Posting to a Blog

To create a blog post, enter the title of the post into the title text box on the Create page on the Posting tab, as shown in Figure 2-19 on the next page. Blogger, and most blogging applications, includes a text editor within the browser for entering text. A **text editor** is a simplified word processor that supports basic text-formatting features, such as the ability to change fonts and bold text, align text, and add bulleted lists. Additional buttons on the text editor allow you to create hyperlinks and upload images and video files. After writing a blog post, you can save it as a draft to come back to later, preview it to see how it will look on the blog when published, or publish it on your blog for everyone to see.

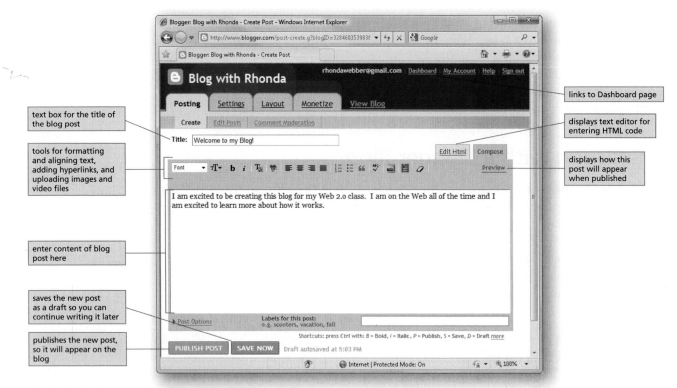

Figure 2-19 Entering a blog post using Blogger's text editor.

Figure 2-19 displays the Compose tab of the text editor. The text editor also includes an option for users to specify formatting for their blog posts using HTML tags, as shown in Figure 2-20, by clicking the Edit HTML tab.

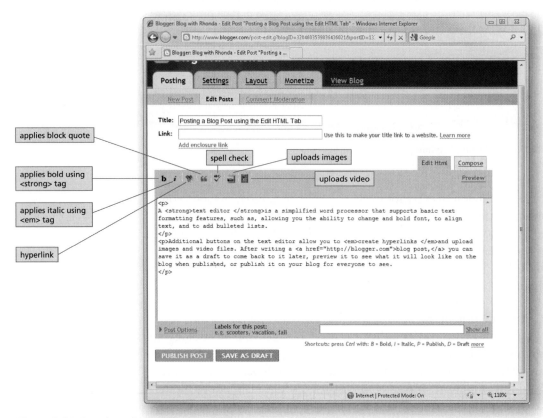

Figure 2-20 Entering a blog post using HTML.

The Edit Posts page on the Posting tab, shown in Figure 2-21, displays a list of all of the posts that appear in your blog.

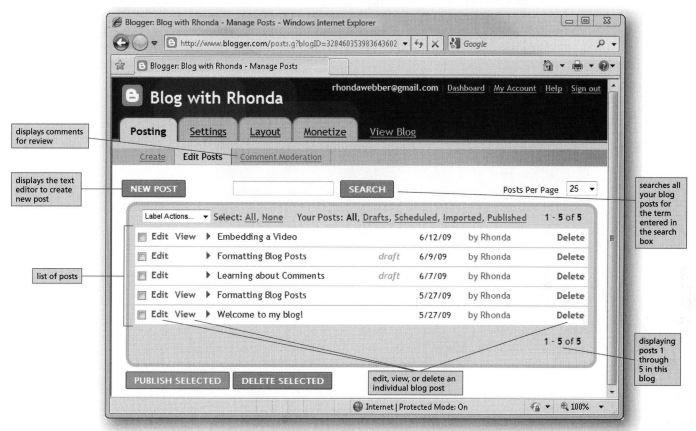

Figure 2-21 Edit posts view in Blogger.

On the Edit Posts page, you can select a previously published post to edit or delete, or you can continue to work on unpublished posts, which are identified by the word "draft" following the title. You can create a new blog post by clicking the New Post button. You also can search for posts that contain a particular word or phrase. If you configured your blog to allow users to post comments, you can review those comments by selecting the Comment Moderation option under the Posting tab.

Configuring a Blog's Settings

The Settings tab contains options for specifying basic information about a blog. A blog's basic settings, as shown in Figure 2-22(a) on the next page, include specifying the blog's title and description, whether the blog should be added to Blogger's blog listings, and whether search engines will be allowed to index the blog whenever a new post is submitted.

If you elect to include your blog in Blogger's blog listings, Blogger may place a link to your blog on its home page, or your blog may appear when a reader clicks the Next Blog link, located in the Blogger header shown in Figure 2-22(b). If you do not add your blog to Blogger's blog listings, readers will have to know your blog's URL in order to view your blog. If you allow search engines to find your blog, content from the blog's posts may appear in their search results.

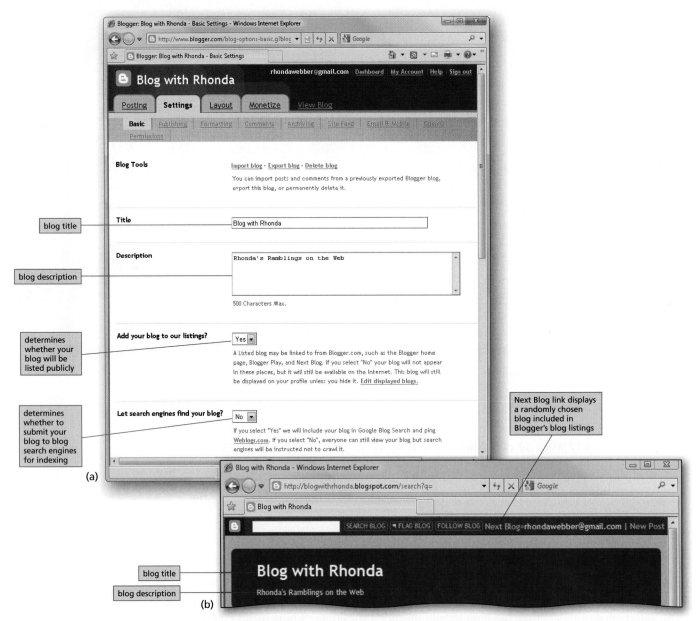

Figure 2-22 Configuring a blog's basic settings (a) and displaying the title and description on the blog itself (b).

You can use the Formatting settings, as shown in Figure 2-23, to specify the number of posts to display on the main page, the format for displaying dates and times, and the format for how archive links will be displayed in the sidebar. This also is where you can set your time zone so that your blog posts appear with the correct time when you publish them.

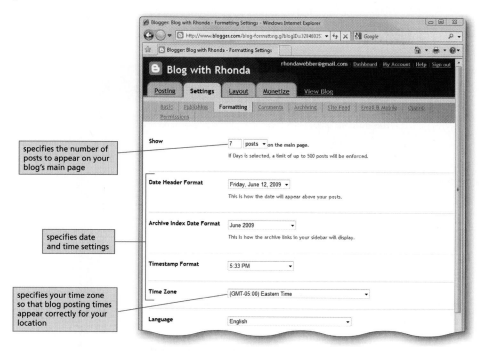

Figure 2-23 Configuring the Formatting settings in Blogger.

You can decide whether or not to display comments on a blog and who has permission to add comments to your blog by using the Comments page on the Settings tab, shown in Figure 2-24. Depending on the purpose of your blog, you could allow anyone to add comments, or you could restrict comments to users who register or to users to whom you give explicit permission to do so.

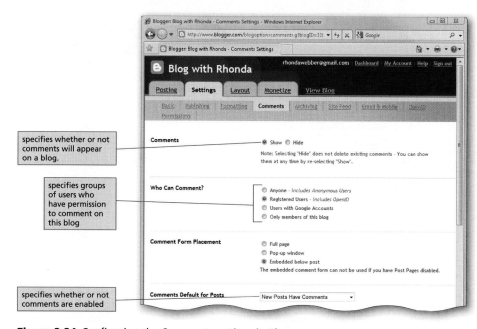

Figure 2-24 Configuring the Comments settings in Blogger.

The Email & Mobile settings, shown in Figure 2-25, allow you to select users to be automatically notified by e-mail when you update your blog. You may also create an e-mail address to which you can send messages that will appear as posts on your blog. With this e-mail address, you can post to your blog by using any e-mail application, including that of your cell phone.

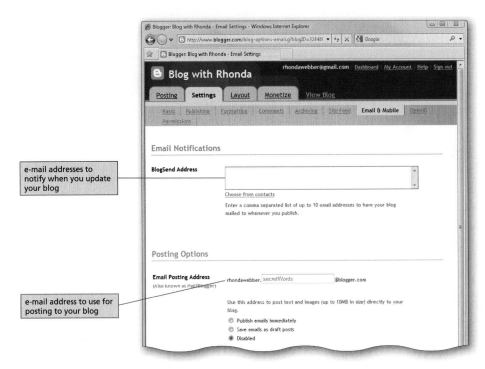

Figure 2-25 Configuring the Email & Mobile settings in Blogger.

Permissions settings, shown in Figure 2-26, allow you to specify who can write new posts to your blog and who can read your blog.

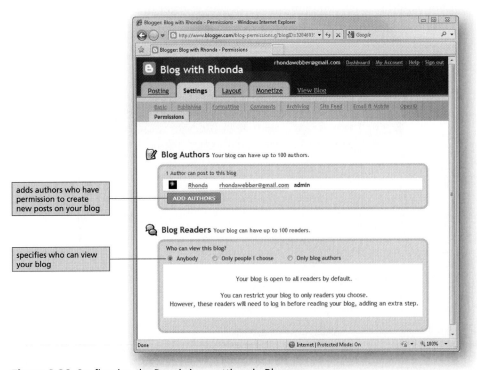

Figure 2-26 Configuring the Permissions settings in Blogger.

If your blog has multiple authors, they all can add new posts to your blog. The Permissions setting is useful when setting up group projects or creating an online community where many people post to the same blog. By default, anyone can view your blog. To restrict access to who can read your blog, you can specify who will have access to it.

Blogger offers a variety of other settings for customizing your blog under the Settings tab. A few of these additional capabilities include:

- Publishing settings to specify whether the blog will be published using the domain provided by Blogger or at a custom domain that you may have purchased and registered

- Archiving settings to specify how often to group past blog posts from a specified time interval (daily, weekly, or monthly) together for easy access based on publication date

- OpenID settings to configure your blog's URL so that it can be used as a common digital identity in order to access other OpenID-enabled sites

Specifying a Blog's Layout

When specifying a blog's layout, you can configure page elements, including the header, footer, blog posts, and sidebar areas of your blog. You also can specify fonts, colors, and a design template for your blog. Some blogs display a copyright or privacy statement in the footer of the blog.

The Page Elements page on the Layout tab, shown in Figure 2-27, offers a rich user experience when configuring the layout of your blog. You simply drag and drop elements to rearrange their locations on the page.

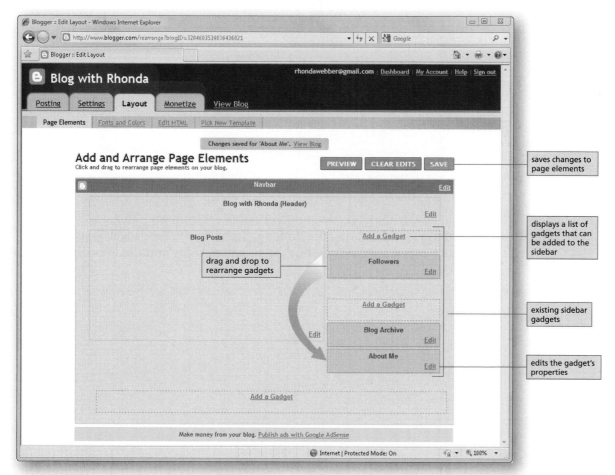

Figure 2-27 Adding and arranging page elements.

Blogger provides the capability to add the latest news headlines, stock quotes, and content from other information providers to your blog. **Gadgets**, sometimes referred to as **widgets** on other blogging platforms, are mini Web applications that instruct the Web server to access content from the application's database or from an external Web site and display the requested information in the blog.

Basic gadgets can simply display custom text or a blog roll, whereas specialized gadgets may display local weather, sports headlines, historical information, or world clocks. When using Blogger, you can choose from hundreds of gadgets to add content to your blog.

You add a gadget to the sidebar or footer area of your blog by clicking an Add a Gadget link and then selecting the desired gadget from the list, as shown in Figure 2-28.

Figure 2-28 Adding a gadget to a blog.

You also can modify the gadget's settings or remove it from your blog. Figure 2-29 displays the settings for configuring the Profile gadget. The Profile gadget appears in a blog's sidebar and displays the blog creator's name and the blog's title and description.

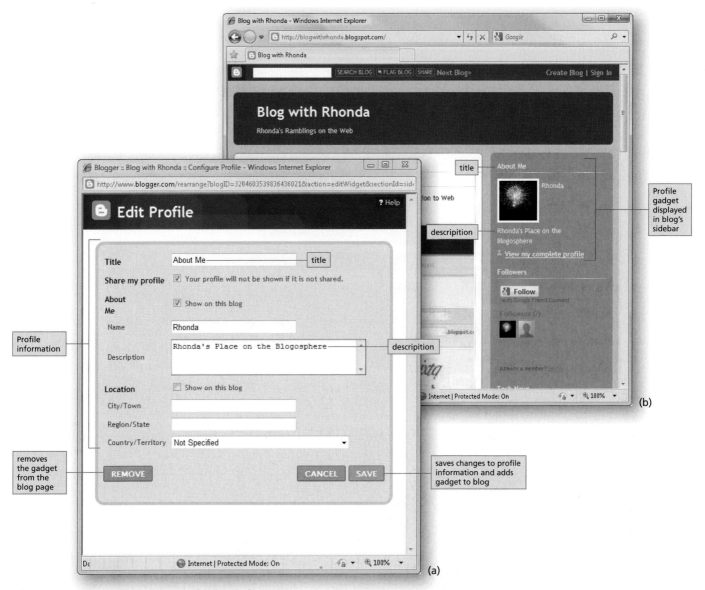

Figure 2-29 Editing (a) and viewing (b) the Profile gadget.

The Fonts and Colors options on the Layout tab allow you to specify custom colors for the background, text, post titles, and other page elements, as shown in Figure 2-30 on the next page. These settings will be applied to all blog posts. Advanced users may customize the appearance of their blogs further by editing the HTML code of the blog's template.

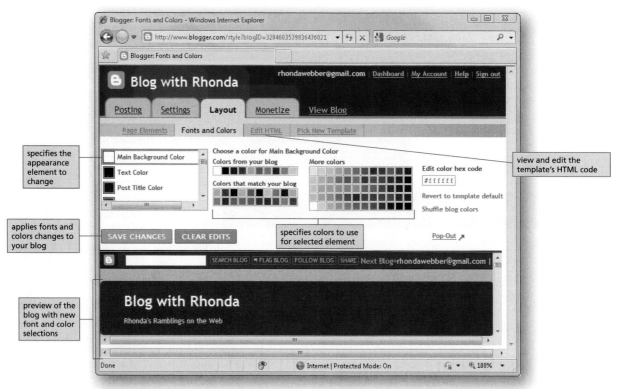

specifies the appearance element to change

applies fonts and colors changes to your blog

preview of the blog with new font and color selections

view and edit the template's HTML code

specifies colors to use for selected element

Figure 2-30 Specifying fonts and colors for a blog.

You also can select a new template for your blog, choosing from a set of predefined options, shown in Figure 2-31, and further customize the template by changing its fonts and colors. Note that by selecting a new template, you discard any changes that you made on the Fonts and Colors page.

saves change and applies new template to blog

predefined template options

select a new template

Figure 2-31 Selecting a new template for a blog.

Blogging with Multimedia

Blog posts can contain more than simple text; adding multimedia makes a blog visually appealing. Bloggers can upload, or transfer, images and videos directly to the blog application's Web server for display on their blogs. Typically, a blogging application, as part of its user interface for uploading files, will prompt the user to locate files on his or her computer and then transfer those files to the server so that they may be referenced within blog posts.

Alternatively, bloggers can follow a similar process to upload images and videos to a third-party multimedia sharing service, such as Flickr or YouTube, and then display the content on their blogs. Each approach has its advantages. Content uploaded to the blog's server is stored with the blog and often does not require any additional steps to display within a blog post. Content uploaded to an external photo- or video-sharing Web site can be viewed on the video-sharing site itself or included in blog posts.

Including Images in Blog Posts

Most blogs are enhanced with the addition of images. A photograph taken with a digital camera may be perfect for making prints or enlargements, but the resulting size of the image usually is too large to display on a blog or Web site. When posting an image to a blog, as shown in Figure 2-32, the blogging application will usually resize the image so that it fits within the blog's content area.

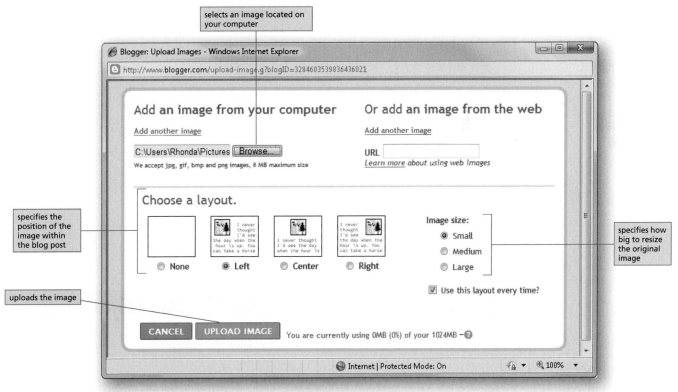

Figure 2-32 Uploading and resizing an image to display in a blog post.

The blogging application Blogger creates a new smaller image from the one that you uploaded to display. Blogger and other blog applications generate HTML for the resized image to allow it to act as a hyperlink to the original image. This allows an image to fit in the blog post and also provide access to the original image, as shown in Figure 2-33 on the next page.

image acts as hyperlink to the full-sized image

full-sized image is too large to display in the browser

Figure 2-33 Clicking the resized image displays the full-sized image in the browser.

File formats commonly used for displaying images on the Web include JPG, GIF, and PNG. JPG is the most popular format for pictures taken with a digital camera. GIF and PNG image formats are often used for screen shots and drawings. JPG, GIF, and PNG all store images in compressed formats. A **compressed image format** is one that reduces the file size with only negligible loss of image quality. In general, the same image stored in a compressed image format will be smaller than if stored in an uncompressed image format. An **uncompressed image format**, such as BMP, stores each pixel individually, results in large files and generally should not be used for displaying images on the Web. Images saved in uncompressed image formats take additional time to download because of their large file sizes. Table 2-2 summarizes common file formats for images and provides suggestions for their use.

Table 2-2 Image Formats			
File Format/ Extension	**Name**	**Compressed?**	**Notes**
BMP	Bitmap	No	This uncompressed file format results in large file sizes. Never use it for displaying images on the Web.
PNG	Portable Network Graphics	Yes	This format is useful for line art, basic screen shots, and drawings.
JPG	Joint Photographic Experts Group	Yes	Digital cameras typically take images using this format.
GIF	Graphics Interchange Format	Yes	Older, proprietary format developed by CompuServe. It is OK to use existing images in this format, but you should create new images using PNG or JPG.

Although you may include images on your blog that you found on the Web by specifying their URLs, in most cases, it is preferable to include your own images on your blog. If you link to an image that someone else posted on the Web, you should investigate the conditions under which the owner of the image permits its reuse. Creative Commons licensing is a common way for content owners to provide permission to reuse digital content and is discussed in Chapter 4.

When linking to an image posted on the Web by someone other than yourself, you also have no control over how long that image will be available. If the Web site hosting the image is down or the owner of the image removes it from the Web, then the image will no longer appear in your blog post. The same is true for videos and other multimedia.

Embedding Multimedia Content on a Blog

Bloggers may upload multimedia content to be hosted on the blogging application's server or access external content that originates from other Web sites. Such external content may include news headlines hosted on a news service Web site, videos or photos posted on sharing sites such as YouTube and Flickr, photo slide shows, or updates from social networking sites such as Twitter.

One way to reference external content in a blog post is to provide a hyperlink in the post to the multimedia content itself. The link may reference content that is stored on the same server as the blog application or on another Web site such as Flickr or YouTube.

Another way to include the content is to embed the content as part of the post or Web page itself. When an image or video is **embedded** in a blog or on a Web page, the image or video appears within the context of the post or page, although the actual data remains on the server that hosts it.

For example, if you were to embed a YouTube video in your blog post, readers could watch the video when visiting your blog. The video continues to be stored on the YouTube server but is displayed as part of your blog post. If the owner of the video chooses to delete it from YouTube, that video would no longer be available to play on your blog. A blog may contain content that originates from multiple Web sites, as shown in Figure 2-34.

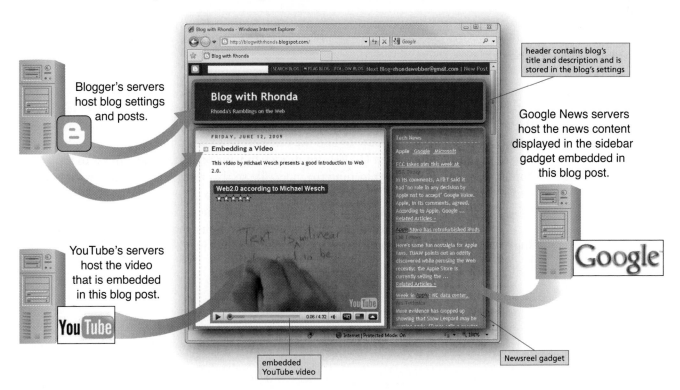

Figure 2-34 Content embedded in a blog may originate from different Web sites.

This blog contains a post with a YouTube video and a sidebar Newsreel gadget that displays news headlines from Google News. The YouTube video and Google News headlines content are stored on their respective servers. To display this page, the Web browser must request content from the Blogger, YouTube, and Google servers, as shown in Figure 2-35.

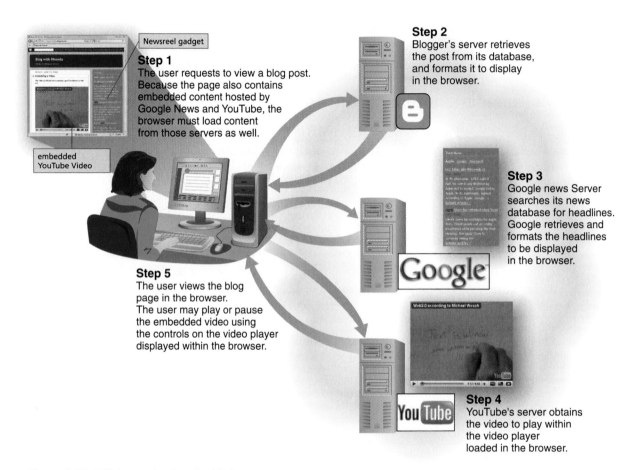

Step 1
The user requests to view a blog post. Because the page also contains embedded content hosted by Google News and YouTube, the browser must load content from those servers as well.

Step 2
Blogger's server retrieves the post from its database, and formats it to display in the browser.

Step 3
Google news Server searches its news database for headlines. Google retrieves and formats the headlines to be displayed in the browser.

Step 4
YouTube's server obtains the video to play within the video player loaded in the browser.

Step 5
The user views the blog page in the browser. The user may play or pause the embedded video using the controls on the video player displayed within the browser.

Figure 2-35 A Web page loads embedded content.

Blogger fetches the blog's content from the Blogger database and returns HTML for the page back to the browser. The request to the Google News server for news headlines queries Google's news database to find the relevant news headlines. The server returns headline content encoded in HTML for display in your browser. The request to the YouTube server begins downloading the video file so that the user can play it with the embedded media player. The user interacts with the video player in the browser through its user interface to play, pause, rewind, or fast-forward the video.

Web sites hosting video content that is available for sharing typically provide the appropriate HTML code with which to embed the video in a blog post, as shown in Figure 2-36.

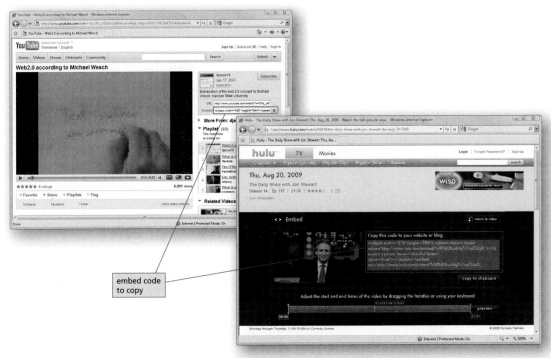

Figure 2-36 Video-sharing sites provide code for embedding video in different ways.

The HTML code may appear after the words "embed" or "share" or may be marked with an angle bracket icon (<>). When embedded in a blog, the HTML code instructs the browser where to obtain the video and how to display it. When writing a blog post that includes embedded video, copy the embed code from the video-sharing Web site and paste it into the blog application's HTML editor, as shown in Figure 2-37.

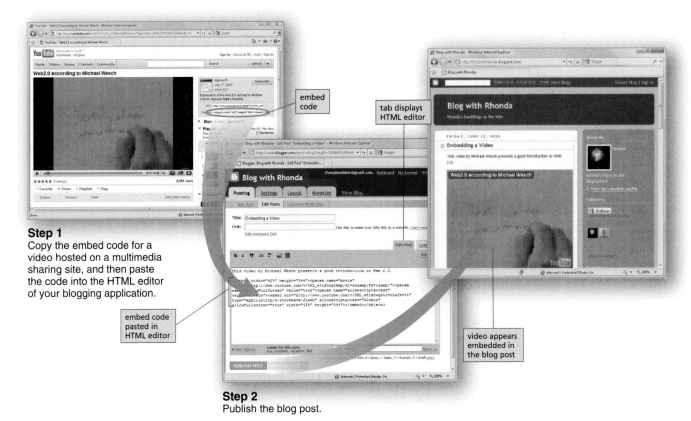

Step 1
Copy the embed code for a video hosted on a multimedia sharing site, and then paste the code into the HTML editor of your blogging application.

Step 2
Publish the blog post.

Figure 2-37 Embedding video in a blog.

| Streaming Video

Streaming video describes a process in which a video player in the browser plays a portion of a video while the rest of the video is still downloading. When streaming content is transmitted to the client computer, some or all of the video is temporarily saved or buffered until it is played. Each video-sharing Web site offers its own video player for downloading and playing video content within a Web browser. Some video players, such as the one provided by the Hulu video-sharing service, shown in Figure 2-38(a), delete the buffered video from the client computer after it has played so that replaying the video requires the client computer to download the video again. In contrast, YouTube's video player,

shown in Figure 2-38(b), takes a different approach to streaming video. It retains the buffered video so that users may freely skip to a previously watched segment of a video without waiting for it to reload.

Most Web-based video players require the use of Adobe Flash or Microsoft Silverlight as their underlying browser presentation technology. Although there are technical differences in these products, both provide the capability to view streaming video within a browser. Flash is a more established product and is in use by many Web sites that use video and animation to provide a rich user experience. Silverlight is a newer product that is increasing in market share.

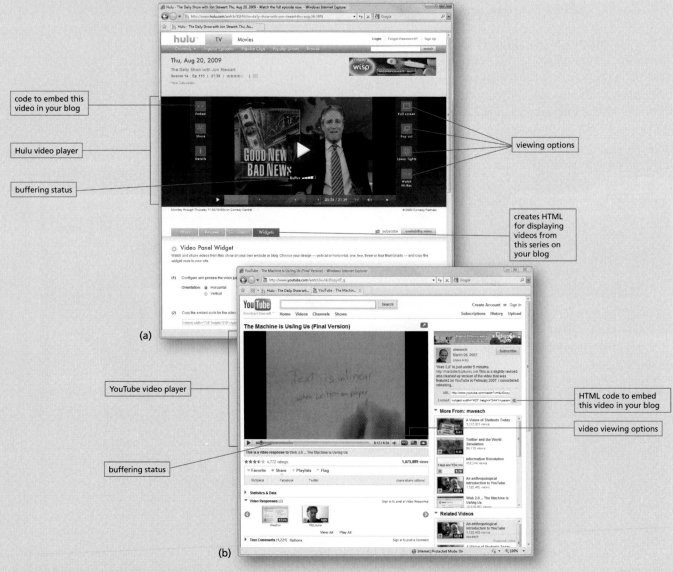

Figure 2-38 Examples of streaming video players built upon Adobe Flash: Hulu (a) and YouTube (b).

Video Blogging

Video blogs are blogs whose posts primarily contain videos recorded by or featuring the owner of the blog. Video blogging became increasingly popular as portable video recording equipment became readily available. Using video for blog posts enables video bloggers to capture what just happened and share those moments with viewers almost immediately or to tell longer stories in carefully edited video essays. Steve Garfield's blog, shown in Figure 2-39, was one of the first video blogs on the World Wide Web.

Figure 2-39 Steve Garfield's blog was one of the first video blogs on the World Wide Web.

Video blogs may include previously recorded video as well as live video. Some bloggers will use their cell phones to capture, broadcast, and post live video and often announce to their readers via social network updates and blog posts when the live broadcast will occur. Qik, shown in Figure 2-40, is a service that enables users with supported cell phones to send live video from their phones to the Qik Web site.

Figure 2-40 Qik streams live video and allows viewers to comment on the video in a chat window while it is being broadcast.

Qik streams the video for viewers to watch live, recording the video as it is being broadcast, and then archives the recorded video on the user's video blog so that others can watch it at a later time. Similar to blogging applications, Qik displays videos in reverse chronological order and gives viewers an opportunity to comment on them. During live broadcasts, viewers can use text chat to communicate with each other and with the person taking the video by entering their messages in the chat window.

Extending a Blog's Value

After creating a blog, your readers need to be able to find it. Registering a blog with different search engines and directories makes it easier for readers to find your blog and can enhance a blog's value. One measurement of success for a blog is the amount of **traffic**, or the number of visitors, that a blog receives. If a blog sells advertising space, advertisers are willing to pay more if they know that their ads will be seen by a large number of people.

Perhaps the most important way to increase traffic to a blog is to ensure that its content is fresh and new so that readers will see updated and interesting information when they return. Frequent posts increase the value of a blog and also, potentially, the number of visitors to it. Additionally, appropriate photos or videos make a blog visually appealing.

Publicizing Your Blog

The simplest way to promote a blog is to tell people about it. Many bloggers include their blog's URL in the signature of their e-mail messages so that it appears at the bottom of every e-mail message that they send. Bloggers frequently update their status messages on social networking sites, such as Facebook, whenever they write a new blog post. They also will include the post's URL so that their friends on their social networks can easily click the link to read the new post.

Bloggers also become known in the blogosphere by being active participants on other people's blogs. They can become identified by the comments that they leave on other blogs. If readers like a particular blogger's comments, readers are apt to read that person's blog as well. Links to a blog from other blogs and Web sites help to publicize the blog. A hyperlink from another Web site to your blog is called a **back link**, or an **inbound link**, whereas a hyperlink from your blog to another Web site is called an **outbound link**. One indicator of the popularity of a blog is the number of inbound links. Many bloggers promote each other's blogs by posting **reciprocal links** on their blogs. By providing a link to another Web site or blog, a blogger is indicating that the other Web site has valuable information that the reader should see.

To help increase traffic, many bloggers will manually **ping** (slang for notify) different search engines to inform them that they updated the content of their blogs. Bloggers often ping several search engines and blog directories whenever they update their blogs so that their new posts will be found. For example, both Google Blog Search and Technorati have pinging services that bloggers can use to inform the search engine when they update their blogs, as shown in Figure 2-41. Both of these search engines track blog updates and share them with other search engines.

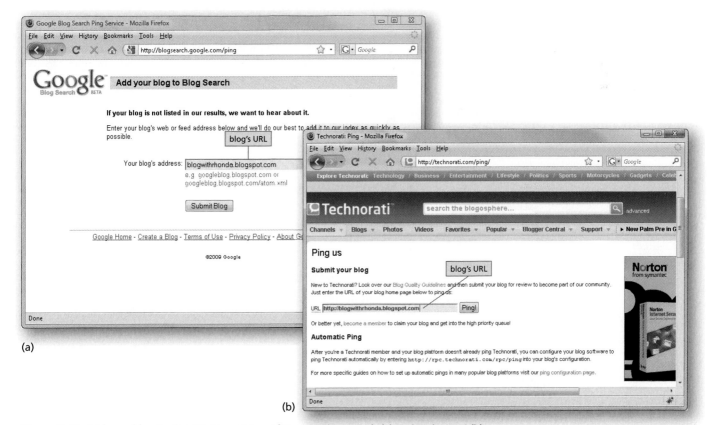

Figure 2-41 Add your blog to the pinging services of Google Blog Search (a) and Technorati (b).

It can take time to manually notify several blog-pinging services about blog updates. Many blogging applications, including Blogger, can be configured to automate the process by notifying a ping server of updates as they happen. Or, bloggers can use a service such as Ping-O-Matic, shown in Figure 2-42, which notifies several blog search engines at once of changes to their blogs. Notifying a ping server of an update to a blog improves how quickly search engines will find and index the new content.

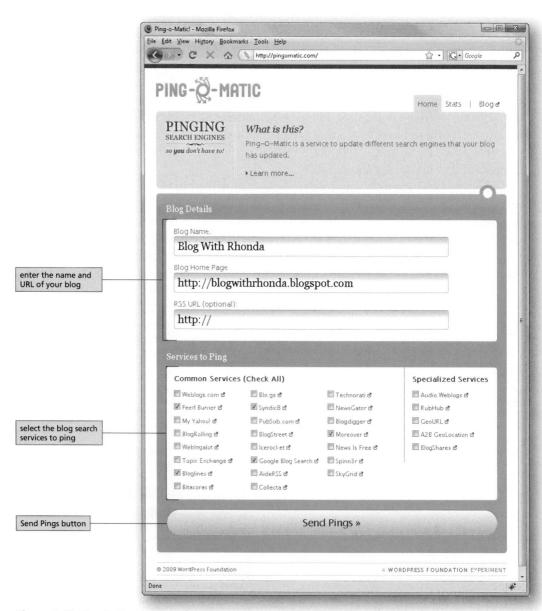

Figure 2-42 Ping-O-Matic can notify multiple search engines of blog changes.

To use Ping-O-Matic, you enter the title and URL of your blog and select the services that you wish to ping. Search engines access the Ping-O-Matic to determine which sites have new content. By limiting the scope of the search, blog search engines only have to index pages containing new content, as shown in Figure 2-43.

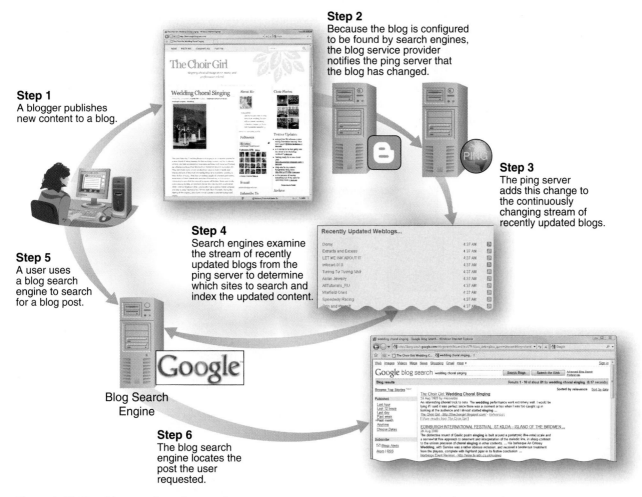

Step 1
A blogger publishes new content to a blog.

Step 2
Because the blog is configured to be found by search engines, the blog service provider notifies the ping server that the blog has changed.

Step 3
The ping server adds this change to the continuously changing stream of recently updated blogs.

Step 4
Search engines examine the stream of recently updated blogs from the ping server to determine which sites to search and index the updated content.

Step 5
A user uses a blog search engine to search for a blog post.

Blog Search Engine

Step 6
The blog search engine locates the post the user requested.

Figure 2-43 How blog search engines work.

SIDEBAR | ## Search Engine Optimization

The process of making a blog or Web site easily discoverable by search engines is called **search engine optimization**. Companies go to great lengths to have their names or products found within the first page of search results. Factors that can improve the position of a blog or a Web page in search engine results include:

- Placing keywords for which a user is likely to search in the page title
- Adding **meta tags** (HTML codes for search engine programs to identify keywords) in the header of a Web page

- Purchasing advertisements for your blog to appear on search engine results pages and other blogs and Web sites
- Having a large number of links from other people's blogs to yours.

Once the contents of a blog have been included in a search engine's results, it is desirable to be listed as close to the top of the search results as possible so that people are more likely to find it. A higher placement within search results is more likely to drive traffic to a blog, since people are more likely to click links that appear on the first few pages of search results.

Making Money from a Blog

Advertising is the main source of revenue for most blogs. The cost of placing an advertisement on a blog is based on its size and placement on the page, as well as the number of readers of the blog. Different-sized ads appear on different parts of the page. **Leaderboard**, or **banner**, ads are horizontally oriented ads that usually appear at the top of a blog near or above the logo. These are the widest ads and are useful for larger-format messages. **Skyscraper** ads are narrow vertical ads often found in the left or right sidebar of a blog. Other ads may be smaller, rectangular, or square in shape. Advertisers may purchase ads for as short as a day, when launching a product or Web site, or for longer periods of time to build brand recognition and awareness on the Web. Popular blogs, such as TechCrunch in Figure 2-44, seek paid advertisements that appear prominently on their front page.

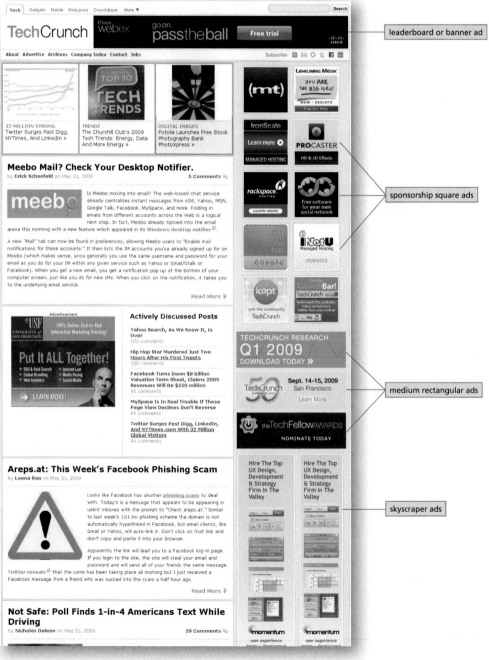

Figure 2-44 Advertising on the TechCrunch blog.

Another source of revenue for blogs comes from context-sensitive text, image, or video advertisements, as shown in Figure 2-45. The content of a context-sensitive ad is related to the content of the page on which the ad appears. Google's AdSense is one of several services that bloggers can use to place context-sensitive ads on their blogs. After signing up with AdSense, a blogger adds Google AdSense advertisements to a blog by including a few lines of code or by using an AdSense sidebar gadget.

Figure 2-45 Context-sensitive ads on TechCrunch.

AdSense ads displayed on a blog are priced at either **cost-per-click** (CPC) or **cost-per-1000-impressions** (CPM). An online advertisement impression consists of one appearance of an advertisement on a Web page. For cost-per-click ads, advertisers pay when users click on an advertisement; for cost-per-1000-impressions ads, advertisers pay when an ad appears 1000 times. For example, if an advertiser says their CPM (cost-per-1000-impressions) is $5, it means that they are paying $5 for their ad to appear 1000 times, which works out to a cost per impression for that ad of $0.005. If a CPM ad appears on your blog, or if a user clicks on a CPC ad, then Google pays you a portion of the advertiser's fee.

TechCrunch uses Google AdSense to display ads on individual blog posts. In Figure 2-45, the context-sensitive ads that appear on the blog are all related to the subject matter of the article.

Blogger offers built-in functionality to make money on your blog by using Google AdSense. Using the Monetize tab, shown Figure 2-46, you can set up AdSense for your blog and configure where the advertisements should be placed.

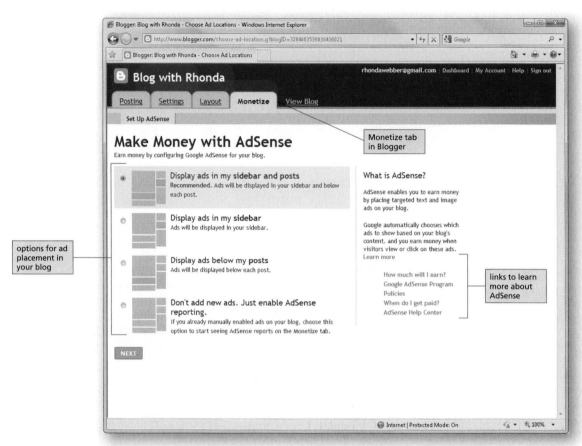

Figure 2-46 Configuring a blog to use AdSense.

Understanding Wikis

Whereas blogs have become a popular tool for individuals and organizations to publish and share their messages online, wikis have become a useful tool for individuals and organizations to organize their information online. A wiki is a collection of Web pages where users can add, discuss, or edit existing content that they, or others, have created.

Blogs and wikis differ in where new content appears when published, who can publish or edit content on the site, and where any discussion about the content takes place. In a blog, posts appear in reverse chronological order, and readers cannot change another person's posts, although they can comment on them. In contrast, contributors to a wiki use a wiki application to enter content on a main page and discuss the content of the main page on an associated discussion page. To add content to a wiki, contributors access a common Web site that contains documents and files that all members of the wiki can edit. Contributors to a wiki typically have to register with the wiki to be able to make changes to an article or to add their own thoughts to the discussion. Unregistered readers of a wiki can review the discussion to understand any issues that the contributors considered when creating the page, although they cannot add comments to it.

Wikis have an open structure that supports creating new pages and linking to existing pages within the wiki. Wikis promote collaboration, as many contributors can edit the same page at different times. The wiki application tracks all changes to a wiki's pages, making it possible to revert back to earlier versions if necessary. Like the World Wide Web, which contains a vast collection of documents connected by hyperlinks, a wiki contains a collection of documents connected by hyperlinks to other documents in the wiki. As a result, wikis are an excellent solution for storing collective knowledge in one central online location. Each time that a contributor adds useful information to the wiki, the wiki as whole becomes more useful. Perhaps the most famous wiki application on the World Wide Web is Wikipedia, an online encyclopedia. Figure 2-47 shows the Wikipedia article on Web 2.0.

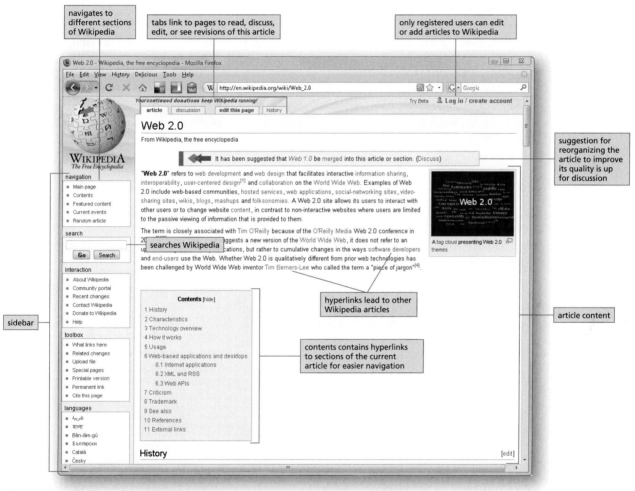

Figure 2-47 Anatomy of a Wikipedia page.

The center of the Wikipedia page displays the article content. Complex articles often have a table of contents containing links to sections within the article. Hyperlinks within Wikipedia articles reference other Wikipedia articles, creating a web of hyperlinks to pages of related information. The sidebar contains links for navigating the Wikipedia site. Unlike a traditional encyclopedia, which is arranged alphabetically, readers can browse Wikipedia's content in multiple ways: by category, timeliness, featured content, or even at random. A search box allows readers to search Wikipedia for articles that mention the terms that they are seeking. Tabs across the top of the page link to the article itself, a discussion among its authors, and the history of revisions made to it.

Wikis have emerged as useful tools for collaboration because they offer searchable, centralized storage for content that is created by multiple authors or needed by multiple users. Content on a wiki can range from articles, to document or spreadsheet attachments, to photographs or video. Wikis can be publicly accessible to everyone, like Wikipedia, or private so that the content is only accessible to a wiki's contributors, as with wikis set up by companies for their employees. Many companies encourage employees to contribute to a wiki to capture and document information about the company's policies, procedures, and products in a central online location. Employees may use wiki pages to share their work activity reports, contacts, user manuals, and other documents with coworkers and project team members. Outside of the workplace, wikis are used for planning events; managing to-do lists and group projects; and sharing information online with friends, members of organizations, and, in the case of publicly accessible wikis, the world.

Table 2-3 details several publicly available Wikis, in addition to Wikipedia. These wikis, some of which are shown in Figure 2-48, serve as topic-specific knowledge bases that rely on user-contributed content.

Table 2-3 Popular Wikis		
Site	**Logo**	**Features**
Wikipedia		Provides an online encyclopedia.
LyricWiki		Provides lyrics for songs by any artist, and features lyrics for iTunes top songs.
ShopWiki		Provides information and buying guides when purchasing different kinds of products.
Wikia		Provides a portal with links to wikis about popular entertainment topics, including comic book characters, video games, sports, television programs, toys, and movies.
WikiBooks		Provides a free library of educational books on natural and social sciences, computing, and humanities subjects.
wikiHow		Provides instructions on how to do almost anything, from avoiding mistakes on a resume to making a poncho from a shower curtain.
WikiTravel		Provides up-to-date travel information for places around the world.

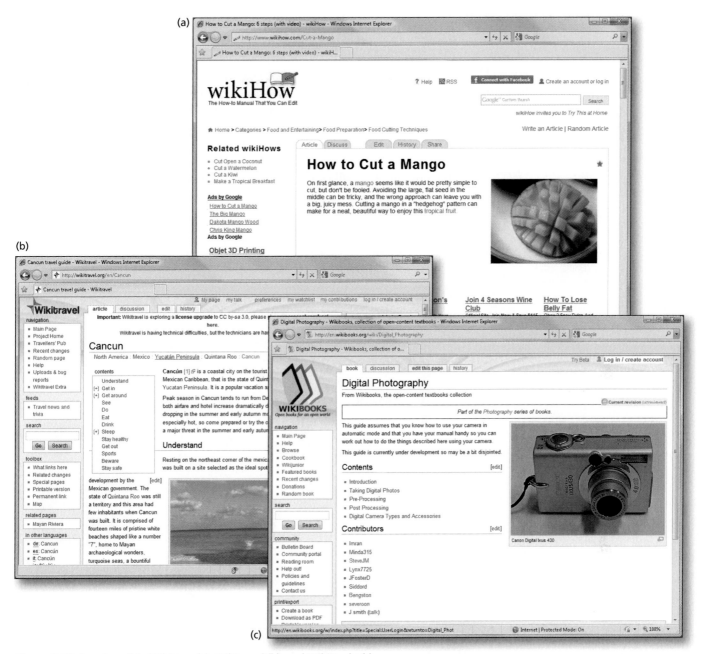

Figure 2-48 Popular wikis: WikiHow (a), Wikitravel (b), and WikiBooks (c).

Web-Based Wiki Applications

Creating or contributing to a wiki requires the use of a browser-based wiki application. The Web server hosting the wiki application accesses an online database to retrieve and update the wiki's content. Many wiki providers host wiki applications on their own servers and allow contributors to create wikis with basic features at no cost. They charge additional fees for increased storage, for associating a custom domain name with the wiki, or for providing dedicated customer support. Hosted wiki applications are popular among small groups and organizations who may not have the resources to maintain the wiki application or the servers needed to run it.

Professional users often want to associate their own domain names (e.g., mycorporatewiki.com) with their blog or wiki Web sites. Typically, custom domain names are shorter and easier to remember than the hybrid domain name assigned by the hosting service. Domain names assigned by hosting services usually contain elements of both the provider's and user's domain name (e.g., http://pbworks.com/mycorporatewiki). Corporations or technically adept groups often will install, configure, and host a Wiki application on their own servers in order to have more control over its features. Some wiki applications are open source applications, supported by a large developer community, whereas others may be the product of a single vendor.

Three of the more popular wiki applications are MediaWiki, PBworks, and Google Sites, shown in Figure 2-49. The choice of which wiki application to use depends on which features are needed.

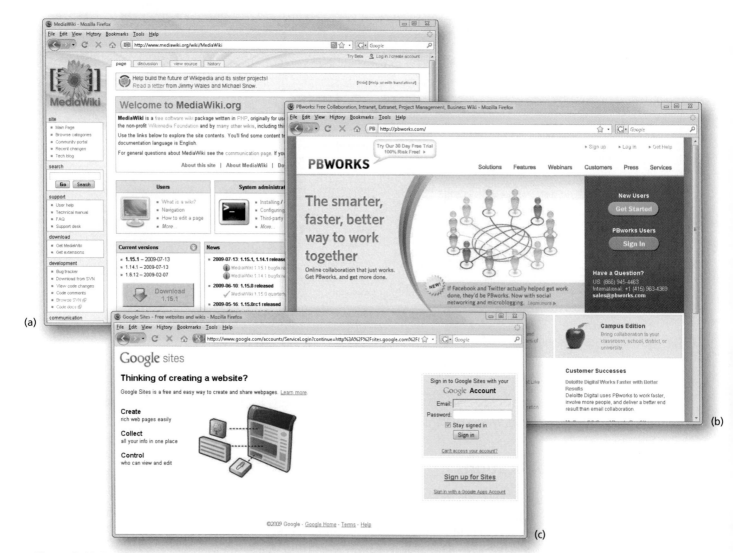

Figure 2-49 Popular wiki applications: MediaWiki (a), PBworks (b), and Google Sites (c).

MediaWiki is a highly configurable, open source wiki application that powers large-scale wikis, such as those shown in Figure 2-48 on the previous page. MediaWiki must be hosted on a Web server owned or leased by the providers of wiki applications created on the MediaWiki platform because MediaWiki does not provide a hosted version for casual users. PBworks is a hosted wiki solution that is popular among educators and casual wiki users because of its intuitive interface and large collection of third-party plug-ins to add extra features, such as spreadsheets, chat rooms, and calendars. Google Sites is a hosted Wiki application that integrates images, videos, spreadsheets, and other content from various Google applications. It is popular among both casual and professional users. Table 2-4 lists several popular wiki applications and describes some of their features.

Table 2-4 Wiki Applications		
Provider	**Logo**	**Features**
Google Sites	Google sites	Provides an easy to use set of tools for creating and sharing web pages. Integrated with Google applications.
MediaWiki	MediaWiki	Provides open source wiki software, originally created to support Wikipedia. You must install and configure the MediaWiki application on your web server in order to use it.
PBworks	PBWORKS	Provides hosted software for creating collaborative work spaces used across several industries. PBworks is popular among educators because of its simplicity and security.
TiddlyWiki	tw.org	Provides personal wiki notebook capabilities in a single HTML file without the need of a web server or an internet connection.
Wet Paint	wetpaint	Provides an easy to use hosted wiki tool which also includes features of blogs, forums, and social networks. Educational wikis are advertisement-free.
WikiSpaces	Wikispaces	Provides a user-friendly and intuitive hosted wiki platform used by business, nonprofit, and educational customers.

Because publicly accessible wikis are apt to have much more traffic than a wiki used by small organizations or college classrooms, they need to be scalable. A **scalable** application is one that can successfully handle the increased processing that is required when the number of simultaneous users increases from hundreds to hundreds of thousands, without degrading in performance. MediaWiki, originally built to power Wikipedia, is designed to handle these high-usage situations.

A contributor must log in to a wiki to add new content or modify existing content. Wiki applications allow readers and contributors to have different levels of access in order to control who can modify parts of the wiki. For example, in PBworks, contributors may take on the following roles:

- Administrators, who can add, manage, and delete wiki content as well as assign wiki and user settings

- Writers, who can edit pages and revert pages to previous versions, upload new files, and create new pages

- Editors, who can do everything that writers can do plus delete pages
- Readers can view pages on a wiki but cannot edit or change them. Readers do not have to log in to view a wiki's pages.

Google Sites allows contributors to take on similar roles: owners can administer a site; collaborators can add or modify content; viewers can read but not change content.

These roles allow wiki administrators to make their wikis available to a large number of people, from those who simply read the content to those who actively contribute to it. Using roles adds additional security to the wiki, as only those who have permission to post may do so.

Interacting with a Wiki

Wikis can be used in many different settings. For example, Figure 2-50 shows a wiki hosted by PBworks that has been implemented in a college information technology course, which allows students to post and share their notes with the class. In this example, students can either create new wiki pages or edit existing ones. Wikis typically have two different modes, the View mode, shown in Figure 2-50, and the Edit mode. The View mode allows readers to view existing information, whereas the Edit mode enables registered contributors to add new posts or edit existing ones.

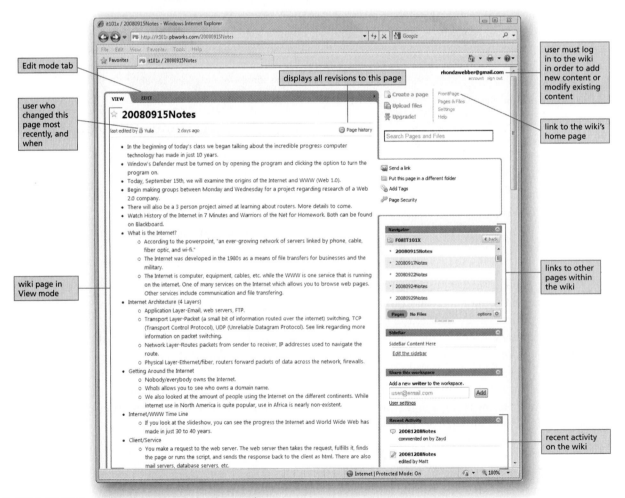

Figure 2-50 Anatomy of a wiki page in View mode.

PBworks allows users to create or edit an article by using a **WYSIWYG** (What-You-See-Is-What-You-Get, pronounced "whizzy-wig") text editor. In Figure 2-51, a wiki contributor named Rhonda adds a phrase to the second bulleted item on the page and then saves the changes to the database.

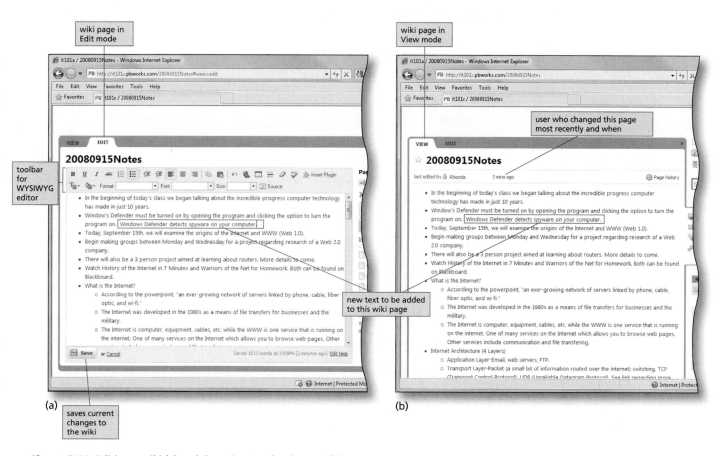

Figure 2-51 Editing a wiki (a) and then viewing the changes (b).

Each time that a contributor makes a change to a wiki, the wiki application saves a new version of the page. If necessary, the wiki administrator can revert back to an earlier version of the page if a contributor adds inappropriate content or accidentally deletes valid content. Version records show exactly who modified a page and when so that changes can be traced back to a specific contributor. Page history is important for public or large-scale wikis, as it allows them to recover from unintended errors, malicious attacks, or vandalism. Figure 2-52 on the next page shows the history of all changes made to the page that Rhonda edited and the exact changes that she made to the latest version.

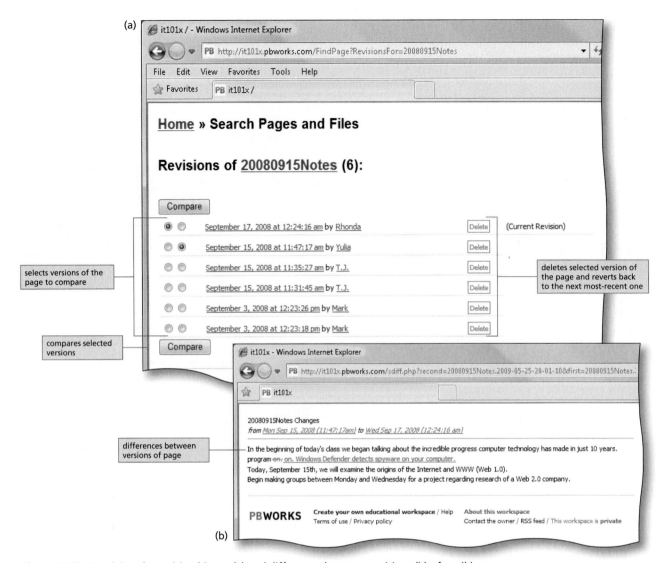

Figure 2-52 Examining the revision history (a) and differences between revisions (b) of a wiki page.

The Revisions page, shown in Figure 2-52(a), displays the dates when contributors made changes to the wiki. Selecting two different versions of the page to compare displays the differences between them, as shown in Figure 2-52(b). An administrator can revert back to an earlier version of a page, deleting all later changes.

When two contributors try to edit the same page at the same time, an **edit conflict** is created. To resolve an edit conflict, many wikis will block the contributor who is attempting to edit the page from being able to do so until the contributor currently editing the page saves changes or remains idle on the page for an extended period of time.

Wikipedia

All of the content found in Wikipedia, the successful online encyclopedia, is generated by its contributors. Wikipedia depends upon people coming together to contribute their expertise on a variety of topics. Over time, the Wikipedia community established policies to guide contributors who support the site by adding and reviewing its articles. Wikipedia has experienced exponential growth since it began and is still growing. In 2010, Wikipedia contained more than 3.1 million articles.

"Wikipedia is first and foremost an effort to create and distribute a free encyclopedia of the highest possible quality to every single person on the planet in their own language. Asking whether the community comes before or after this goal is really asking the wrong question: the entire purpose of the community is precisely this goal."

Jimmy Wales, cofounder of Wikipedia

Anyone who registers as a Wikipedia contributor can create or edit an article on Wikipedia. Every article must be approved before it can be published. Wikipedia, like many other online wikis, encourages beginners to become familiar with using the wiki editor to create or modify content by experimenting with text in the site's Sandbox page. The **Sandbox page**, shown in Figure 2-53, is a page that is dedicated to learning how to use the wiki application software and does not affect the content of actual pages.

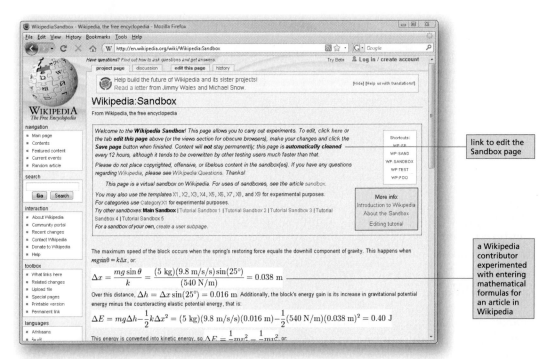

Figure 2-53 Wikipedia's Sandbox page.

New Wikipedia articles are first posted in a private section of each user's account, where reviewers can read them. After reviewers provide feedback and the author makes corrections, the article can be moved to the live Wikipedia site for everyone to see. Discussions about an article take place on the article's Talk, or Discussion, page, shown in Figure 2-54.

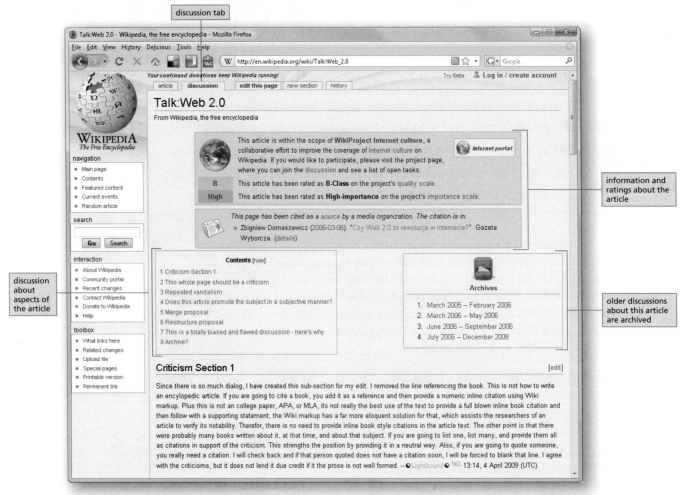

Figure 2-54 A Wikipedia Talk page.

The Talk page often contains critical reviews of the article, suggestions for how to improve it, or questions about its accuracy. Comments should be objective and on topic. The Talk page also is a place to discuss the rationale for edits to an article, such as when a user reverts back to an earlier version of an article. Authors use the Talk page to propose details for moving, reorganizing, or merging content with other Wikipedia articles.

Google Wave

Google Wave is an integrated collaboration tool from Google that combines features from blogs, wikis, instant messaging, and e-mail. Google Wave, shown in Figure 2-55 on the next page, has multiple streams of communication, called **waves**, to which users may add, edit, or share each other's comments at the same time. A wave is composed of smaller messages called **blips**.

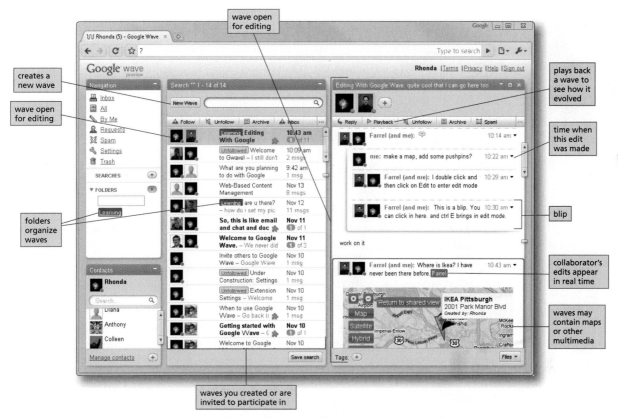

creates a new wave

wave open for editing

folders organize waves

wave open for editing

plays back a wave to see how it evolved

time when this edit was made

blip

collaborator's edits appear in real time

waves may contain maps or other multimedia

waves you created or are invited to participate in

Figure 2-55 Google Wave combines elements of blogs, instant messaging, wikis, and multimedia for creating collaborative documents.

As with a wiki, participants in a wave can edit another person's comments; as with a blog, participants can respond to a message that another person wrote. Wave participants can reply anywhere in the message, edit the content, and add participants from their Google Contacts list at the same time, without getting locked out. Similarly to a wiki's revision history, playing back the wave shows how the conversation evolved from when it began and displays who said what and when they said it. Updates to the wave take place in real time and may be shared online. Google Waves can be embedded into blogs and other Web sites.

Google Wave is a hybrid collaboration tool that represents the evolution and convergence of several Web 2.0 online publishing and communication applications.

Summary

Blogs and wikis are two Web 2.0 tools that facilitate the process of creating and sharing online content. The underlying three-tiered architecture of Web applications, while transparent to the user, provides the technical foundation that enables users to enter and manage their content through online applications. Blogging has become a popular tool for individuals and organizations to publish and share their messages online. Blogs usually are authored and maintained by individuals, whereas wikis often reflect the knowledge of an entire community. Several blogging services, including Blogger and WordPress, provide either hosted or custom configurations for users to create blogs. Wikis are built as a collection of linked Web pages, any of which contributors can edit and discuss. Wikis are a useful collaboration tool and are used to create centralized online resource banks, document group processes, or plan projects.

Both blogs and wikis enable collaboration and communication and have contributed to the transformation of the World Wide Web into a social Web where users share their knowledge, ideas, and opinions.

Think

Submit responses to these questions as directed by your instructor.

1. Name three ways that blogs and wikis are similar. Name three ways in which they are different.

2. What are the three tiers in a three-tiered architecture, and what is the significance of each?

3. Other than for this class, why might you create your own blog?

4. To what do permalinks on a blog permanently link? Why are permalinks needed?

5. What is the significance of the World Live Web?

6. Name two ways that blogging has changed the way that people share and report news and information.

7. How does Google AdSense help bloggers make money from their blogs? What are two things that you can do to drive traffic to your blog?

8. What is search engine optimization and why is it important?

9. Describe two advantages and two disadvantages of using a hosted wiki application or installing and managing wiki software such as MediaWiki on your own Web server.

10. What are two key features of a wiki that make it a useful collaboration tool?

11. Describe a group that you are involved in, for which a wiki could improve how information is gathered or shared among its members.

12. What steps does Wikipedia take to ensure the quality of its articles?

13. Why do you think Wikipedia is so successful if anybody can post or change almost anything?

Watch

Watch the video for Chapter 2 on the Online Companion at scsite.com/web2. Be prepared to answer or discuss the questions posted on the Online Companion as directed by your instructor.

Try

Visit the Online Companion at scsite.com/web2 and follow the steps as you complete the tutorials for this chapter.

Tutorial 2-1 Create a Blogger Blog and Post to It
In this tutorial, you will learn to create a Blogger blog and add a post.

Tutorial 2-2 Configure the Appearance and Settings of Your Blog
Blogger has many features for customizing the appearance of a blog. In this tutorial, you will learn to change the appearance and settings of your blog.

Complete these exercises on the blog that you created for this class.

1. Write a short post introducing yourself on your blog. Write about three of your favorite Web sites.

2. Add a photograph of yourself to your blog if you're comfortable doing so.

3. Search the Web for a recent article about a company that uses wikis for collaboration. Write a blog post containing a link to the original article and a summary of its main points in your own words.

4. Use a search engine to find a list of some of the most popular blogs. Add a Links gadget to the sidebar of your blog, and share hyperlinks to two popular blogs with readers of your blog.

These activities encourage you to explore Web 2.0 sites and applications on your own. Submit your responses as directed by your instructor.

1. Perform a Google Blog Search and a Technorati search for the same topic. How similar are the results?

2. Research some of the differences in features between Blogger and WordPress. Write a blog post or speak to what you have learned.

3. If your blog is configured to be indexed by Google, use Google Blog Search to search for a unique keyword or phrase that you wrote in one of your posts, and see whether Google Blog Search or another blog search engine can find it.

4. YouTube provides the ability to record short videos directly from a Webcam as one of the site's options for uploading videos. If you have access to a Webcam, use this feature to create a short video greeting that you upload to YouTube and embed in a new post on your blog. In order to complete this exercise, you will need to create an account on YouTube if you don't already have one, and you will need access to a Webcam.

5. Using Google Sites, PBworks, or one of the other Wiki providers in Table 2-4, set up a wiki for a student organization, group project, or class in which you are involved, and explain to your group the benefits of using it.

6. Use a search engine to find an article about how to create a new article on Wikipedia. Read it and give it a try.

7. Create an account on one of the Web sites that uses wikis listed in Table 2-3. Find its Sandbox page and use it to modify some text.

8. Use the Paint application, on the Windows operating system, or another photo-processing program to resize and save a picture taken from a digital camera in various formats (BMP, GIF, JPG, PNG). Compare the file sizes and quality of the images that result.

Collaborate

If your instructor set up a class wiki, complete these exercises.

1. Add your name, your Google ID (or Gmail address), and the URL of your blog to a roster page that your instructor created on your class wiki.

2. Together with members of your class, write your own Wikipedia-style article about blogs, wikis, Web 2.0, or another topic on a page on the class wiki that your instructor created. Because this is a wiki, you should feel free to edit or rearrange the sentences that your classmates wrote so that the article appears as if one person wrote it. Use the Discussion page to describe why you made the changes you did. Remember that the wiki software keeps track of changes and previous versions of each page, so your instructor will be able to tell exactly what contribution you made to the article and when you made it.

3 | Syndicating Content

Overview

People who regularly follow many different blogs or Web sites may spend a lot of time checking each one to see whether anything has changed since their last visit. One way to simplify this task is to automate the process of checking for new content. By separating the content of a blog or a Web site from the formatting used to display it, that content can be used by various software applications and on many different devices.

Blogs and Web sites can share content using a process known as syndication. **Syndication** is the process of making a summary of a Web site's information available to other Web sites and applications. Syndicated content is delivered to Web sites and applications via a Web feed. A **Web feed** represents the list of items, such as blog posts, news headlines, and other frequently updated Web content, that are being shared. Web feeds make up-to-date content automatically available to people and sites that request it. A Web site that has a Web feed is said to syndicate its content. A Web feed distributed as audio or video is known as a podcast.

Users may interact with syndicated content from their favorite Web sites by using a feed reader application, by using a Web browser or cell phone, or by embedding the content in the sidebar of a blog. **Feed reader** applications and devices access the Web feed of each of the blogs and Web sites that has been subscribed to by the user and deliver any new content. Figure 3-1 on the next page shows the TechCrunch blog and several different ways that users can access its content.

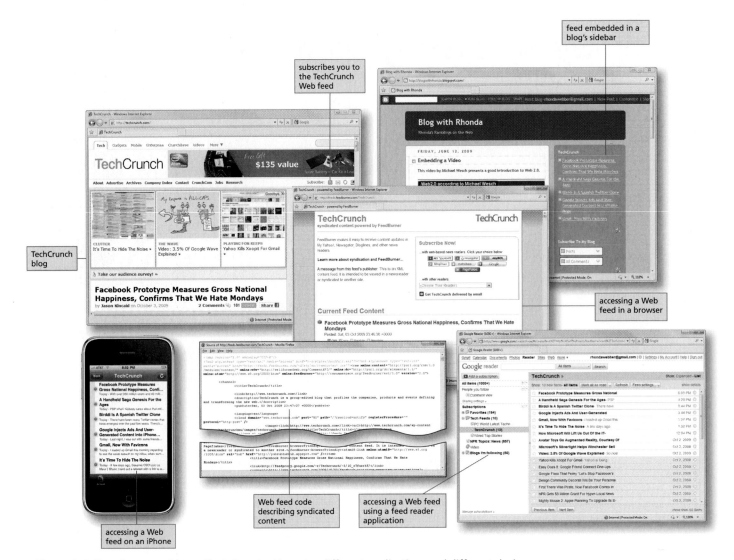

subscribes you to the TechCrunch Web feed

feed embedded in a blog's sidebar

TechCrunch blog

accessing a Web feed in a browser

accessing a Web feed on an iPhone

Web feed code describing syndicated content

accessing a Web feed using a feed reader application

Figure 3-1 Users interact with syndicated content by using different applications and different devices.

The content from the TechCrunch blog is published as a Web feed. Because the Web feed itself is coded in a way that describes just the content without any information as to how it is displayed on the TechCrunch blog, its information may be shared easily on other blogs or viewed in a browser or in a feed reader application. Users may also access Web feeds via feed reader applications running on Internet-enabled cell phones. Web sites that embed syndicated content access the feed and display its information as part of the site.

Exploring Web Feeds

RSS, most commonly known as an acronym for **Really Simple Syndication,** is one of the first and most popular types of Web feeds for syndicating frequently updated Web content. An RSS feed contains a summary of information about the blog or Web site and the list of items that are being syndicated, including the URL, title, author, and publication date of each item. RSS began as a way for news sites to make their stories available for publication on other blogs and Web sites and to facilitate the process for bloggers to follow many blogs without having to manually check for updated content. As syndication became popular, Web sites from news providers to social networks have turned to syndicating content. Web sites that provide feeds usually display an orange Web feed icon, shown in Figure 3-2. Variations on the icon include an orange box with the letters RSS or XML instead of the feed icon.

Figure 3-2 An orange icon is the symbol for Web feeds.

"When people ask me what RSS is, I say it's automated web surfing. We took something lots of people do, visiting sites looking for new stuff, and automated it. It's a very predictable thing, that's what computers do—automate repetitive things."

Dave Winer, Father of RSS

Without syndication, users have to check each of their favorite sites individually to see whether they have been updated, as shown in Figure 3-3. For those who follow more than a few Web sites with regularity, this has the potential to become a time-consuming process.

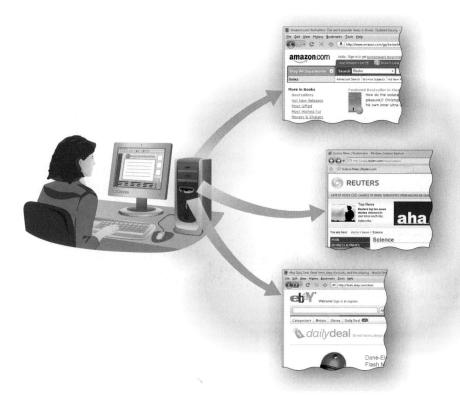

Figure 3-3 Without using feeds, a user has to visit favorite Web sites individually to see what is new.

Users can automate the process of manually checking sites for updates by using a feed reader application. The **publish/subscribe model,** shown in Figure 3-4 on the next page, illustrates how a feed reader application checks a user's subscribed feeds for updated information and ensures that users receive the newly published content to which they subscribe.

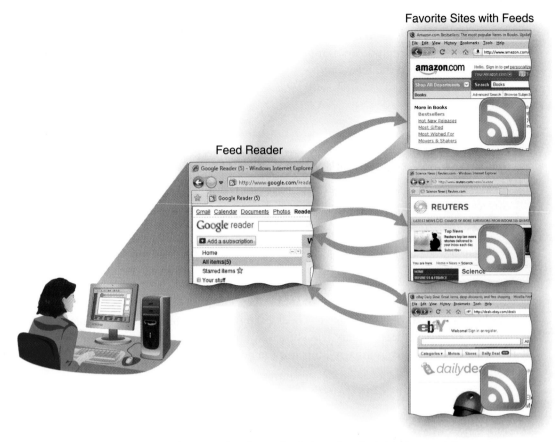

Figure 3-4 Using a feed reader, the user subscribes to feeds from favorite Web sites, and the reader checks for updated content.

The presence of a feed icon in the browser indicates that a site publishes its content using a feed. Clicking on the feed icon provides the user with the URL for the site's feed. Users enter the URLs for the feeds of frequently visited Web sites in a feed reader application in order to subscribe to their content and receive updates when new content is published. Instead of visiting each site in a Web browser, users simply launch a feed reader application such as Google Reader, shown in Figure 3-5, which checks a user's subscribed feeds for updated information.

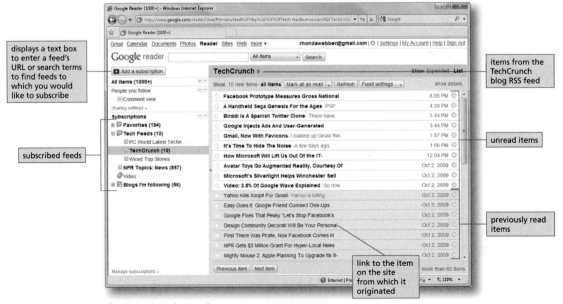

Figure 3-5 Viewing feeds in Google Reader.

The feed reader displays the feed's content by showing links to each of the items on the site from which they originated. Periodically, the feed reader examines the contents of the file given by the feed URL that the user specified. If the feed contains new information, the feed reader downloads the new content.

Finding Feeds

Many bloggers syndicate their blogs' content as Web feeds. Because blog search engines, such as Google Blog Search and Technorati, update their listings based on a blog's Web feed, you can use them to find blogs that syndicate their content. While blog posts are a popular type of syndicated content, Web feeds also deliver other types of frequently updated Web content. Figure 3-6 shows several Web sites that contain feeds.

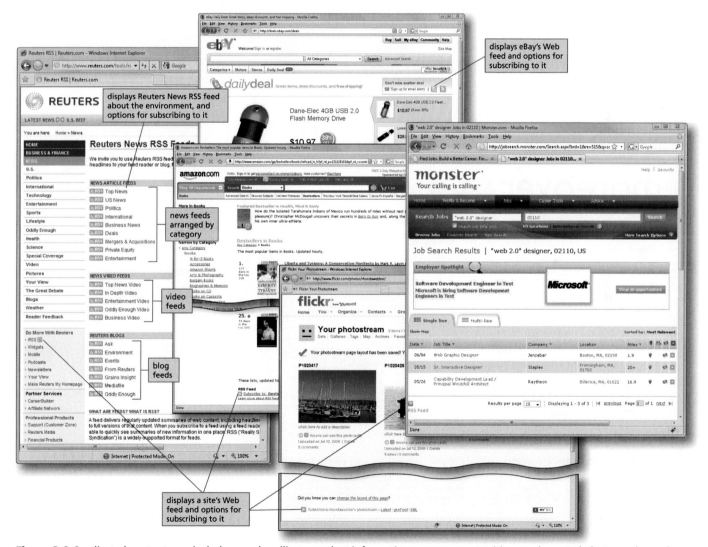

Figure 3-6 Syndicated content may include news headlines, product information, career opportunities, newly posted photographs, and bestselling books.

Users may sign up to receive feed information from a variety of sources. News sites such as Reuters syndicate news headlines. Monster provides an RSS feed with job postings, eBay alerts users of daily deals via Web feeds, and Amazon uses its Web feed to keep users informed about its bestsellers list. Flickr's feed notifies users whenever their friends share a new photo on Flickr. You also can find feeds that are registered with syndicated content directories such as Syndic8 or Moreover, shown in Figure 3-7.

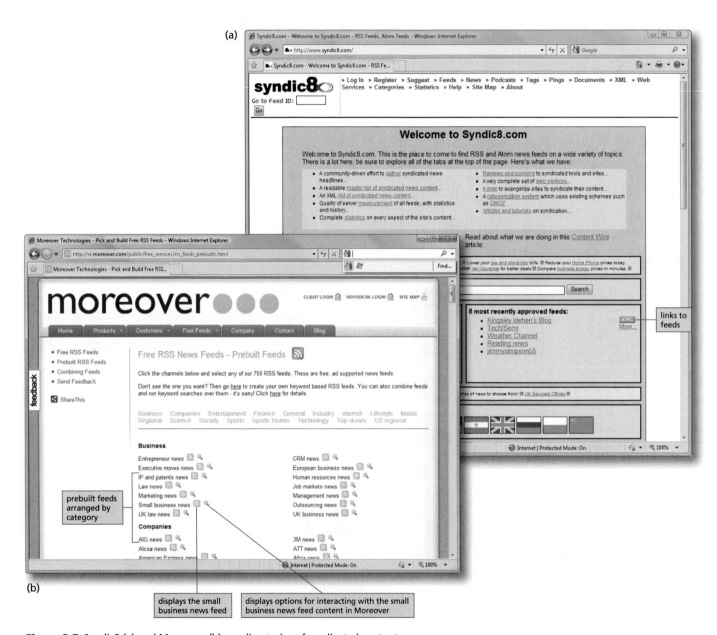

Figure 3-7 Syndic8 (a) and Moreover (b) are directories of syndicated content.

Additionally, some search engines offer the results of a search query as a Web feed. For example, Google News allows users to subscribe to the results of a search query as an RSS feed. Rather than search Google News every day for stories related to the housing market, you can subscribe in your feed reader to a feed containing the results of a Google News search on that topic. The feed reader will automatically access the updated feed content from Google News and display the most recent items. Figure 3-8 shows the results of a Google News search on the term "housing market."

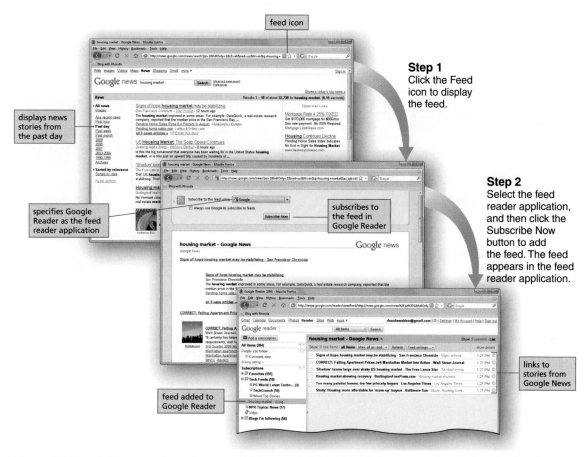

Figure 3-8 Google News search results are available as an RSS feed to which you can subscribe in a feed reader.

To subscribe to the latest news about the housing market, the user enters "housing market" in Google News and subscribes to the feed containing the search results, using Google Reader. The search results are displayed in Google Reader. When the user returns to Google Reader at a later time, Google Reader will check the latest search results about the housing market from Google News.

Subscribing to and Reading Feeds

You can subscribe to and read feeds in many different ways, as shown in Figure 3-9 on the next page. You can read feeds online by using your Web browser or a Web-based feed reader application. You also can embed or view the content of a Web feed on a blog's sidebar by using a Web gadget provided by the blogging application or a third-party developer.

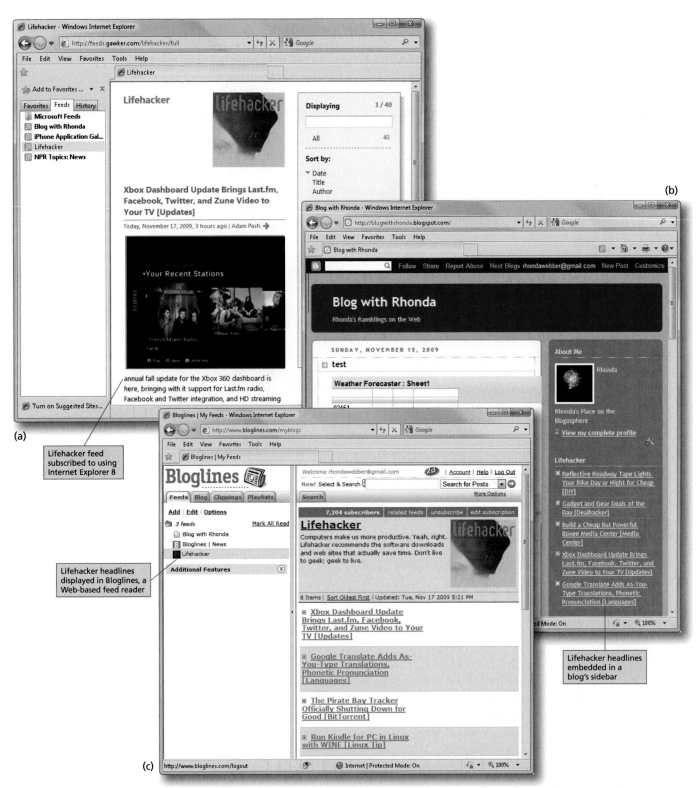

Figure 3-9 Reading feeds in a browser: subscribed feeds in Internet Explorer (a), using the Bloglines Web-based feed reader (b), and embedded in a blog's sidebar (c).

You can also access feeds from a variety of applications installed on devices that are connected to the Internet, as shown in Figure 3-10. For example, you can use a Windows desktop gadget to display content from feeds on your Windows desktop. Many cell phones have feed reader applications that can download and display updated feed content.

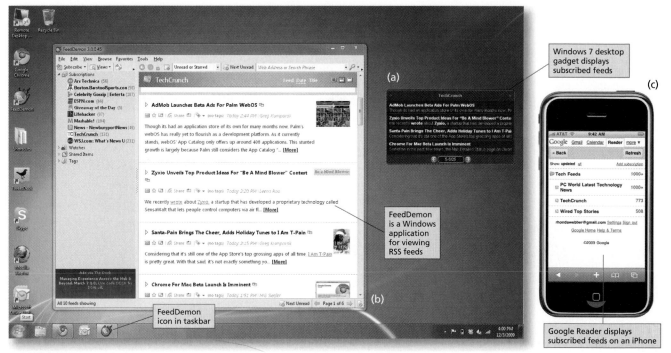

Figure 3-10 Accessing feeds using different applications: a Windows desktop gadget (a), the FeedDemon Windows client application (b), and Google Reader on a mobile phone (c).

Subscribing and Reading Feeds Using a Web Browser

The ability to subscribe to a feed is standard in many Web browsers, although the methods for subscribing may differ. When you subscribe to a feed using a browser, the feed information is stored with the browser on the hard drive of the computer. Subscribing to Web feeds by using a browser is convenient—you do not need to use an additional application to manage your subscribed feeds. One drawback is that your feed subscription information is limited to that specific browser and computer. If you use another computer, you will not be able to access your subscribed feeds unless you subscribe to them again on the new computer.

Every browser visually presents Web feeds differently, even though the list of items being syndicated is the same. This is because the feed itself is represented in **XML** (Extensible Markup Language), which uses code to describe the title, content, and publication date of each item but does not supply instructions for how to display the items. Because the underlying XML does not contain any formatting information, each Web browser applies its own style when displaying feed information. How to understand the XML for a Web feed is described later in this chapter.

SUBSCRIBING USING INTERNET EXPLORER   Internet Explorer has supported Web feeds since version 7. To subscribe to a feed in Internet Explorer, click the Subscribe to this feed link when viewing the feed in the browser. Specify a name and location for the feed, and then click Subscribe. The newly subscribed feed will appear in the list of feeds in the Feeds tab of the Favorites Bar. Internet Explorer includes a task pane that allows you to interact with the data by filtering or sorting its contents, as shown in Figure 3-11.

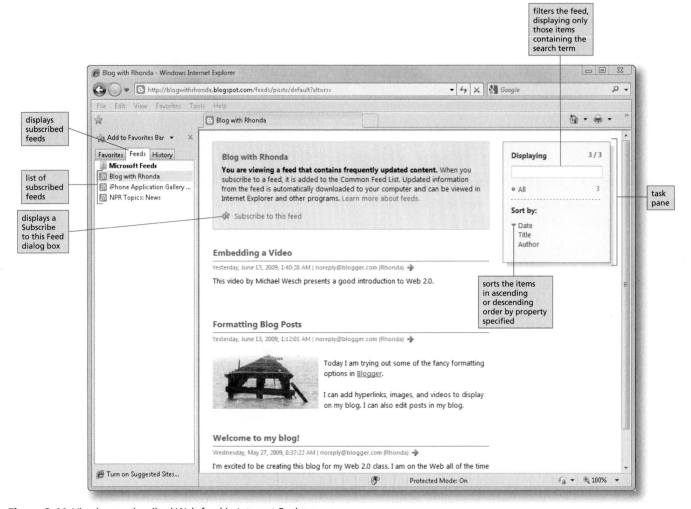

Figure 3-11 Viewing a subscribed Web feed in Internet Explorer.

SUBSCRIBING USING FIREFOX   In Firefox, subscribed feeds are called live bookmarks. Each **live bookmark** is the title of a blog post from the feed, and clicking the live bookmark takes you directly to the permalink of that blog post. Each time that you launch Firefox, it updates live bookmarks automatically by accessing the latest information from the blog or content provider's feed. To subscribe to a feed as a live bookmark in Firefox, click the Subscribe Now button when viewing the feed in the browser. Firefox will display a dialog box asking you to choose whether to add the bookmark to the Bookmarks Menu or Bookmarks Toolbar. If you select the Toolbar, Firefox displays feed items in the Bookmarks Toolbar, as shown in Figure 3-12.

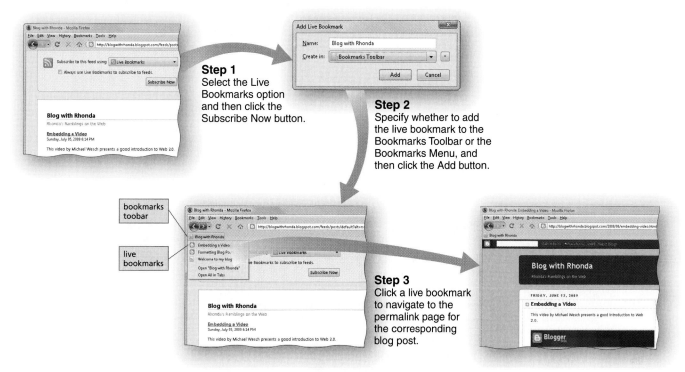

Step 1
Select the Live Bookmarks option and then click the Subscribe Now button.

Step 2
Specify whether to add the live bookmark to the Bookmarks Toolbar or the Bookmarks Menu, and then click the Add button.

bookmarks toobar

live bookmarks

Step 3
Click a live bookmark to navigate to the permalink page for the corresponding blog post.

Figure 3-12 Viewing a subscribed Web feed in Firefox as a live bookmark.

SUBSCRIBING USING SAFARI Apple's Safari browser also supports Web feeds. When you view a feed in Safari, a sidebar offers options for searching, sorting, and filtering items in the feed, as shown in Figure 3-13. Safari's sidebar is similar to the task pane found in Internet Explorer. To subscribe to a feed in Safari, add it as you would add any bookmark, using the Add Bookmark option.

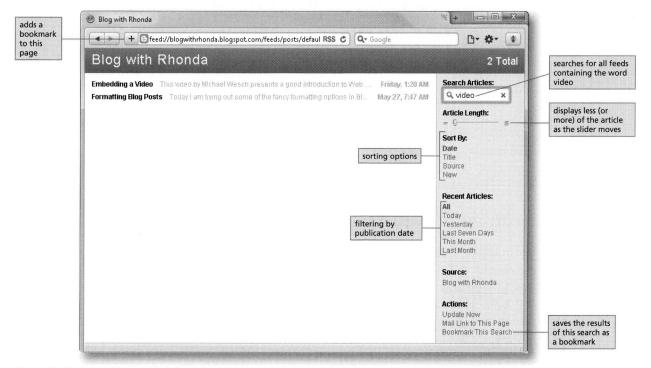

adds a bookmark to this page

searches for all feeds containing the word video

displays less (or more) of the article as the slider moves

sorting options

filtering by publication date

saves the results of this search as a bookmark

Figure 3-13 Subscribing to Web feeds in Safari.

Some Web browsers display a feed icon in the address bar if a Web site offers a Web feed. Clicking the feed icon gives you options for subscribing to each feed, as shown in Figure 3-14.

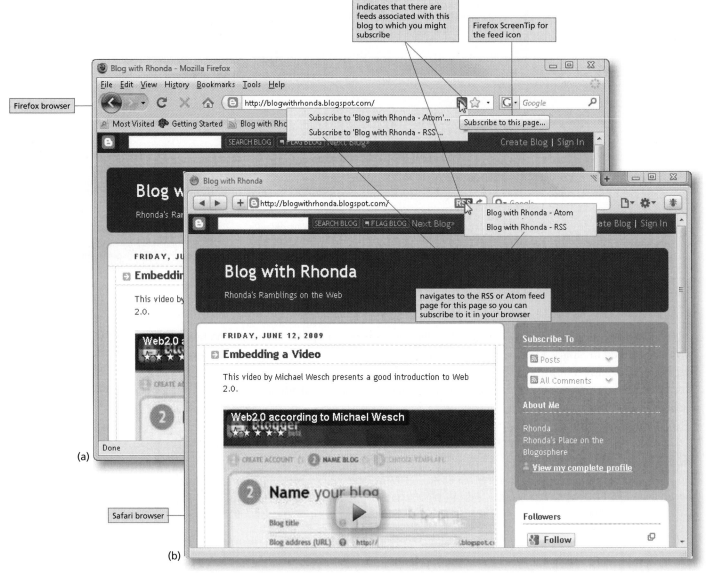

Figure 3-14 Discovering Web feeds in Firefox (a) and Safari (b).

Features of Web-Based and Client Feed Readers

Feed reader applications allow you to subscribe to feeds and manage the posts that you have read. Web-based feed readers, such as Google Reader, shown in Figure 3-15, are popular because all of the feed information is stored online and is, therefore, available on any computer or mobile device with a browser and an Internet connection. Client feed readers, which are applications installed on a laptop or desktop computer, store feed information locally.

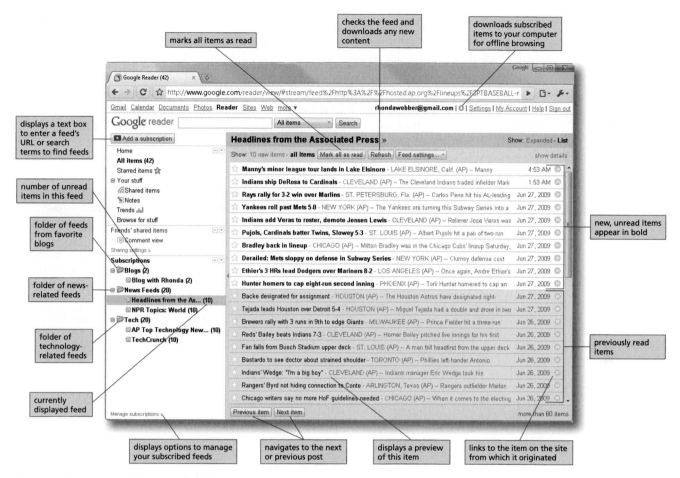

Figure 3-15 Features of Google Reader.

To subscribe to a feed using a feed reader application, enter the feed's URL in a dialog box, often labeled Add or Subscribe to a feed. Once you have subscribed to a feed, the feed reader usually will display a content summary containing the title and the first few lines of the description. If you are interested in reading more, click the title of the item to access the complete article.

Feed readers manage the content that you have read and have yet to read. The titles of new unread content are displayed in bold. Once new content has been read, the article's title is no longer displayed in bold. If the number of unread items in your reader is overwhelming, you can choose to mark everything as read. To read an article in Google Reader, click the title for a preview or the double arrow icon to navigate to the Web site from which it originated.

Feed readers also can display content from multiple feeds, which allows you to quickly scan information contained within each feed. To assist with feed management, you can use folders to group related feeds. You might have one folder for feeds from news sites and another from favorite blogs.

Cell phones, client feed readers, and some Web-based feed reader applications may be configured to download new information from your subscribed feeds directly to your device so that you can read them without having to be connected to the Internet. This feature is called **offline browsing**. Some features, such as adding new subscriptions, may not work if there is no Internet access. Feed reader applications usually will download only text content; images and video will not be available without Internet access. Some feed readers will mark articles that you read while offline and update your account with this information when you go back online.

WEB-BASED FEED READERS   Web-based feed reader applications, such as Google Reader or Bloglines, give you access to your feeds within a browser window. You first must create an account in order to use a Web-based feed reader. Many feed reader applications support similar features: adding and searching for feeds, suggesting sample feeds to which you might want to subscribe, organizing feeds in folders, and tracking the items that you have and have not yet read. Each of these Web-based applications also allows you to view your feeds with a cell phone. In addition to these standard features, Table 3-1 summarizes some of the features of popular Web-based feed reader applications.

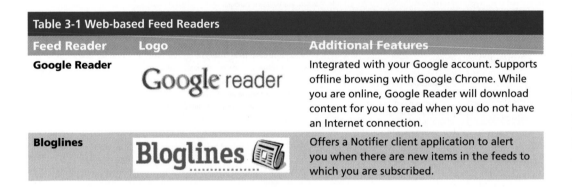

Table 3-1 Web-based Feed Readers		
Feed Reader	**Logo**	**Additional Features**
Google Reader	Google reader	Integrated with your Google account. Supports offline browsing with Google Chrome. While you are online, Google Reader will download content for you to read when you do not have an Internet connection.
Bloglines	Bloglines	Offers a Notifier client application to alert you when there are new items in the feeds to which you are subscribed.

Google Reader also has a feed-searching capability that assists users in finding feeds, shown in Figure 3-16.

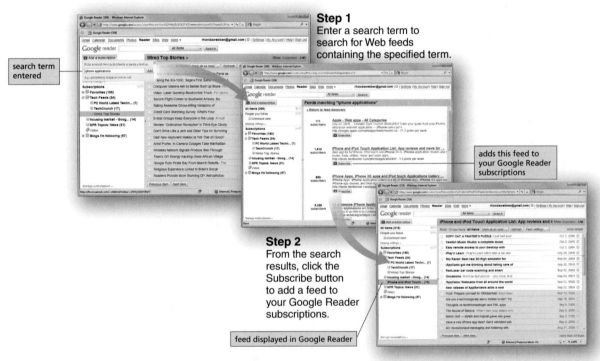

Figure 3-16 Searching for feeds in Google Reader.

If you do not know the exact URL for a feed to which you would like to subscribe, you can enter a search term in the Add a Subscription box, and Google Reader will suggest feeds related to the search term to which you could subscribe.

CLIENT FEED READERS In addition to subscribing to a feed using a browser or a browser-based reader, you can also download a feed reader program and install it on your computer. FeedDemon, FeedReader, and Microsoft Outlook are three popular client feed reader applications. In addition to standard features of feed readers discussed earlier, some client feed readers automatically can download the associated images and text to your computer so that you can browse the feeds when you do not have an Internet connection. Table 3-2 summarizes some of the features of popular client feed reader applications.

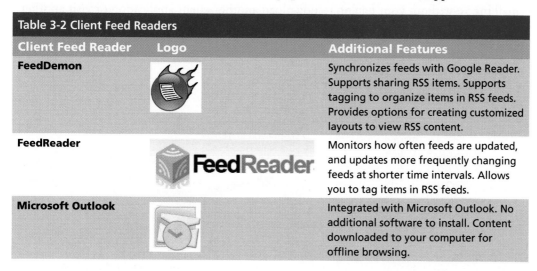

Table 3-2 Client Feed Readers		
Client Feed Reader	**Logo**	**Additional Features**
FeedDemon		Synchronizes feeds with Google Reader. Supports sharing RSS items. Supports tagging to organize items in RSS feeds. Provides options for creating customized layouts to view RSS content.
FeedReader		Monitors how often feeds are updated, and updates more frequently changing feeds at shorter time intervals. Allows you to tag items in RSS feeds.
Microsoft Outlook		Integrated with Microsoft Outlook. No additional software to install. Content downloaded to your computer for offline browsing.

FeedDemon is a popular free feed reader application for the Windows operating system and is available for downloading from the NewsGator Web site. FeedDemon has many of the same features as a Web-based feed reader. Although FeedDemon, shown Figure 3-17, is installed locally, it can synchronize your subscribed feeds with instances of FeedDemon running on other computers, as well as with Google Reader.

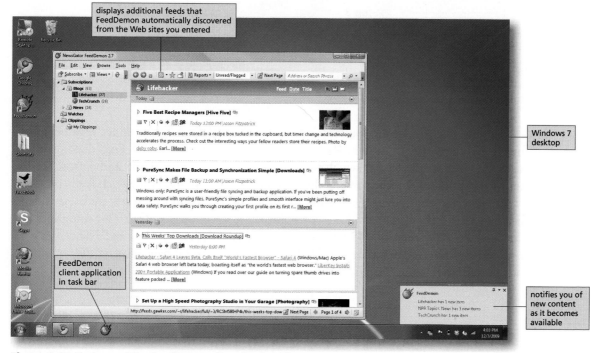

Figure 3-17 Features of the FeedDemon client feed reader.

The FeedDemon client application regularly polls your subscribed feeds and alerts you when new content is available by displaying a notification message in the lower corner of your Windows desktop. Because FeedDemon is an application installed on your computer, you can access it from the icon in the taskbar on the Windows desktop when it is running.

You also can subscribe to Web feeds within Microsoft Outlook, shown in Figure 3-18. Microsoft has included feed reader capabilities in Outlook since Outlook 2007. An advantage to subscribing to Web feeds from within Outlook is that they appear within your e-mail inbox, without your having to download another client application or visit another Web site. Outlook checks the feed periodically and downloads new items as they become available.

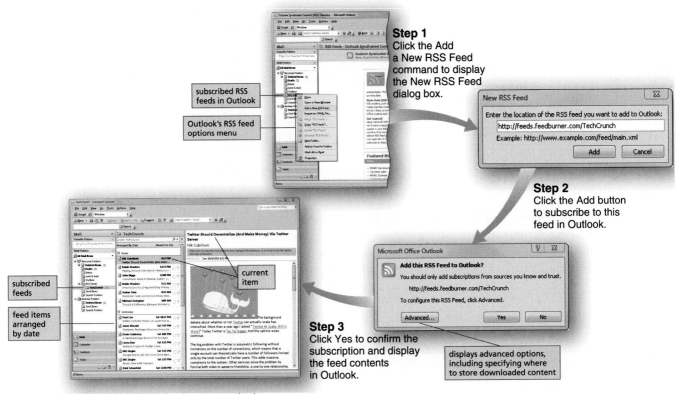

Figure 3-18 Subscribing to RSS feeds using Outlook.

To subscribe to a feed in Outlook, right-click the RSS feeds folder under your personal folders and select the Add a New RSS Feed command. In the New RSS Feed dialog box, enter the URL for the feed to which you want to subscribe and click the Add button. Advanced options include specifying the location on your computer to which feed content will be delivered and specifying whether to automatically download images, audio, or video files associated with feed items. After reviewing these selections, confirm your subscription. The feed will appear in the RSS feeds folder in the far-left pane of Outlook. The center pane contains the feed items arranged by date, and the far-right pane displays the content of the selected feed item.

You can search the Web to find additional client feed reader applications that run on various operating systems, including Windows, Mac OS X, and Linux, and cell phones, including Blackberry, Android, and iPhone. Although client feed readers all offer the same basic functionality, their user interfaces will differ. The data that feed reader applications display is the same regardless of whether you subscribe to Web feeds using a browser, a Web-based application, a client application, or a cell phone. One feed reader application is not necessarily better than another; how you choose to interact with feeds is a matter of personal preference based on your individual needs and working style.

Embedding Feed Content in Blogs and Web Sites

Blogs can display syndicated content from a Web feed by using sidebar gadgets. You can configure a feed gadget by specifying the feed's URL, the number of items to display, and appearance options such as feed title, font, and color. When the blog containing the gadget is loaded or refreshed, the gadget will access, format, and display the latest syndicated content from the feed. Figure 3-19 shows a sidebar gadget that displays items from the Associated Press News Headlines Web feed. The title of each item in the Web feed is a hyperlink to the article on the blog where the content originally appeared.

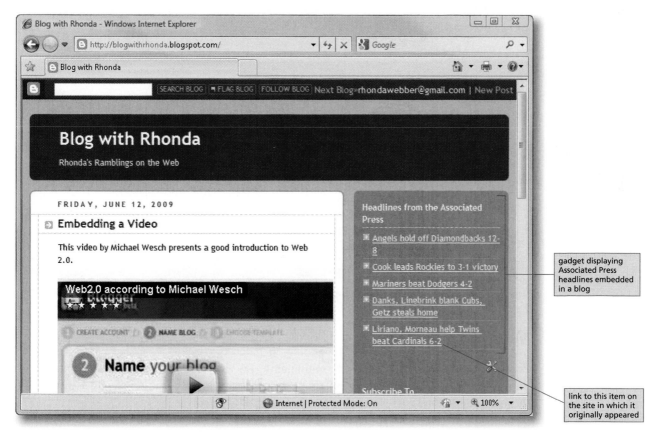

Figure 3-19 A blog with embedded feed content.

Publishing Web Feeds

Bloggers may configure their blogs to generate a Web feed. Blogger defaults to automatically creating feeds for the blogs that it hosts. Blogger also defaults to syndicating the full content of each post, rather than only the first paragraph, as shown in the Site Feed page under the Blogger Settings tab (Figure 3-20). As a result, the entire post will be available in the user's feed reader. Some blogs that often contain very lengthy posts will opt to syndicate only the first paragraph of each post.

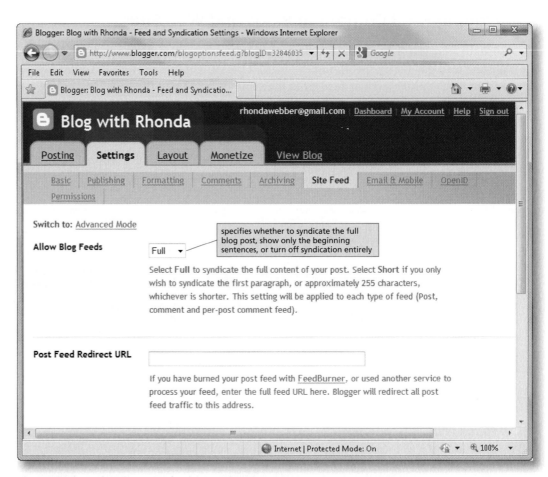

Figure 3-20 Configuring a site feed using Blogger.

Managed Feeds

Professional bloggers often use a feed-managing service such as FeedBurner to publish their feeds and provide information about how users interact with their feeds. Figure 3-21 shows a blog and its corresponding feed, managed by FeedBurner.

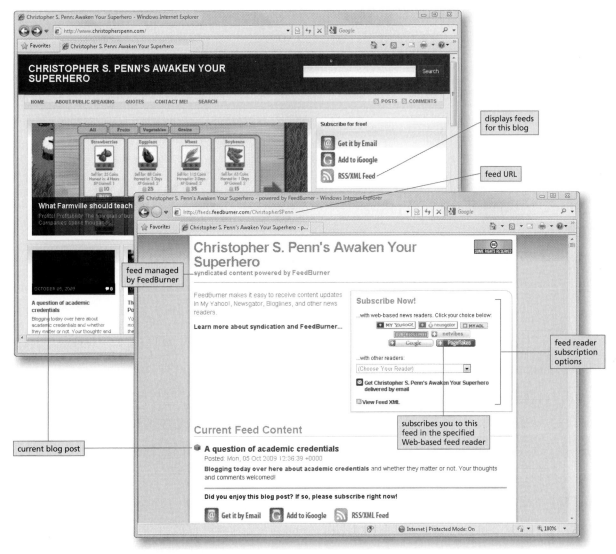

Figure 3-21 Subscribing to a managed feed.

Feed managing services regularly update Web feeds as bloggers publish new content to their blogs, and they simplify the process of subscribing to a feed when using a Web-based feed reader. FeedBurner offers several Web-based feed readers from which you can choose to subscribe to a feed. To subscribe to a managed feed using a Web-based reader, select the desired feed reader listed under the Subscribe Now section of the feed page. To subscribe to the feed using a feed reader that is not listed, enter the feed URL in the feed reader application as you would when subscribing to any feed using that application.

Feed-managing services also provide content producers with **metrics**, or quantitative results from periodically measuring and assessing Web traffic and usage, that summarize how users interact with a feed's content. Most bloggers want to know how many people subscribe to their feeds, because increased readership may also mean increased revenue if a blog displays advertisements. Under the Analyze tab shown in Figure 3-22 on the next page, FeedBurner informs bloggers of their blog's **reach**, which is a term used to describe the total number of people who have viewed or clicked on the content in a blog. A higher reach suggests that users are actually reading and engaging with blog content and not simply skimming it.

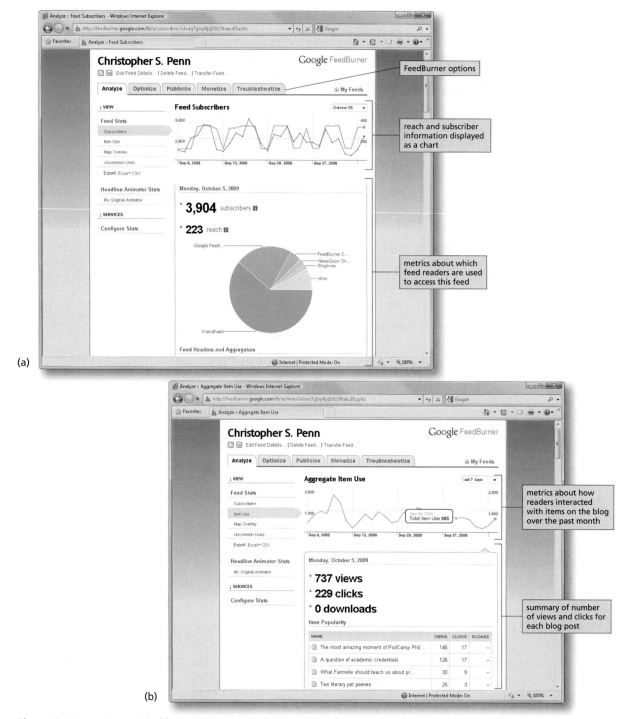

Figure 3-22 Metrics provided by FeedBurner include the number of subscribers (a) and which items have been viewed (b).

Some users may view a blog's content without actually subscribing to it because they found it via a blog search engine or because it appeared in a blog's sidebar. These users are also included in the measurement of a blog's readership. FeedBurner also provides metrics about the various Web-based feed reader applications that are used to access this feed. For individual blog posts, FeedBurner measures the number of views, the number of times that an individual blog post was displayed, the number of times a user clicked on a link within a post, and the number of clicks that each blog post received over a period of time. FeedBurner also provides the URLs of the referring pages from which users accessed the single blog post.

In addition to these capabilities bundled under FeedBurner's Analyze tab, the Optimize tab gives options for displaying a feed with easy subscription options using a variety of feed reader applications. The Publicize tab provides services for content publishers to add custom logos and provides gadgets to facilitate subscribing to a blog using a variety of readers. The Monetize tab provides instructions for activating Google AdSense to include ads as part of the Web feed. The Troubleshootize tab gives hints for correcting problems, for example, if FeedBurner does not update the feed file correctly after new content is posted.

Using a feed-managing service can provide simplified functionality for the user and valuable metrics for the professional blogger as to how users are interacting with their feeds.

Web Feeds Incorporated into Applications

A variety of Web-based applications incorporate data from Web feeds to present it visually in ways that traditional feed readers cannot. For example, news maps, such as the one shown in Figure 3-23, display information from news feeds on a map. These sites rely on an extension of RSS, called GeoRSS, that adds geographical location information (latitude and longitude coordinates) to items in an RSS feed.

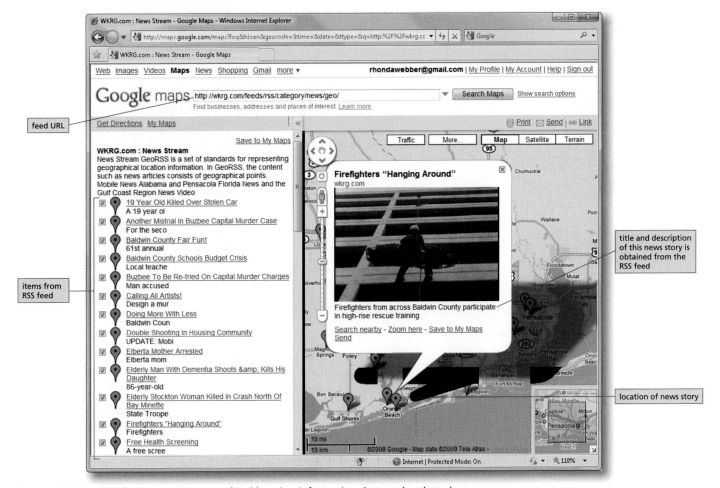

Figure 3-23 GeoRSS feeds contain geographical location information that can be plotted on a map.

Alltop is a feed reader application that visually displays content from Web feeds in a magazine format. The site relies on RSS without requiring the user to know anything about it. After creating an account on Alltop, users may create a personal MyAlltop page to display feeds of interest selected from among the hundreds of feeds that Alltop monitors. Alternatively, users may view popular content from feeds taken from all over the Web. Figure 3-24 shows the MyAlltop page with feeds selected by Dave Winer, who is considered to be the father of RSS.

Figure 3-24 Dave Winer's MyAlltop page.

Alltop provides a rich user experience for reading feed content. Placing the cursor over a headline title displays the first few sentences of the news story or blog post. You can click the title to read the story on the site from which the story originated or click the feed title to visit the feed's Web site. To ensure that only actively updated content is displayed on Alltop, the site monitors updates to all of the feeds that it follows and removes those feeds that have not been updated within four weeks.

Formats for Web Feeds

The information contained in an RSS feed and how it is represented has evolved since RSS was first developed in 1999. The most widely used version of RSS is called RSS 2.0. The creators of RSS declared RSS closed to further modifications so that developers could continue to write applications using this specification and to promote RSS as a technology for syndicating content. Because there would be no further enhancements to the RSS format after version 2.0, the door was opened for others to create new syndication formats that might be able to implement additional features.

As blogging and the use of syndicated content gained popularity, some limitations were found in the RSS format. **Atom** is a newer, evolving, open source format that is an alternative to RSS. First developed in 2003, Atom builds on the ideas behind RSS, but also provides a way to identify additional information not found in RSS feeds.

RSS and Atom are two different formats used to syndicate content. RSS is simpler, well known, and has a history of wider use; Atom is becoming popular because it was designed to syndicate content across many operating systems, browsers, and devices. As an open source format, Atom is supported by a community that advocates for its continued development.

The distinction between the RSS and Atom feed formats typically is transparent to the user. In fact, many applications for reading feeds (such as Google Reader) and applications for generating feeds (such as Blogger and WordPress) support both formats. For example, WordPress defaults to the RSS format to syndicate blog content but allows Atom syndication as an option. Google's Blogger uses the newer Atom format by default but offers the RSS format as an option. Many content producers, such as the *New York Times*, also syndicate their content in both formats, as shown in Figure 3-25.

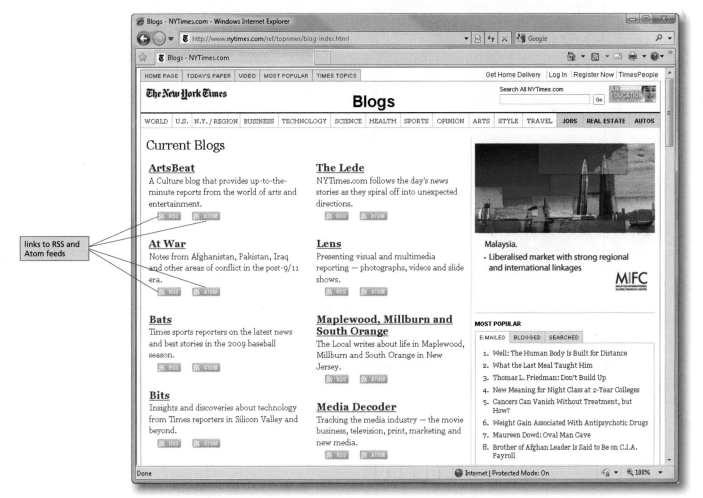

Figure 3-25 The *New York Times* syndicates blog content in both RSS and Atom formats.

Finding Your Blog's RSS and Atom Feeds

You can find the URL of the RSS feed for a Blogger blog by appending
`/feeds/posts/default?alt=rss` to the blog's URL. To find the URL for the
Atom feed for a Blogger blog, append `/feeds/posts/default?alt=atom` to the
blog's URL. Figure 3-26 shows the RSS feed for a Blogger blog. Other than a different
ending to its feed URL, the Atom feed looks exactly the same when displayed in the
browser. Only the underlying XML is different, as the next section explains.

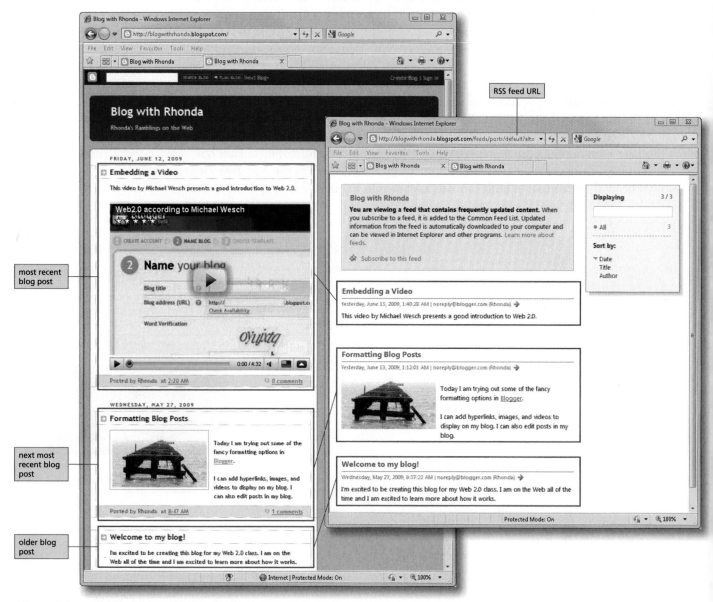

Figure 3-26 A Blogger blog and its RSS feed.

Representing Web Feeds in XML

XML (Extensible Markup Language) is the underlying technology used for describing content syndicated using RSS and Atom feeds. XML uses descriptive keywords, or **tags**, to describe information. Both RSS and Atom follow a set of rules that specify the names and sequence of XML tags used to describe their content. In XML, as in HTML, tags are special keywords placed between angle brackets (for example, `<title>`) that describe a piece of information. Like HTML, each piece of information is preceded by an **opening tag** and is followed by a **closing tag**. A closing tag is specified by a slash before the tag name, such as `</title>`. Whereas HTML tags, such as `<b>` for bold and `<p>` for paragraph, specify how to display content in a Web browser, XML tags such as `<pubDate>`, used to identify a publication date, describe data but do not offer formatting instructions.

To view the underlying XML of an RSS feed, right-click in the browser window and select View Source or View Page Source. Firefox displays the XML in the browser as one very long line of text. XML-formatted data is intended for software applications, not humans, to read and process. Software applications such as feed readers and sidebar gadgets that display syndicated content rely on XML as the format for describing and sharing information between applications.

The Structure of RSS and Atom Feeds

RSS and Atom feeds are the most common types of content represented in XML. Understanding their internal structure provides additional insights into the relationship between the feed and the origin of the data that it contains and into how feeds may be used to share data with both client and Web applications on a variety of devices.

Figure 3-27 illustrates some of the XML tags and the relationship between them used to represent RSS feeds. Every RSS feed, whether it describes blog posts, news headlines, or job postings on Monster.com, is described using these tags.

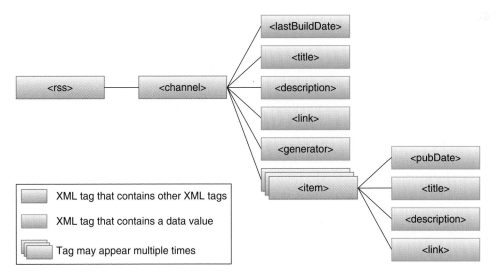

Figure 3-27 Tags used in the structure of an RSS feed.

The structure of an XML document must follow strict rules in order for other applications to make use of its data. Figure 3-28 shows how this structure is implemented in XML for an RSS feed. To make the XML easier to read, the text has been reformatted by adding color to the tag names and by aligning the pairs of beginning and ending tags. Some less common tags also have been omitted for clarity.

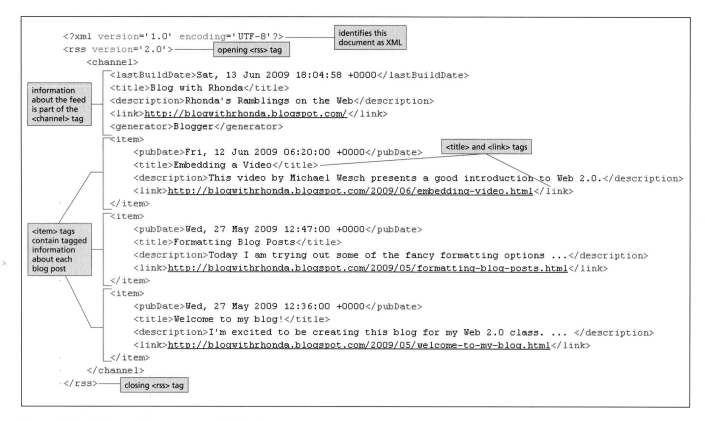

Figure 3-28 XML is used to represent an RSS feed.

The file begins with an `<?xml>` declaration specifying that the contents of the file are given in XML. The `<rss>` tag indicates that this feed is in RSS format. The tags between `<rss>` and `</rss>` describe the feed. In XML, tags such as `<title>` and `<link>` simply contain the information that they describe, whereas other tags, such as `<item>`, enclose tags themselves. The `<channel>` tag, which appears once in a feed, contains information about the feed's last build date (when it was last generated), title, description, and link as well as the name of the Web application that generated the XML for the feed. The `<channel>` tag also contains a list of items, each given by its own `<item>` tag, describing the publication date, title, description, and link for each item in the feed.

In the XML of a Web feed, the presence of the `<feed>` tag indicates that a feed is in Atom format. Figure 3-29 illustrates some of the XML tags and the relationship between them used to represent Atom feeds.

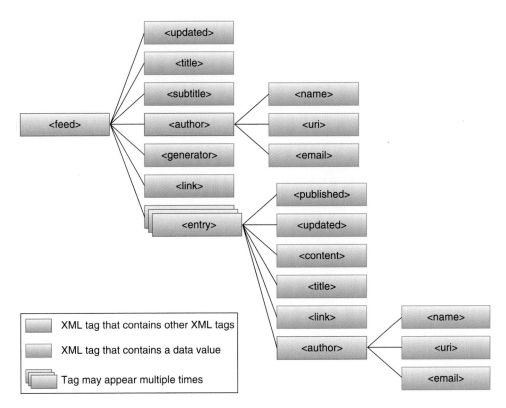

Figure 3-29 The structure of an Atom feed.

As with the RSS feed format, the XML tags between `<feed>` and `</feed>` represent information about the feed itself and each entry, or item, that the feed contains. Atom uses a different set of tags to convey information about syndicated content than does RSS. The additional tags defined for Atom feeds enable it to represent more complex information than is possible using the RSS format. Figure 3-30 on the next page shows how this structure is implemented in XML for an Atom feed. Some optional tags have been removed for clarity.

```
identifies
this
document
as XML ─────────── <?xml version="1.0" encoding="utf-8"?>
                  <feed xmlns='http://www.w3.org/2005/Atom'>
<feed> tag            <updated>2009-06-13T14:04:58.426-04:00</updated>
identifies            <title type='text'>Blog with Rhonda</title>
this feed as          <subtitle type='html'>Rhonda's Ramblings on the Web</subtitle>
an Atom-              <link rel='alternate' type='text/html' href='http://blogwithrhonda.blogspot.com/'/>
formatted             <author>
feed                      <name>Rhonda</name>
                          <uri>http://www.blogger.com/profile/06881506583152915864</uri>      <author> tags contains
<feed> tag                <email>noreply@blogger.com</email>                                  information about the
contains              </author>                                                               content's author
other                 <generator version='7.00' uri='http://www.blogger.com'>Blogger</generator>
tags with             <entry>
information               <published>2009-06-12T02:20:00.004-04:00</published>
about the                 <updated>2009-06-13T01:40:28.411-04:00</updated>
feed                      <title type='text'>Embedding a Video</title>
                          <content type='html'>This video by Michael Wesch presents a good introduction to Web 2.0. ... </content>
                          <link rel='alternate' type='text/html'
                              href='http://blogwithrhonda.blogspot.com/2009/06/embedding-a-video.html'
                              title='Embedding a Video'/>
                          <author>
                              <name>Rhonda</name>
                              <uri>http://www.blogger.com/profile/06881506583152915864</uri>
                              <email>noreply@blogger.com</email>
                          </author>
                      </entry>
                      <entry>
                          <published>2009-05-27T08:47:00.008-04:00</published>
                          <updated>2009-06-13T01:12:01.247-04:00</updated>
                          <title type='text'>Formatting Blog Posts</title>
<entry> tags,             <content type='html'>Today I am trying out some of the fancy formatting options ...</content>
enclosed in               <link rel='alternate' type='text/html'
the <feed>                    href='http://blogwithrhonda.blogspot.com/2009/05/formatting-blog-posts.html'
tag, contain                  title='Formatting Blog Posts'/>
tagged                    <author>
information                   <name>Rhonda</name>
about each                    <uri>http://www.blogger.com/profile/06881506583152915864</uri>
blog post                 </author>
                      </entry>
                      <entry>
                          <published>2009-05-27T08:36:00.001-04:00</published>
                          <updated>2009-05-27T08:37:22.991-04:00</updated>
                          <title type='text'>Welcome to my blog!</title>
                          <content type='html'>I'm excited to be creating this blog for my Web 2.0 class. ...</content>
                          <link rel='alternate' type='text/html'
                              href='http://blogwithrhonda.blogspot.com/2009/05/welcome-to-my-blog.html'
                              title='Welcome to my blog!'/>
                          <author>
                              <name>Rhonda</name>
                              <uri>http://www.blogger.com/profile/06881506583152915864</uri>
                              <email>noreply@blogger.com</email>
                          </author>
                      </entry>
                  </feed>
```

Figure 3-30 XML is used to represent an Atom feed.

Exploring Podcasts

A **podcast** is a series of audio or video files that are broadcast to a computer or personal media player over the Internet by publication in an RSS feed. A single episode of a podcast series also is called a podcast. Users subscribe to a podcast series by using a

podcast reader application, sometimes called a podcatcher or media aggregator, to manage their subscriptions. Apple's iTunes, shown in Figure 3-31, is a popular podcast reader application that allows you to download and manage your podcast subscriptions.

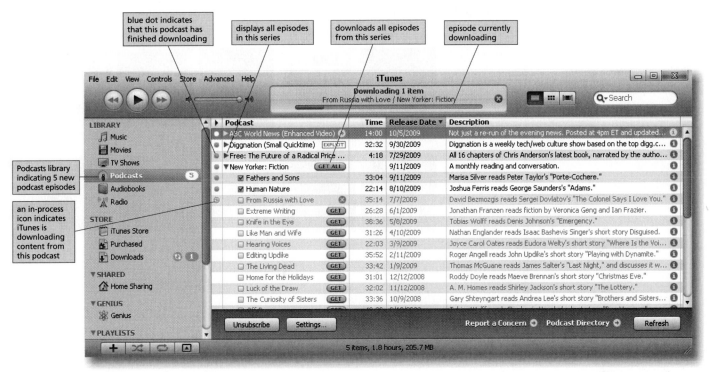

Figure 3-31 Subscribing to podcasts in iTunes.

Your subscribed podcasts can be found in the Podcasts library in iTunes. iTunes downloads audio or video content to your computer and tracks which episodes have been listened to or viewed.

Podcasting became popular at the same time that personal media players such as Apple's iPod were becoming the preferred portable device for listening to music. Although the term podcast was inspired by the popularity of the iPod, podcast sometimes is defined as an acronym for "Personal On Demand broadcast." Once personal media players developed the capability to display video, podcasting became a natural format for distributing video content on a small screen. You do not need to have an iPod in order to view or subscribe to podcasts. Manufacturers of many portable media players, such as the iPod and the Zune, provide online podcast directories, as shown in Figure 3-32 on the next page, for users to select podcasts from to download and synchronize with their devices.

Figure 3-32 Zune users can select podcasts from the Zune Web site.

You can download and watch or listen to podcast episodes directly from the Web site on which they are posted, or you can use Web-based applications to listen to, view, and manage your podcast subscriptions. If you watch or listen to podcasts on your computer, you need to have a media player application, such as Windows Media Player or Quick-Time, installed. Podcast files are usually stored in a compressed format, such as MP3 for audio or MP4 for video.

Podcasting has changed the way that many people think about multimedia. In contrast to audio and video offerings from traditional media and entertainment companies, podcasts provide content to watch whenever you want and wherever you are. The tools for creating and publishing podcasts are readily available. Although specialized recording equipment produces better results, an amateur can create an audio or video file of reasonable quality for a podcast by using a cell phone, digital camera, or video camera that fits in a shirt pocket. Multimedia files can be stored online for free or at a low cost.

Podcasting has become a channel for both traditional and new media to broadcast to their listeners and viewers, as shown in Figure 3-33. Traditional media outlets such as National Public Radio and ABC News make audio or video editions of their broadcasts available—in part or in their entirety—as podcasts for viewers to listen to and watch on demand. The creators of Digg, a news-ranking Web site, host the weekly DiggNation podcast, featuring highlights of articles posted on Digg each week.

Figure 3-33 A variety of podcasts are available featuring both new and traditional media sources: NPR (a) and ABC (b) make their news broadcasts available as podcasts, and DiggNation (c) is a podcast based on the Digg news ranking Web site.

Features of Podcast Readers

Like a feed reader application, a podcast reader simplifies the process of checking each podcast to which you are subscribed to see whether new audio or video content is available. Client podcast readers installed on your computer, such as iTunes, will download to your computer's hard drive the multimedia content for the podcasts to which you are subscribed and can then synchronize this content with your portable media player. Figure 3-34 illustrates the process of subscribing to and downloading podcasts using a client podcast reader such as iTunes.

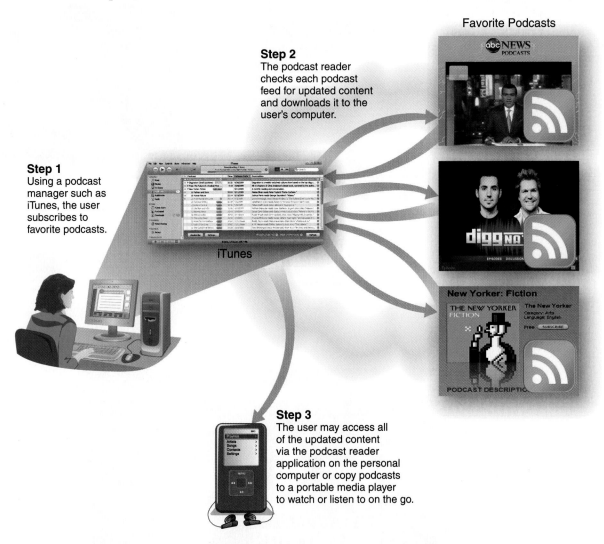

Step 2
The podcast reader checks each podcast feed for updated content and downloads it to the user's computer.

Step 1
Using a podcast manager such as iTunes, the user subscribes to favorite podcasts.

iTunes

Favorite Podcasts

Step 3
The user may access all of the updated content via the podcast reader application on the personal computer or copy podcasts to a portable media player to watch or listen to on the go.

Figure 3-34 Podcast readers automatically check for new content and download it to your computer.

Each time that your portable media player is connected to your computer, the software that manages your music and other multimedia content can also copy podcast files to it. By synchronizing a portable media player with your desktop podcast reader, your portable media player will always have the latest episodes for you to watch or listen to on the go.

SUBSCRIBING WITH CLIENT PODCAST READERS You can find podcasts to subscribe to through content provider Web sites and online podcast directory sites, as well as the Apple iTunes Store. Unlike music or videos, which often must be purchased, subscribing to podcasts is almost always free.

Apple iTunes, shown in Figure 3-35, is a popular client podcast reader that must be installed on your computer before you can subscribe to or watch podcasts. iTunes also synchronizes content with Apple's iPod and iPhone media players.

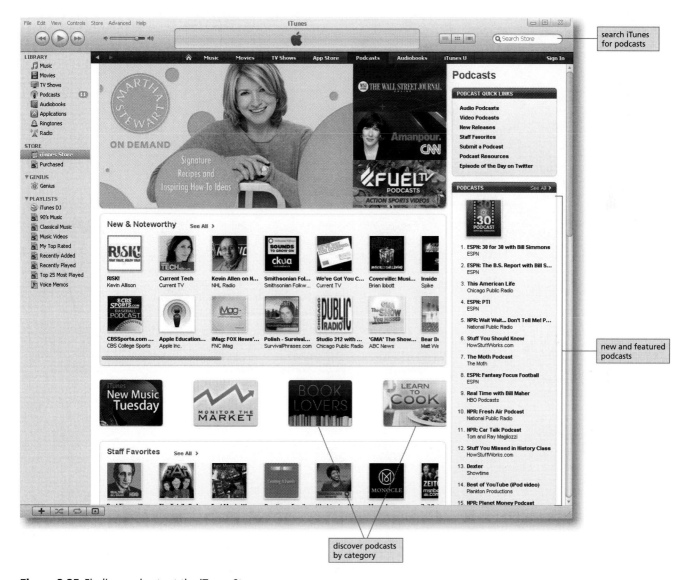

Figure 3-35 Finding podcasts at the iTunes Store.

New and featured podcasts are displayed on the front page of the Podcasts tab in iTunes. You can search iTunes for specific podcasts of interest or browse the site to find podcasts by category. After selecting a podcast or category of podcasts, you can subscribe to the entire series or select individual episodes of the podcast to download from the podcast's details page in iTunes, as shown in Figure 3-36.

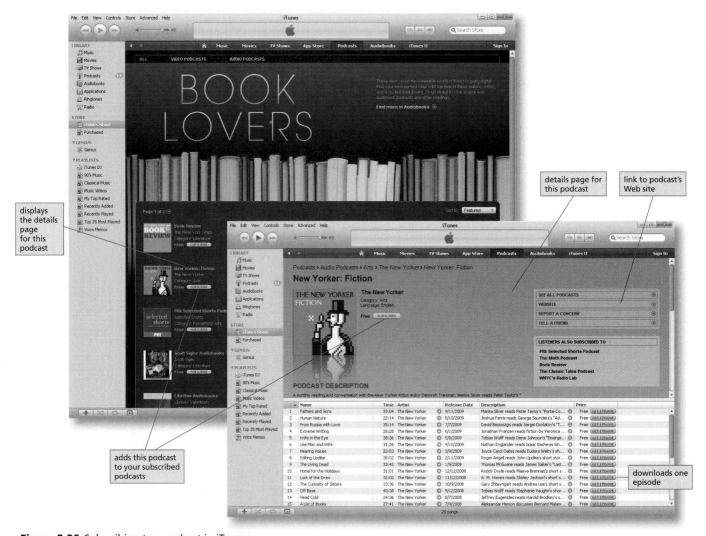

Figure 3-36 Subscribing to a podcast in iTunes.

When you subscribe to a podcast, you give iTunes permission to access the podcast's multimedia files and download them to your computer. Each time that you launch iTunes, it will automatically check the podcasts to which you are subscribed and download any new episodes. You can manually subscribe to the podcast whether or not it is included in the podcasts section of the iTunes store, as shown in Figure 3-37.

Figure 3-37 Subscribe to a podcast manually in iTunes.

Some client feed readers, such as FeedDemon, shown in Figure 3-38, include support for podcasts and will synchronize with various personal media players.

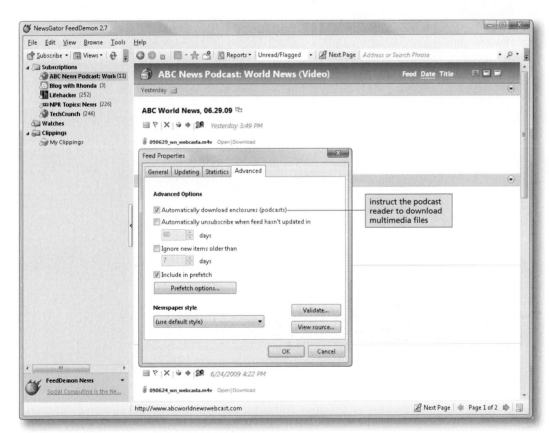

Figure 3-38 Subscribe to a podcast with FeedDemon.

When subscribing to a podcast, you may need to explicitly set the feed properties of a subscribed feed so that the application automatically will download the multimedia files.

SUBSCRIBING USING WEB-BASED PODCAST SERVICES Web-based podcast services, such as Odeo, shown in Figure 3-39, contain directory listings of audio and video podcasts. The site manages your podcast selections and provides streaming audio or video of each podcast episode in your browser. Using Odeo, you can access podcast episodes without having to install any client applications or specialized media players on your computer.

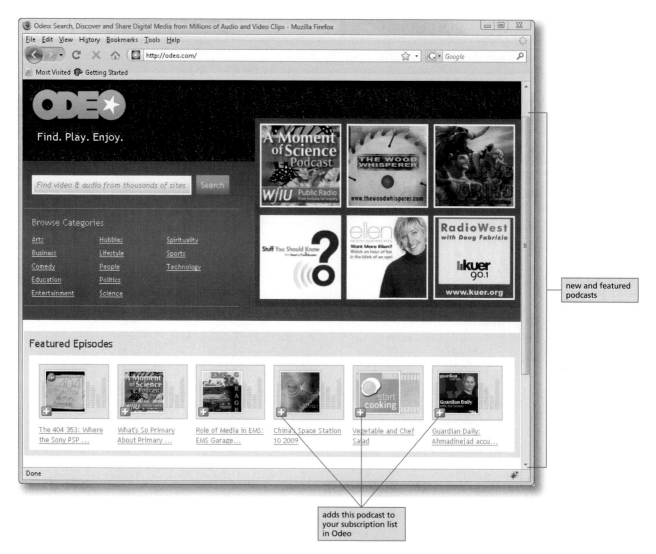

Figure 3-39 Odeo is a Web-based podcast directory and subscription management service.

After creating an account on Odeo, you can subscribe to podcasts and receive alerts when new episodes become available. Each podcast listed with Odeo has its own page from which you can subscribe to the podcast, watch new episodes as streaming audio or video within your browser, or add episodes to a playlist, as shown in Figure 3-40.

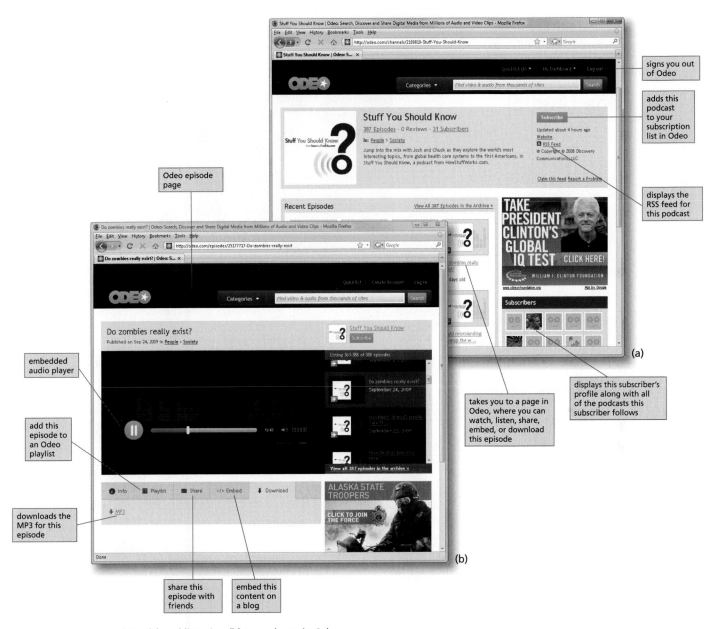

Figure 3-40 Subscribing (a) and listening (b) to podcasts in Odeo.

Odeo uses an embedded media player to stream the audio or video within the Web browser. You can embed a favorite audio or video on your own blog or Web site by using the provided embed code, or you can manually download a multimedia file to your computer.

Odeo also has elements of an online community—for example, you can rank and share your favorite podcast episodes with friends. Your profile contains a list of all of the podcasts to which you are subscribed. Odeo lists your profile along with those of all others subscribed to a particular podcast. You can click on a subscriber's profile to see the other podcasts to which he or she has subscribed.

SUBSCRIBING TO MANAGED PODCASTS   Feed managing services offer one-click subscription to podcast content when subscribing using iTunes or other client and Web-based podcast readers. In addition to managing Web feeds, FeedBurner, shown in Figure 3-41, manages audio and video podcast feeds.

Figure 3-41 Subscribing to a managed podcast.

To subscribe, simply click the desired application. You can always subscribe manually by entering the podcast's URL in the Subscribe to a Podcast option in the podcast reader application of your choice.

Anatomy of a Podcast Feed

A podcast is an RSS feed with additional information about the multimedia file associated with each episode. Podcasts follow the XML specification for RSS feeds, with one addition: each item also contains an enclosure tag that describes the URL of the associated multimedia file, its length in bytes, and its type (audio or video). Figure 3-42 displays the RSS feed for the Stuff You Should Know podcast, with some tags omitted for clarity.

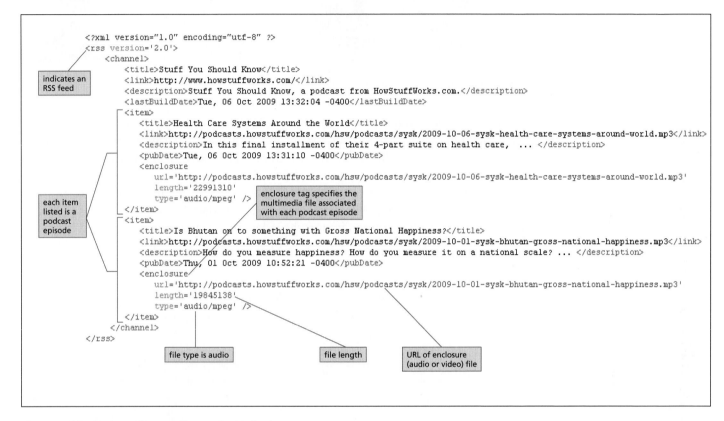

Figure 3-42 XML is used to specify a podcast's feed.

The podcast feed uses the same tags as the RSS feed does, except that there is an `<enclosure>` tag within each `<item>` tag. Applications use the file length to ensure that there are no errors during the download process by checking the number of bytes downloaded against the reported length of the file.

Creating Podcasts

Podcasting makes it possible for anyone who can create audio or video recordings to host their own show on the Internet by syndicating the multimedia content to subscribers. Politicians have used podcasts to communicate with voters. College teachers create podcasts of lectures so that students can download and listen to them again later. Trainers distribute screencasts, which are videos of actions on a computer screen, instead of printed instructions to demonstrate how to use software applications.

Creating podcasts requires basic equipment for recording and editing digital audio and video. Most laptop computers have built-in Webcams and microphones, as well as recording software that you can use to create audio and video files for podcasting. You also may use additional hardware to create the multimedia for your podcast episodes, such as the devices shown in Figure 3-43 on the next page.

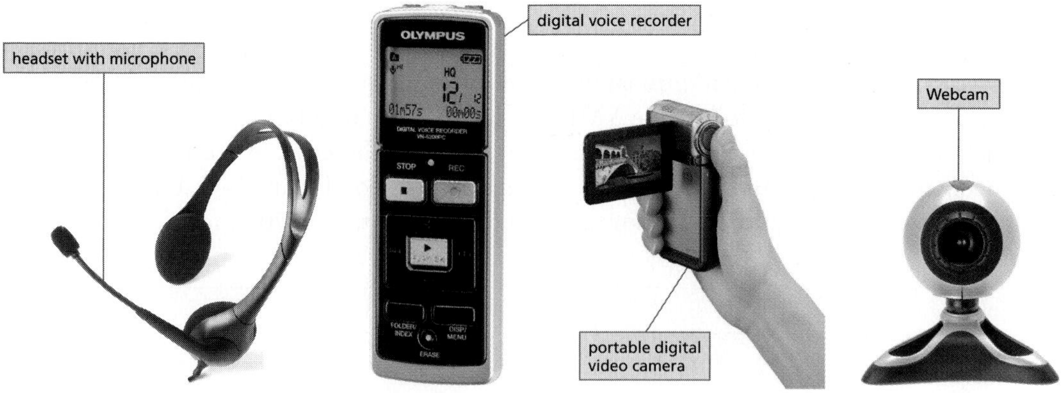

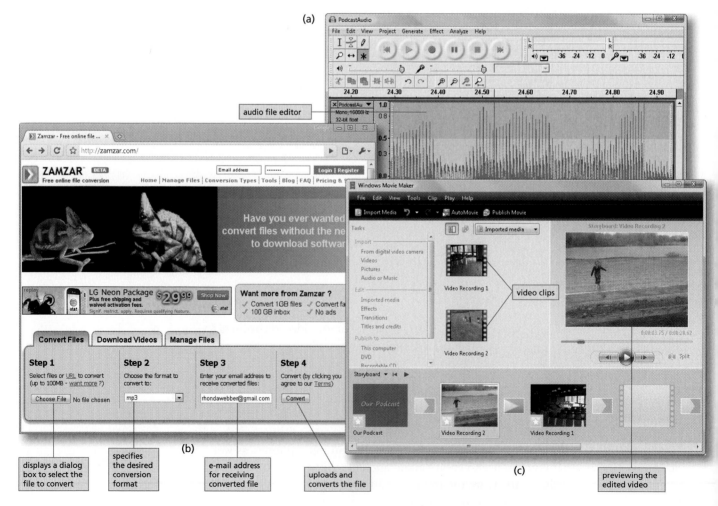

Figure 3-43 Equipment for creating a podcast.

Creating video requires a video camera or a Webcam to record the video. Creating an audio file requires a voice recorder or headset with audio recording software on your computer to create the audio. These devices can connect directly to a USB port on your computer, enabling easy transfer of the multimedia files for later editing.

Once you have created an audio file, audio-editing software, such as Audacity for Windows, shown in Figure 3-44(a), or GarageBand for Mac can be used to edit the file. After a video is recorded, you can import the video into an application such as Windows Movie Maker, shown in Figure 3-44(c), or iMovie on the Mac to edit it.

Figure 3-44 Software for editing and converting podcasts: Audacity (a), Zamzar (b), and Windows Movie Maker (c).

Just as television and radio broadcasts have short introductions that make them recognizable as part of a series, consider adding a short audio or video clip to append at the beginning of each podcast episode. Also consider creating a short clip with credits or a link to the podcast's Web site at the end of each episode. This helps to make a podcast episode recognizable as one episode of a podcast series.

After creating the audio and video files, you will need to save them in a compressed format for distribution. If the application that you are using to edit the multimedia does not support saving the files in the desired format, you will have to convert the files from one format to another. A Web-based service such as Zamzar, shown in Figure 3-44(b), allows you to upload files and convert them to an alternative format that you specify. Because podcast files must be saved in a compressed format, you might convert the WAV audio format to MP3 or the WMV video format to MP4. Once the files have been converted, you are ready to upload them to your blog host, a podcast application, or a Web server.

Configuring Blogger to Support Podcasts

Many people who create podcasts use a blogging application to post and archive each episode of a podcast. They also configure the blog to generate the podcast's RSS feed. A blog post describing a podcast episode is called **show notes**, which usually contain an outline or summary of the episode, a list of hyperlinks to Web sites mentioned in the episode, and a direct link to the podcast's audio or video enclosure.

To configure your Blogger blog to generate a podcast feed, you must configure the settings to add the enclosure information based on the video content that you specify. Setting the Show Link Fields option, located on the Formatting page of the Setting tab, to Yes generates enclosure tags for blog posts with multimedia, as shown in Figure 3-45.

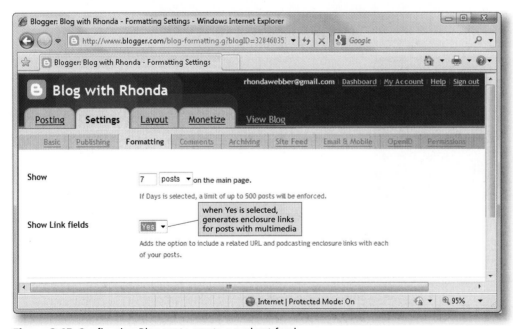

Figure 3-45 Configuring Blogger to create a podcast feed.

The next step is to write a new blog post that will contain the show notes for your podcast episode along with its video file. When you upload your video to Blogger, Blogger will convert it into two different formats: an MP4 version for the podcast feed and a Flash version to display in the show notes blog post. The upload and file conversion may take several minutes to complete. Blogger will display the URL for the enclosure and its media type above the blog post. When the video completes processing, it will be displayed within the blog editor, as shown in Figure 3-46.

Figure 3-46 Uploading a video to Blogger as a podcast episode.

After you publish the post, the video will be embedded as part of the show notes for this episode on your blog, as shown in Figure 3-47. The video also will be specified as an enclosure in the RSS feed so that podcast readers can download it. In most blogs, the title of a blog post acts as a permalink to that post. If you leave this value blank, Blogger will use the permalink of the post as the destination of the hyperlink for the title. You might also specify the URL of the blog or Web site for the podcast if that site contains additional information for the viewer about the podcast series.

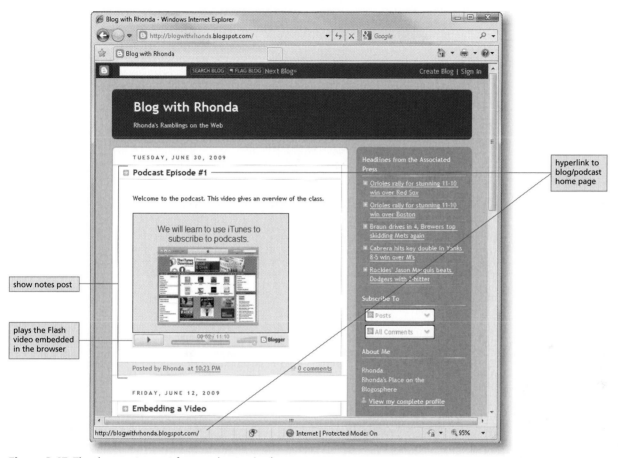

Figure 3-47 The show notes post for a podcast episode.

Summary

Syndication is a way to distribute new Web content to users without requiring them to visit the Web sites from which the content originates. By separating the formatting of the content from the content itself, Web feeds provide a standard way to describe news headlines, blog posts, and other frequently changing Web content. Syndication also makes it possible to share content with other blogs, Web sites, and applications. Users can subscribe to feeds using a Web browser or using a feed reader application that runs in a browser, on a computer, or on a cell phone. The browser or feed reader application checks for new content from the feeds that it monitors and notifies users when new information is available. Content publishers syndicate their content as feeds using either the RSS or Atom formats, represented in XML, which can be utilized by different programs or applications.

Podcasts are RSS feeds in which each episode contains an enclosed multimedia file. Podcasting has become a popular way for both traditional and new media providers to syndicate audio and video content over the Web. Podcasts can be listened to or watched online, on personal computers, or on portable media players.

Think

Submit responses to these questions as directed by your instructor.

1. How can you recognize if a Web site syndicates its content using RSS?

2. What is the advantage of using a Web-based feed reader rather than a Web browser to manage your RSS feeds?

3. How is reading RSS feeds different from reading e-mail messages? What are three features common to most feed reader applications, regardless of whether they are Web-based or client applications?

4. Examine the RSS feed for your Blogger blog. What is the URL of the feed?

5. The FeedDemon client feed reader application offers the ability to synchronize your subscribed feeds with other computers on which FeedDemon is installed. Web-based feed readers such as Google Reader do not have (or need) this capability. Why?

6. What are three metrics that FeedBurner provides for managed feeds and podcasts? How might these be of interest to bloggers and podcasters?

7. Examine the URL of an RSS feed that is the result of a Google News search on a topic of interest. How is the search term included in the feed's URL?

8. What three pieces of information are specified in a podcast's enclosure tag, and how does a podcast reader make use of them?

9. How is a podcast different from an audio or video file published on a Web site?

Watch

Watch the video for Chapter 3 on the Online Companion at scsite.com/web2. Be prepared to answer or discuss the questions posted on the Online Companion as directed by your instructor.

Try

Visit the Online Companion at scseries.com/web2 and follow the steps as you complete the tutorials for this chapter.

Tutorial 3-1 Subscribe to an RSS Feed Using Google Reader
In this tutorial, you will learn how to subscribe to an RSS feed using Google Reader. You will also search for feeds. You will organize your feeds in Google Reader using folders, read a feed, mark all items in a feed as read, and then unsubscribe from a feed.

Tutorial 3-2 Add an RSS Feed to Your Blog's Sidebar
One characteristic of Web 2.0 applications is that they support sharing data between Web sites. In this tutorial, you will you will add the Subscription Links gadget to your blog to allow readers to subscribe to your blog's feed. You will use the gadget to subscribe to your feed in Google Reader. You will embed content from a feed in the sidebar of your blog using the Feed gadget.

Complete these exercises on the blog that you created for this class.

1. Use Google Reader to subscribe to several feeds for sites that you frequently visit. Write a blog post about your experience after using a feed reader every day for a week. What are at least two benefits and drawbacks of using a feed reader?

2. Use a search engine to find a recent article about how a specific company uses RSS or Atom feeds to make information available to its employees or customers. Write a blog post that summarizes your findings. Include a hyperlink to the original article as part of your blog post.

These activities encourage you to explore Web 2.0 sites and applications on your own. Submit your responses as directed by your instructor.

1. Try using a Web-based aggregator other than Google Reader. How do the two compare? Write a short review of each.

2. Find feeds on a variety of topics of interest and subscribe to them using Google Reader or your favorite browser. When you subscribe to a feed in Safari or Internet Explorer, use the task pane to filter or sort the items. If you have a cell phone that has a feed reader application, subscribe to a feed on your phone.

3. Set up your own page at Alltop. How does this site make use of RSS feeds?

4. Use FeedBurner to create a managed feed for your blog. Ask several people to subscribe to its Web feed. Check the FeedBurner page at one-week intervals to investigate the usage of your feed. How can you promote your feed to get better numbers?

5. Download FeedDemon and install it on your computer. Subscribe to several feeds. How is reading feed content using a desktop application different from using a browser-based feed reader application? Which do you prefer?

6. Subscribe to and view a podcast by using a podcast client application as well as by using a Web-based service such as Odeo. How is the process similar? How is it different? What is an advantage and a disadvantage of each?

7. Use a podcast reader to subscribe to and download a podcast on a topic of interest to you. If you have iTunes on your computer, look for podcasts available in the iTunes Store. Otherwise, subscribe to a podcast available from one of the sites mentioned in this chapter. If you have an iPod or other portable media player, transfer the files to that device. Was the process of transferring the files difficult? (Note: To automatically synchronize downloaded podcast episodes on your iPod, you must use iTunes on the computer with which your iPod is registered.)

Collaborate

If your instructor set up a class wiki, complete these exercises.

1. Share the link to a Web feed that you think your classmates will find interesting by adding it to a directory page of student-suggested Web feeds on your class wiki.

2. Create a collaborative study sheet about this chapter. At your instructor's direction, post or answer a question about a topic related to Web feeds, XML, or podcasts to the study sheet page for Chapter 3 on your class wiki. Review the questions posed by your classmates before adding your own to be sure that you do not repeat a question that appears already. Edit or correct a response from one of your classmates.

4 | Organizing Information

Overview

Information traditionally stored in physical formats has become widely available in digital formats. Photographs, music, video, newspapers, books, and magazines are now commonly digitized and stored online for users to access and share with others. As the amount and types of such content multiplies, the ability to organize digital information for easy retrieval becomes increasingly important. **Tagging** is the process of assigning short, descriptive labels to digital information for the purposes of identification and organization. A **tag** is a keyword that you might assign to describe pictures, Web pages, blog posts, e-mail messages, videos, or other digital documents to make them easier to find at a later time. You can categorize digital information by using one or many different tags.

Assigning tags to information stored on the World Wide Web is a collaborative process. As different people use the same tags to describe images, Web sites, and blog posts across the Web, some tags will be used more than others. Commonly used tags essentially can serve as links between items that would otherwise not be related.

Many online services and Web applications support tagging, as shown in Figure 4-1 on the next page. Tagging enables users to organize their own content in ways that make sense to them so that they and other users can find it.

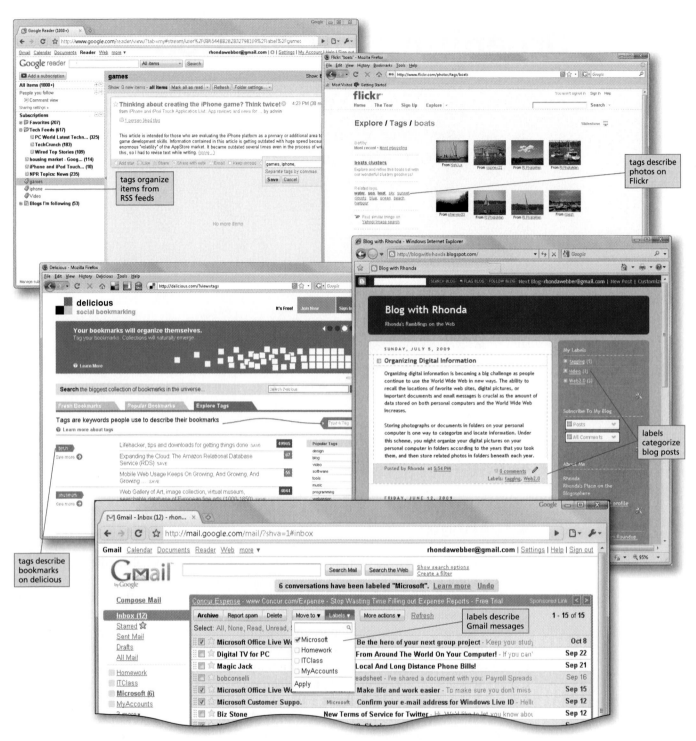

Figure 4-1 Many online services support tagging.

Gmail, Blogger, and Google Reader all allow users to add tags, or labels, to describe e-mail messages, blog posts, and feed items. Flickr is an online photo-sharing Web site where users can upload, share, and tag photos. Delicious is a social bookmarking site. **Social bookmarking** is the process by which users post the URLs of their favorite Web sites online, add tags and additional commentary, and share that content with other users.

Organizing Digital Information

The Internet is the backbone for delivering digital information from one computer to another. Whereas handwritten letters, printed books, and DVDs can be physically transported from one place to the next, the digital versions, such as e-mail messages, PDF documents, and YouTube videos, are not constrained by size or distance. Efficiently organizing digital information on the virtually unlimited shelf space of one's hard drive or a server on the Internet so that messages, documents, videos, or other digital information may be easily located and retrieved becomes an important task.

There are two popular approaches to organizing digital information: hierarchical and nonhierarchical. A **hierarchical** organization arranges and classifies each item in a relationship to the others as being above, below, or at the same level, such as in an outline, or as files within folders stored on your hard drive. A **nonhierarchical** organization allows information to be categorized in an unlimited number of ways by using tags, or labels, to describe items. Unrelated items become related to each other when they are described with the same tags. Locating information with nonhierarchical organization involves searching for a tag and examining all of the information associated with that tag. Figures 4-2 and 4-3 (on the next page) show two different Web sites that provide access to Web content: Dmoz is a hierarchical directory of Web content, and Delicious provides nonhierarchical access to Web content.

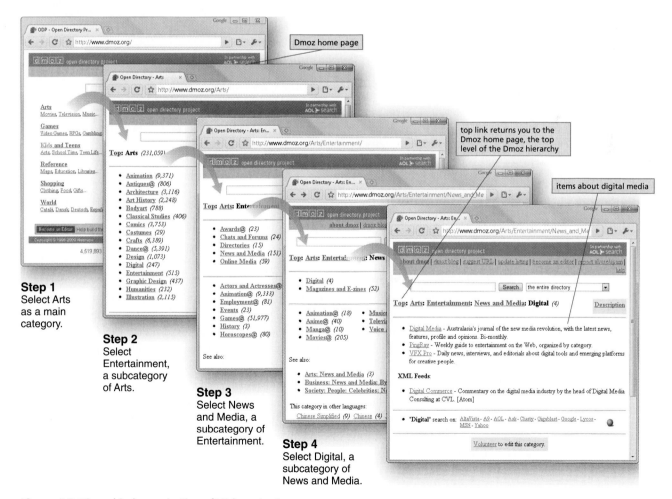

Step 1
Select Arts as a main category.

Step 2
Select Entertainment, a subcategory of Arts.

Step 3
Select News and Media, a subcategory of Entertainment.

Step 4
Select Digital, a subcategory of News and Media.

Dmoz home page

top link returns you to the Dmoz home page, the top level of the Dmoz hierarchy

items about digital media

Figure 4-2 Hierarchical organization of Web content.

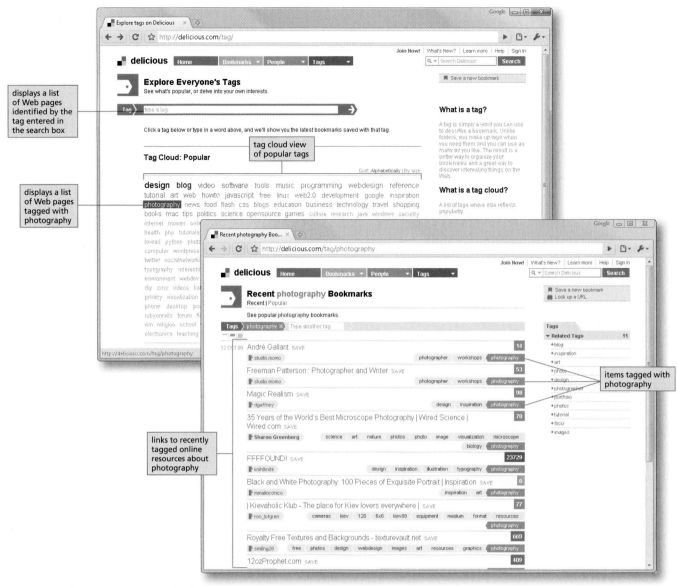

Figure 4-3 Nonhierarchical organization of Web content.

Users of Dmoz, a systematic, open directory of Web content shown in Figure 4-2, who are interested in articles about Entertainment must click the Arts topic and then find Entertainment as a subtopic of the Arts topic. Users would continue following links to lower levels of the hierarchy until they reach individual articles. The top-level home page lists the three most popular subtopics of Arts. The Top link at any level returns the user to the top-level home page.

Users of Delicious, a nonhierarchical directory of Web content shown in Figure 4-3, see a tag cloud view of popular topics on the Delicious Explore Everyone's Tags page. A **tag cloud**, or tagroll, is a visualization in which more popular or more frequently used tags are displayed in a larger font size. Many tag-based Web sites display their most popular tags using a tag cloud, in which each tag is a hyperlink to a Web page that has been associated with that tag.

Clicking the "photography" tag displays a list of bookmarks, or tagged Web pages, about photography. Entering a keyword in the search box will result in a list of links to pages that have been tagged with your keyword.

Organizing Information on Your Computer

Storing photographs or documents in folders on your personal computer is one way to categorize and locate those photos and documents. For example, you might organize digital pictures on your personal computer in folders according to the years in which they were taken. Using this method, each photo can be stored in exactly one folder.

In Figure 4-4, pictures from a trip to San Francisco are stored in a folder named SanFrancisco, and pictures from a visit to a basketball game were stored in a folder named Celtics. Both of those folders are located in a folder named 2008 to indicate the year in which the photos were taken. The 2008 folder is located in the Pictures folder.

Figure 4-4 Arranging photos in folders.

This method of storing information in folders inside of other folders is hierarchical. To find a particular picture, you must start at the topmost folder, the Pictures folder, and then navigate to different folders within folders until you find the picture that you are looking for, because each picture only can appear in a single folder. Placing folders inside of other folders is an efficient way to logically organize photos by year or location but can increase the number of steps that it takes to find a desired picture. Another limitation of this method of storing pictures is that you can only identify a picture based on the year and the location where it was taken.

Suppose, however, that you want to organize pictures of boats taken during all of your vacations. Because pictures are stored in folders, you might create a folder called Boats and copy every picture of a boat to the Boats folder. You might also want to leave a copy of the picture in a folder named for the place where you took it since that is another way to remember and locate the picture. This method of organizing the boat photos would result in multiple copies of the same picture being stored on your hard drive, which is not an efficient use of its storage. If you decided to edit, color-correct, or crop any of those photos, you would then have to replace all of the copies with the edited version in order to keep everything synchronized. The task of storing multiple copies of hundreds of pictures on your hard drive would quickly become unmanageable.

As an alternative, you could assign tags to your photographs. Assigning multiple tags to a picture could make it easier to locate based on any number of associations that you have with the picture. For example, you might tag a picture from the SanFrancisco folder with the keywords "sanfrancisco," "boats," and "marina," as shown in Figure 4-5.

Figure 4-5 Assigning multiple tags to a picture.

Often, tags that contain more than one word are written without spaces, because some tagging applications use spaces to separate multiple tags in a list. To keep "San" and "Francisco" together as a single tag, rather than as two separate tags, the words are combined, removing internal spaces. Other tagging applications use commas or semicolons to separate tags and would treat the tag "San Francisco" as a single tag.

Figure 4-6(a) shows how you might assign these tags to the picture in Figure 4-5 in Windows. Windows uses a database to associate each tag with the name of the picture. Windows can search the tagged pictures in your Pictures folder by their tags and display all of the pictures given a particular tag. Figure 4-6(b) displays all of the pictures tagged with the tag "boats."

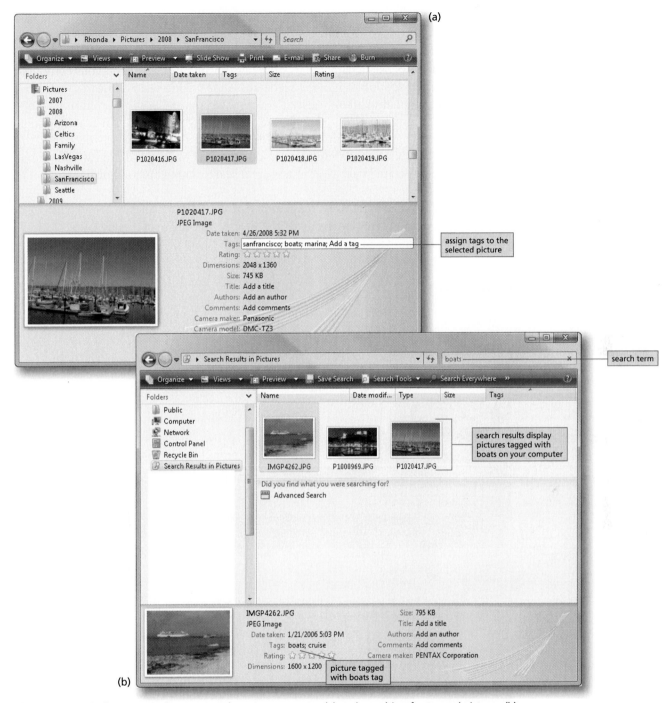

Figure 4-6 Assigning tags to pictures stored on your computer (a) and searching for tagged pictures (b).

Note that tagging does not rely on a hierarchical structure, whereas storing photos in folders on your computer did. When tagged, photos can be located by their tag names, not by the folders in which they are stored.

Tagging Information on the Web

When the information that you are tagging is located on the World Wide Web instead of on your computer's hard drive, new opportunities for organizing, locating, and sharing digital information emerge. On the Web, you can tag items, such as e-mail messages or items in your news reader, for personal use. You can tag items that you share with others, such as your blog posts or photographs. And, finally, you can tag articles or content of interest that you find on the Web and share those items, and their associated tags, with others. Just as Windows uses a database to store tags for pictures stored on your computer, Web applications that support tagging use a database for storing tags for a variety of content contributed from many different users.

By tagging items with multiple descriptive keywords, you can associate a single item with many different tags. In the physical world, a single item can only be stored in a single location, like a book on a shelf or a photo in an album. In the digital world, the same item can be associated with several tags, and searching by any one of the tags can access the item.

Last.fm is a Web site where users may categorize music and artists by using tags. For example, Last.fm users have described The Beatles with tags such as 60s, Rock, and Classic Rock, as shown in Figure 4-7.

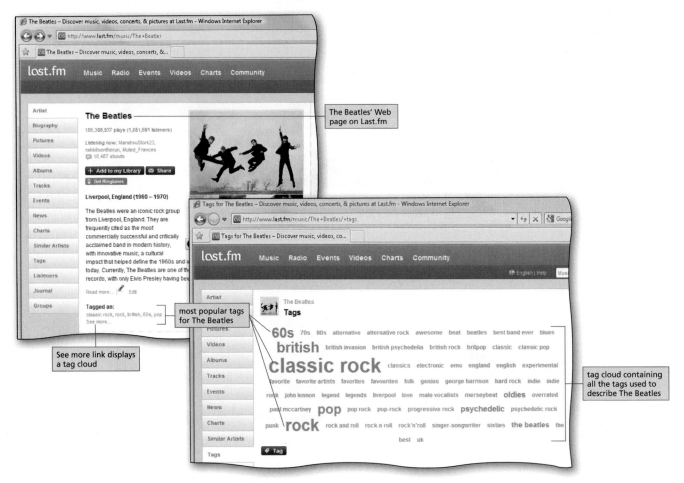

Figure 4-7 Many tags are associated with The Beatles on Last.fm.

The Beatles' page on Last.fm displays the most popular tags that users chose to describe the musical group, along with a link to a page with a tag cloud. The tag cloud includes all of the tags used to describe The Beatles. The most popular tags are shown in a larger size.

Searching with tags can be an alternative to searching with a traditional search engine. A tag-based search may provide different results than those obtained by a standard search engine. Results of a tag search contain items for which people have taken the time to associate tags, whereas a search engine's results are the results of a computer program that matches keywords. A tag search provides a list of items that other users described using the same tag. You can view all of the items that a particular user tagged. For any given item, you can display all of the tags applied by all users who tagged it.

One disadvantage of relying on tagging for organization is the potential ambiguity of any given tag. The same tag may have different meanings in different contexts. For example, the tag "Lincoln" might refer to the Civil War president, the expensive car, the capital of Nebraska, or the tunnel in New York City. To avoid confusion, it is often useful to assign many different tags to describe a particular item.

LABELING E-MAIL MESSAGES IN GMAIL   Gmail enables users to organize e-mail messages with tags. In Gmail, and in most Google applications, the term **labels** is used to refer to tags. Unlike e-mail applications that allow you to group individual messages in, at most, one folder, assigning labels allows you to group and identify Gmail messages based on any number of descriptive labels, as shown in Figure 4-8.

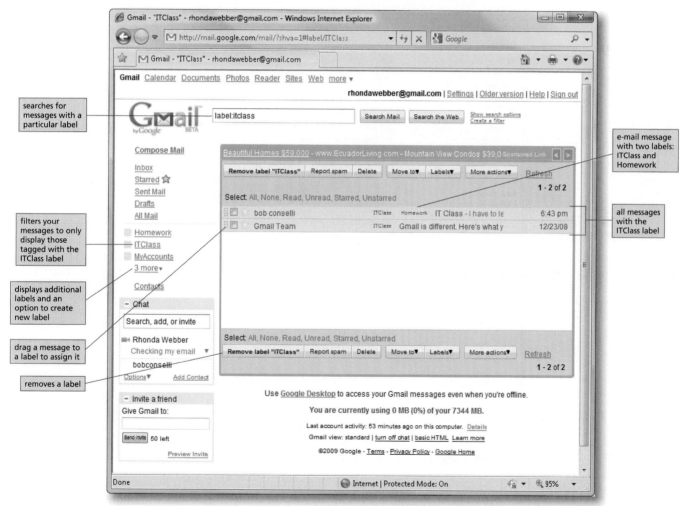

Figure 4-8 Labeling e-mail messages in Gmail.

Clicking the ITClass label, located in the list of the most popular labels, filters all of the messages to only display those messages assigned the ITClass label. **Filtering** is the process of displaying any collection of tagged items that share the same label or tag.

Using Gmail's drag and drop interface, you can assign labels to e-mail messages by dragging a message to a label or by dragging a label to a message. In Figure 4-8, the message from Bob Conselli has two labels assigned to it: ITClass and Homework.

TAGGING IN GOOGLE READER   Google Reader uses both folders and tags to help you organize your Web feeds. As you learned in Chapter 3, feeds can be placed in multiple folders. In Google Reader, tags allow you to organize items in your subscribed feeds. Both folders and tags let you sort and label items in your feeds: use folders to organize items from an entire subscribed feed, and use tags to identify items within a subscribed feed. Items belonging to a feed in a particular folder will automatically be tagged with that folder name. For example, in the previous chapter, you created a Favorites folder for your favorite feeds. Figure 4-9 shows how to add a tag to a post in a subscribed feed in Google Reader.

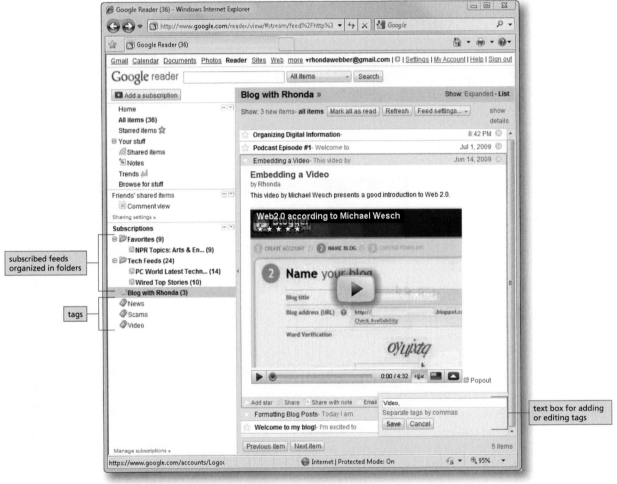

Figure 4-9 Tagging an individual post in Google Reader.

For example, as you read posts from your subscribed feeds, you might use the tag "Video" to tag those posts of interest about videos that you might want to refer back to at a later time. Clicking the Video tag under Subscriptions in Google Reader will display all posts from your current subscriptions to which you assigned this tag. Tags apply to individual posts across all feeds, whereas the feeds themselves are categorized and stored in folders. Figure 4-10 shows several posts from different feeds tagged with "Video."

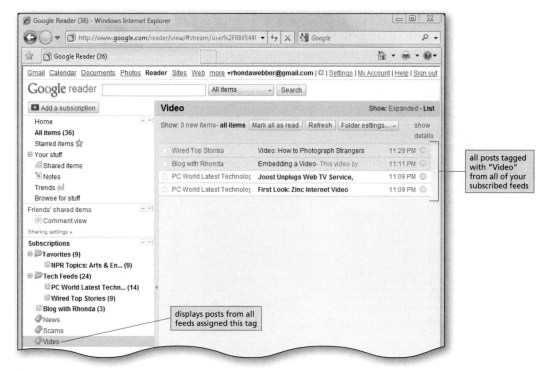

Figure 4-10 Displaying tagged posts in Google Reader.

TAGGING BLOG POSTS USING BLOGGER Tagging blog posts enables readers to easily find related posts. In Blogger, you can add labels, or tags, to a blog post by entering them in the Labels for this post text box when you create or edit a blog post, as shown in Figure 4-11.

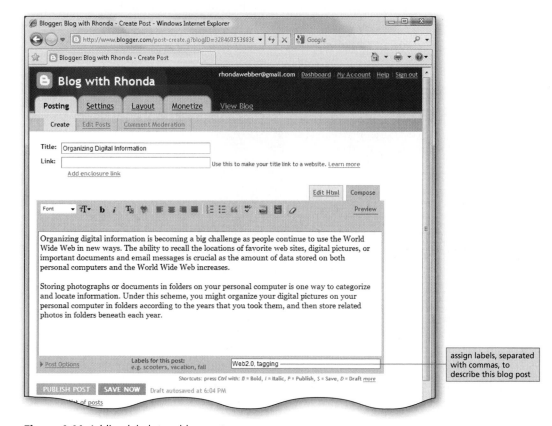

Figure 4-11 Adding labels to a blog post.

By adding the Labels gadget to your blog's sidebar, your blog can display all of the labels that you assigned to your blog posts, as shown in Figure 4-12.

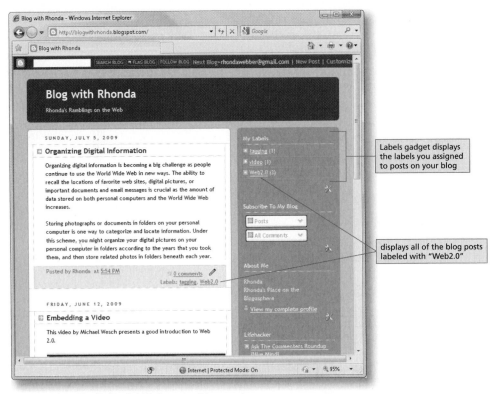

Labels gadget displays the labels you assigned to posts on your blog

displays all of the blog posts labeled with "Web2.0"

Figure 4-12 Displaying labels for your blog posts.

Each label, whether located beneath the posts or in the Labels gadget, is a hyperlink to a page that displays all of the posts on your blog with that label, as shown in Figure 4-13.

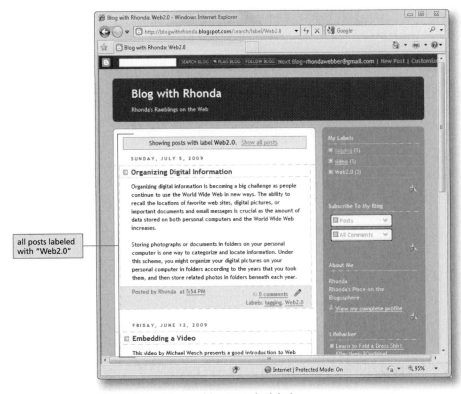

all posts labeled with "Web2.0"

Figure 4-13 Filtering blog posts by label.

Tagging as a Means of Collective Organization

Tagging is a useful way for many different people to collectively organize related information from different sources. By assigning the same tags, it becomes easy to create associations between pictures, documents, or other digital information that would be otherwise unrelated. There is no single correct way to apply tags to digital information. Tags should be descriptive and should capture the important elements of the items being tagged. Most importantly, users should assign tags that they find meaningful.

For example, fans might take digital pictures at a college football game, upload them to Flickr, and agree to assign the photos with a very specific tag such as "FalconsOct3." By searching for this tag on Flickr, you will find all of the pictures that everyone took at the game. Fans now have access to photos of the event taken by others in attendance. Using a common tag creates organization among otherwise unrelated photos taken by different people attending the same event.

In contrast to a **taxonomy**, which is a methodical, scientific way of unambiguously classifying information, among the Web 2.0 community, the term **folksonomy** has emerged to describe the collective result of different people individually applying tags to the same online content. Different "folks" can organize information using taxonomies or categories that are personally meaningful. This collaborative process of tagging digital content allows each person's individual use of tags to enhance the value of the classification as a whole for all who use it.

Consider how three different users might create a simple folksonomy to classify pictures on a photo-sharing Web site, where they can add tags to other users' photos. In this scenario, Users 1, 2, and 3 upload Photos 1, 2, and 3, respectively. As shown in Figure 4-14 and indicated by solid lines, User 1 initially tags Photo 1 with "boats" and "san francisco." User 2 initially tags Photos 1 and 2 with "san francisco." User 3 initially tags Photo 3 with "sailing."

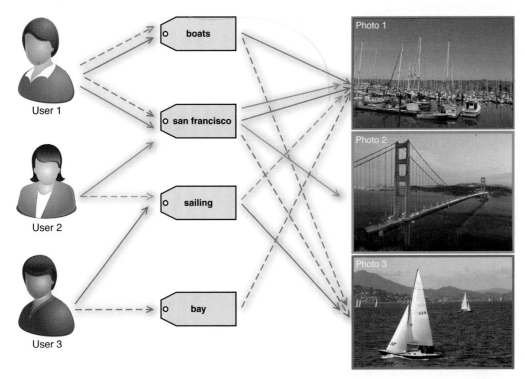

Figure 4-14 Creating a folksonomy.

As indicated by dashed lines, User 1 adds the "boats" and "san francisco" tags to Photo 3; User 2 adds the "sailing" tag to Photo 1; User 3 adds the "bay" tag to Photo 1. Collectively, three users described Photo 1 with the tags "boats," "san francisco," "sailing," and "bay." One user described Photo 2 with the tag "san francisco." Two users described Photo 3 with "boats," "san francisco," and "sailing."

The collective descriptions are more complete than those given by any single user, yet each user's choice of tags is individually meaningful. Additionally, it is apparent that the "san francisco" tag, having been used three times, is the most popular tag in this folksonomy. The tags "boats" and "sailing" are used twice, and the tag "bay" is used only once. Because Users 1 and 2 both tagged Photo 1 with "san francisco," greater importance is given to that tag in describing Photo 1.

Users who contribute to folksonomies by tagging items such as photos or videos on Flickr, blog posts, or Web sites on Delicious engage in a collective effort to categorize digital information in meaningful ways.

Using Tagged Data

Tagged data enables the capability of recommending products to potential customers. **Collaborative filtering** is a method whereby predictions are made about one user's interests by collecting and analyzing data from many users. For example, Last.fm uses related tags to recommend music to listeners. By analyzing tag usage to determine user preferences, Last.fm might recommend that users who like The Beatles will also like the Rolling Stones. Companies such as Amazon use collaborative filtering to recommend products to customers based on the purchases of other customers. These systems rely on the theory of the wisdom of crowds. This theory suggests that in large diverse groups, the group as a whole will make better decisions and predictions, or know more about a topic, than any one individual. As the size of the crowd grows, the quality of the information being tagged or recommended is thought to improve.

In The Commons section of the Flickr Web site, Flickr has gathered publically available images from the Library of Congress and museums around the world for users to add tags and comments. Figure 4-15 displays a photo of President Abraham Lincoln from The Commons section of Flickr.

Figure 4-15 The Commons invites collective tagging of content from libraries and museums around the world.

In addition to making historical and cultural photos widely available, the goal is to take advantage of the collective wisdom of many Flickr users to collaborate and catalog this information by adding tags, descriptions, and comments to these photos. This collective intelligence will make the photos easier to find on the site and benefit researchers looking for information about a particular photo.

Sharing and Tagging Photos on Flickr

Flickr is a popular Web site for uploading, sharing, and organizing digital pictures and videos. Flickr is based on the premise that people who use the World Wide Web want to share their digital pictures online. Adding tags to photos allows others to locate and view the shared pictures. Flickr provides the platform for users to upload and share photos via a computer, e-mail messages, or a cell phone. Pictures posted to Flickr then are available through a number of additional channels, including RSS feeds, e-mail messages, blogs, and maps.

Interacting with Flickr

You first must create an account on Flickr in order to use the service. Because Yahoo! owns Flickr, Flickr accounts are linked to a Yahoo! ID, which also allows access to other Yahoo! applications such as Yahoo! Mail. After creating an account and establishing privacy settings, you can begin to upload pictures to Flickr and assign tags, as shown in Figure 4-16.

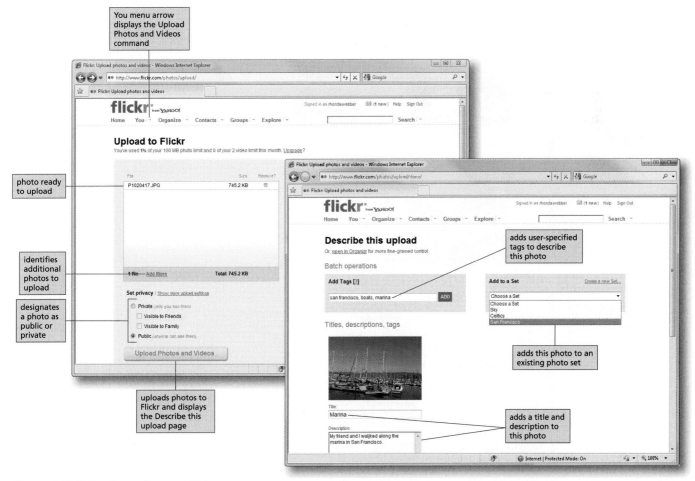

Figure 4-16 Uploading a picture to Flickr.

After identifying the pictures on your hard drive to upload to Flickr, you can designate a picture as public (available for all users to view) or private (available to users designated as friends or family to view). You then can add tags, titles, and descriptions for each and organize them into sets. Your collection of pictures on Flickr is called a **photostream**. Flickr adds your pictures to your photostream as you upload them and displays the most recently uploaded pictures first. A photostream has no organization other than by the date and time that the pictures were added.

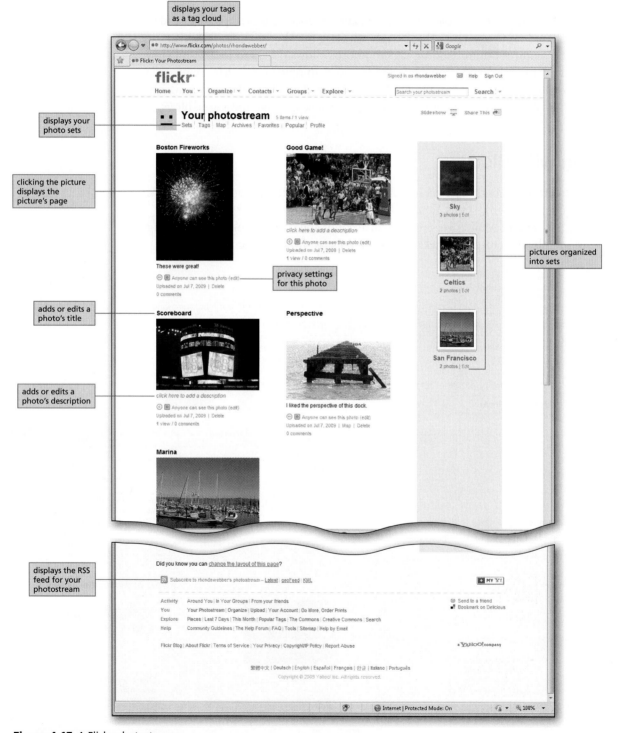

Figure 4-17 A Flickr photostream.

Clicking on a photo from your photostream page displays that photo's page on Flickr, as shown in Figure 4-18.

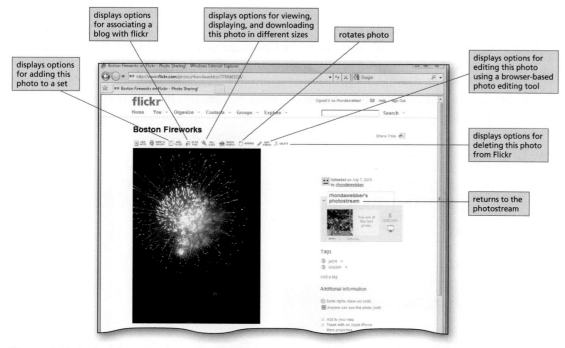

Figure 4-18 Options for managing a photo in Flickr.

Options for managing the photo include adding it to a set, posting it to a blog, cropping or editing it, viewing or downloading, displaying it in different sizes, or deleting it from Flickr.

Flickr creates square, thumbnail, small, medium, and large copies of the images that you upload. The All Sizes link on the photo page displays the Available sizes page, shown in Figure 4-19.

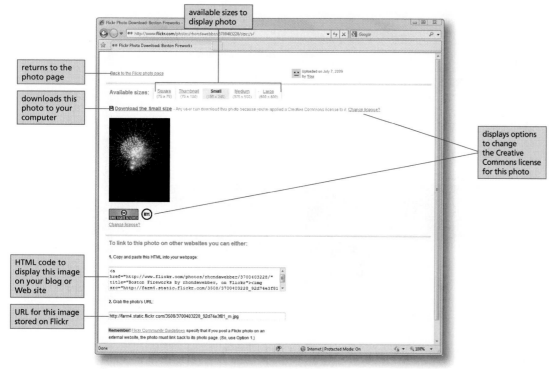

Figure 4-19 Flickr creates copies of your photos in different sizes.

The Available sizes page provides options for downloading the photo in different sizes, along with the HTML code needed to display the photo at each size on a blog or Web site. The Available sizes page also contains options for changing the Creative Commons license for your photo. Creative Commons licenses are discussed in a sidebar on page 145.

After uploading your photos, you can organize them into sets based on the location or event at which photos were taken, such as a Celtics game or a trip to San Francisco. You might choose to organize otherwise unrelated photos based on a common characteristic. Figure 4-20 shows how to add the Marina photo to a set called Sky, which contains photos with interesting skies. Note that the photo of the Marina also belongs to the San Francisco photo set.

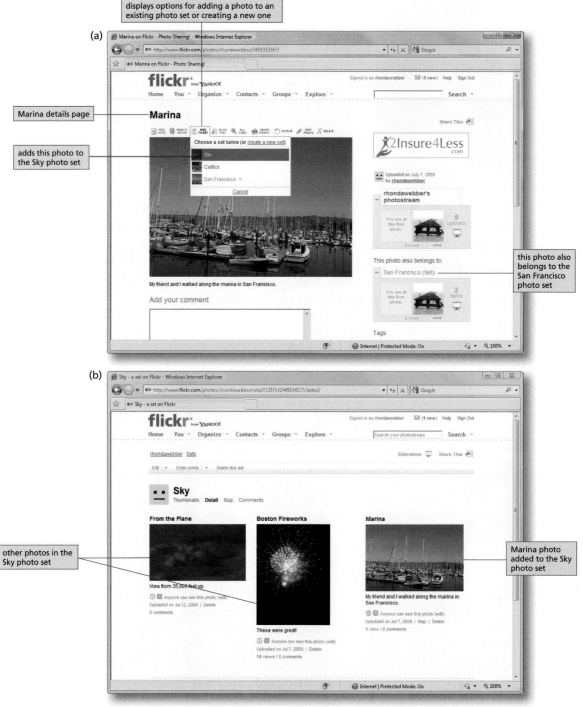

Figure 4-20 Adding a picture to a set (a) and the resulting photo set (b).

You also can view all of your assigned tags as a tag cloud, shown in Figure 4-21. Clicking the Tags link on your photostream page displays all of the tags used to describe your pictures.

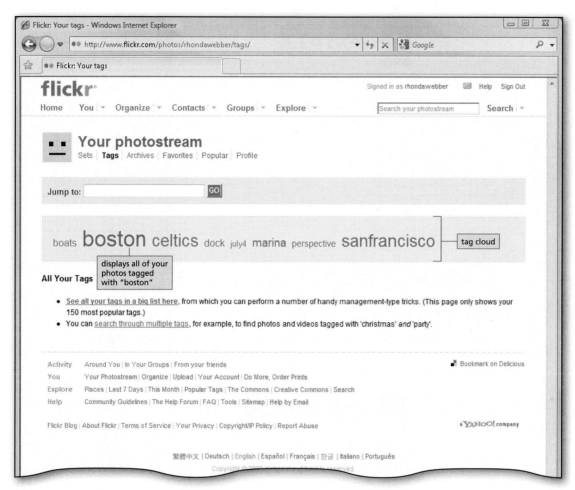

Figure 4-21 Your tags displayed as a tag cloud.

Clicking "boston" in the tag cloud displays the Your photostream / Tags / boston page, which shows all of Rhonda Webber's pictures that are assigned the tag "boston," as shown in Figure 4-22(a) on the next page. Clicking the public content tagged with boston link displays the Explore / Tags / boston page, which presents all of the public photos on Flickr that are tagged with the word "boston," as shown in Figure 4-22(b).

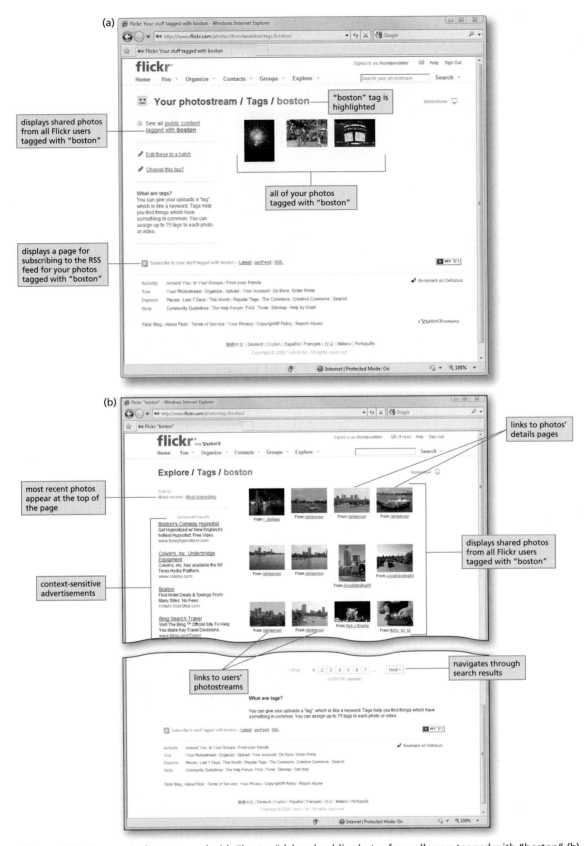

Figure 4-22 One user's photos tagged with "boston" (a) and public photos from all users tagged with "boston" (b).

The photos are sorted so that the most recent photos appear at the top of the page. Each picture links to its respective details page, and the usernames link to the users' photostreams. Flickr also displays context-sensitive advertisements on the Explore / Tags page.

SIDEBAR | Creative Commons

Bloggers often look for photos to accompany blog posts that they are writing. It is illegal to include any photo hosted on Flickr, or any other Web site, on a blog without obtaining permission from the owner of the photograph. Doing so violates copyright laws. The person who took the photo owns its copyright and may specify conditions on how it can be used.

Many Web 2.0 sites often allow content providers to specify their terms of use through **Creative Commons**, a licensing mechanism that offers alternatives to traditional copyright. Creative Commons is a nonprofit organization that facilitates the process of legally using and sharing the work of others; that work can be any form of printed or digital media.

There are several different criteria for attribution under Creative Commons licensing. Table 4-1 summarizes the four categories of licenses available under Creative Commons. Each item licensed through Creative Commons can have a combination of license conditions from each of these four categories.

For example, you may allow commercial uses of your work but not allow other users to modify it.

This combination is referred to as the Creative Commons Attribution-No Derivative Works license. Such a license would allow an author to use your photo on the cover of a book that will be for sale, as long as you are given attribution and the photo is used as you took it, without modification.

By specifying a Creative Commons license for your photos, you allow others to legally use the pictures in blogs and Web sites, PowerPoint presentations, and other published media according to the criteria that you set. You allow your work to be shared (copied, distributed, or transmitted) or remixed (adapted for other purposes) under the terms of the license that you specify.

Flickr holds the world's largest collection of photos licensed with Creative Commons, with more than 100 million licensed images. By default, Flickr uses the most restrictive Creative Commons license, the All Rights Reserved license, for photos uploaded to the site. The All Rights Reserved license does not allow any reuse whatsoever of Flickr photos. This license is applied until you change it. To share your photos, you must explicitly change the license to allow free sharing and remixing, with attribution.

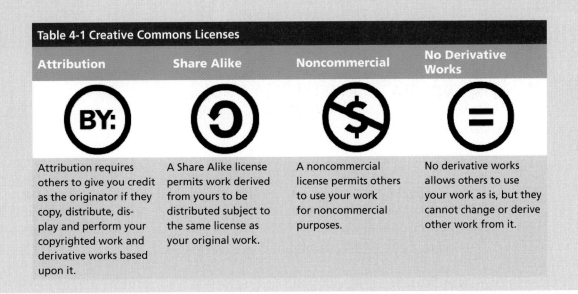

Table 4-1 Creative Commons Licenses			
Attribution	**Share Alike**	**Noncommercial**	**No Derivative Works**
Attribution requires others to give you credit as the originator if they copy, distribute, display and perform your copyrighted work and derivative works based upon it.	A Share Alike license permits work derived from yours to be distributed subject to the same license as your original work.	A noncommercial license permits others to use your work for noncommercial purposes.	No derivative works allows others to use your work as is, but they cannot change or derive other work from it.

Advanced Flickr Features

ADDING A FLICKR BADGE TO YOUR BLOG Flickr provides a tool to create a badge for your blog or Web site. Flickr uses the term **badge** to describe a configurable gadget that you can use to display some of your Flickr photos as a collage on your blog's sidebar. You can access the badge tool from the Help / Tools page that is linked from the bottom of your photostream page. Figure 4-23 displays the steps required to create a Flickr badge and embed it in a blog's sidebar.

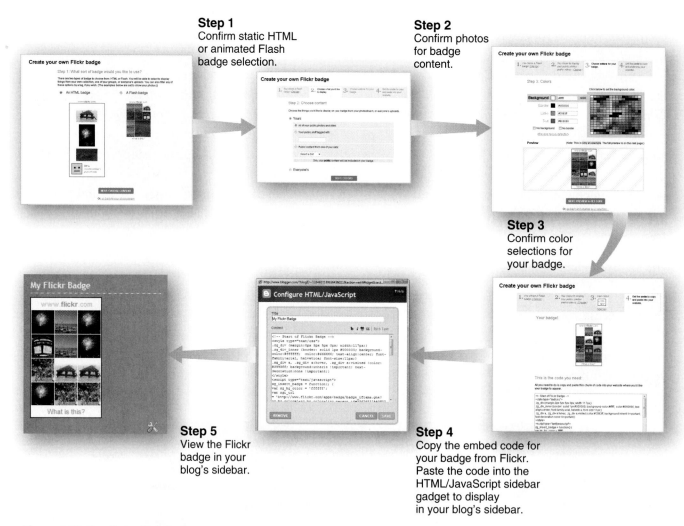

Step 1 Confirm static HTML or animated Flash badge selection.

Step 2 Confirm photos for badge content.

Step 3 Confirm color selections for your badge.

Step 4 Copy the embed code for your badge from Flickr. Paste the code into the HTML/JavaScript sidebar gadget to display in your blog's sidebar.

Step 5 View the Flickr badge in your blog's sidebar.

Figure 4-23 Creating a Flickr badge.

The blog also includes a Flickr photo embedded in a post. The HTML code necessary to display this photo is provided on the Available sizes page for the photo in Flickr. After selecting the desired size of the photo that you wish to include, copy and paste the HTML code to your blog post. According to Flickr's Community Guidelines, a Flickr photo posted on another Web site must provide a link back to its photo page on Flickr. The HTML code includes the hyperlink back to Flickr.

SYNDICATING YOUR PHOTOS USING RSS Flickr offers RSS feeds of an individual user's photostream, photos assigned a specific tag, or a tag search of photos from all users. When you subscribe to one of these feeds, your feed reader will notify you when there are new photos with a tag of interest. You can subscribe to RSS feeds for your contacts' photostreams in order to be notified when your contacts upload new pictures to Flickr. Figure 4-24 displays the RSS feed page for all recent uploads to Flickr tagged with "boston."

Figure 4-24 Syndicating Flickr photos as an RSS feed.

SETTING CREATIVE COMMONS LICENSES

The process for setting the Creative Commons license for a Flickr photo is straightforward, as shown in Figure 4-25. First, navigate to the photo's page on Flickr, and then click the edit link after the currently applied license. Select the desired license and click the Save button.

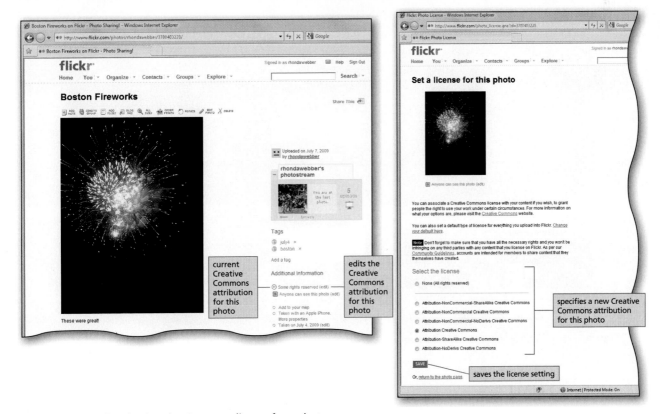

Figure 4-25 Setting the Creative Commons license for a photo.

ADDING GEOTAGS   Flickr allows users to apply a specialized type of tag to their photos, known as a geotag. A **geotag** contains the latitude and longitude coordinates of where a photo was taken in order to plot it on a map. You can use this metadata to find and locate photos taken at a particular location. Using geotags, you also can associate your pictures with others that were taken in the same or a nearby location.

In Flickr, you can display the map feature by clicking the Organize menu arrow on your photostream page and then clicking Your Map. The simplest way to apply a geotag to a photo in Flickr is to zoom the map to the location where the photo was taken, as shown in Figure 4-26, and then drag and drop the photo onto the map.

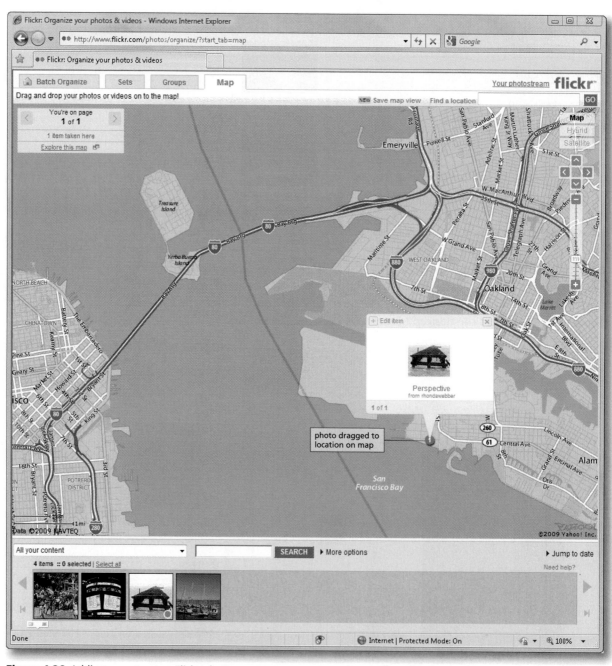

Figure 4-26 Adding a geotag to a Flickr photo.

When a picture has geotags, it becomes possible to search for it based on its location information as well as its tag information. Flickr's geotag-enabled search page is accessed by clicking the Explore menu arrow on your photostream page and then selecting World Map. This search page allows you to enter a descriptive tag as well as a location, and it will find photos that match the specified tag taken in the corresponding location. Figure 4-27 shows the results of a geotag search for everyone's uploaded photos that were tagged with "diner" and taken in Massachusetts. Flickr converts the location Massachusetts into its corresponding latitude and longitude coordinates in order to perform the search.

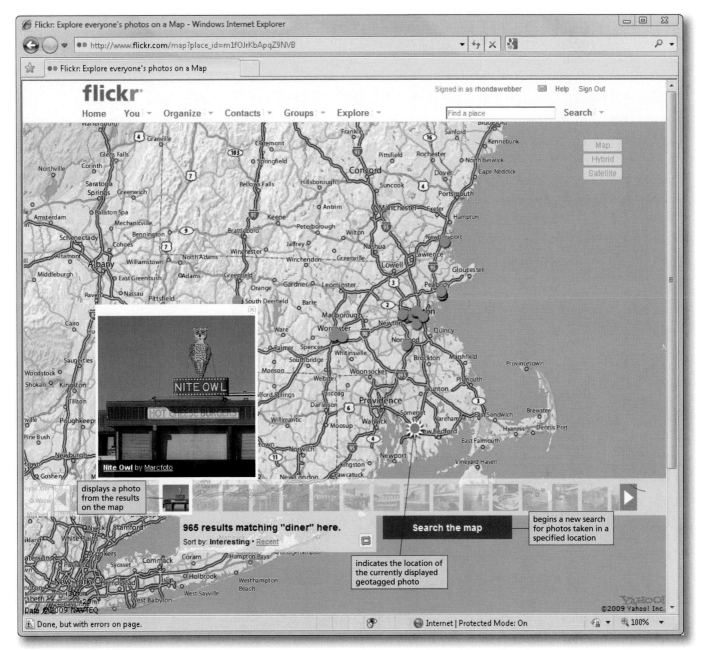

Figure 4-27 A geotag search for photos of diners in Massachusetts.

SIDEBAR | # How Do Web 2.0 Companies Make Money?

Many Web 2.0 companies do not charge people to access their online information services. For example, there is no charge for your Gmail account or to store your bookmarks on Delicious or to create a blog using Blogger. Google is one of many companies that relies on advertising as a source of income. Flickr, owned by Yahoo!, does not charge for the basic use of its photo-sharing services. Through online advertising programs, Web sites host advertisements and receive payment for displaying the ads based on the number of impressions or clicks that they receive. Flickr also includes context-sensitive ads on pages that display users' photographs.

Flickr is one of many Web 2.0 companies that, in addition to displaying ads, makes use of a freemium business model. **Freemium** is a business model in which an information service provider offers basic features to its users at no cost and charges a premium, or fee, for additional features or services.

The term freemium implies a combination of both free and premium services. The freemium business model often uses ads to support the cost of the site for free users and relies on the fact that the nonpaying users will either become paying customers or tell other people about the service, expanding the potential for new paying customers. Paying customers receive added value or an improved user experience while using the site.

Flickr gives away its core functionality for free: users do not pay anything to view, upload, tag, or organize photos. Flickr imposes limits on the number of photos and videos that holders of free accounts can upload in a month and does not allow such users to download high-resolution images. Flickr gives away its core functionality for free and offers premium services that include unlimited uploads and storage, access to high-resolution files, and ad-free browsing, as shown in Figure 4-28 (a).

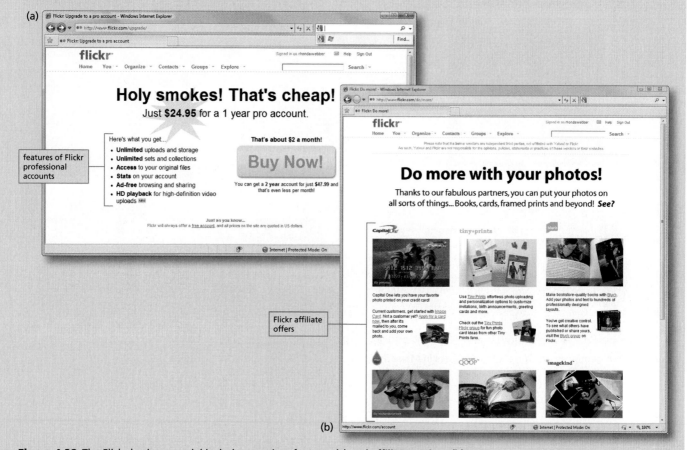

Figure 4-28 The Flickr business model includes premium features (a) and affiliate options (b).

How Do Web 2.0 Companies Make Money? *(continued)*

It is estimated that less than 20% of Flickr's customer base is paying customers. The cost for Flickr to host any individual customer's photos is negligible; the only real cost is that of the storage space for an individual user's photos.

As an additional source of revenue, Flickr has partnered with other companies, known as affiliates and shown in Figure 4-28 (b), who provide photo-printing services. Customers may purchase prints or create greeting cards, mugs, and other gift items from their photos through any of Flickr's affiliates. This **affiliate marketing** is beneficial to both Flickr and its partner companies that produce the goods from Flickr photos. Each affiliate company makes a profit from the items that it sells. Flickr also receives a portion of the proceeds from the sale of these items in exchange for allowing its affiliates to sell products featuring Flickr photos.

Social Bookmarking with Delicious

Delicious was one of the earliest Web 2.0 sites to offer social bookmarking, a service that enables users to use tags to bookmark, or save, the locations of their favorite Web pages or resources online. A bookmark contains the title and URL for items such as Web pages, blog posts, Flickr photos, online documents or spreadsheets, audio or video files, or any other resource posted on the Web that is accessible through a URL.

Web browsers, samples of which are shown in Figure 4-29, use different terminology to refer to your collection of favorite Web sites. Internet Explorer calls them **favorites**,

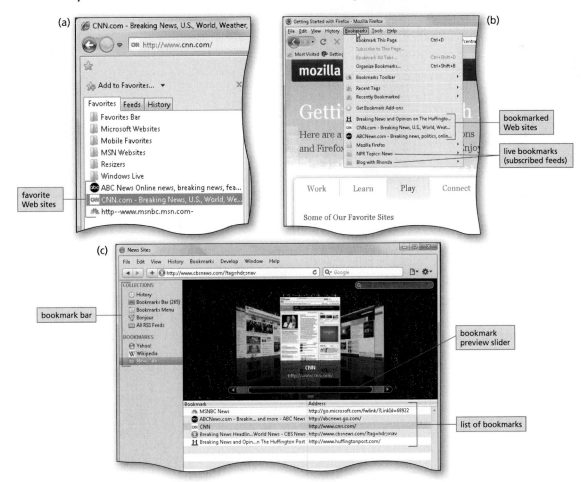

Figure 4-29 Accessing bookmarks and favorites in various browsers: Internet Explorer (a), Firefox (b), and Safari (c).

whereas Mozilla Firefox, Apple Safari, and Google Chrome call them **bookmarks**. This text uses the terms favorites and bookmarks interchangeably. When you save a bookmark from your browser, the browser stores the URL and title of the page in a file on your computer.

Your bookmarks are available to you only on the computer and in the browser in which they were originally saved. This may be problematic if you use different computers to browse the Web, perhaps at home, at work, or in a computer lab at school. In addition, if you use multiple browsers on a particular computer, you would need to copy your bookmarks from browser to browser if you wanted them to be available in all of the browsers that you use. Finally, you can only save one bookmark in one folder at a time. Consider the process of creating a favorite for a YouTube video about social bookmarking, as shown in Figure 4-30.

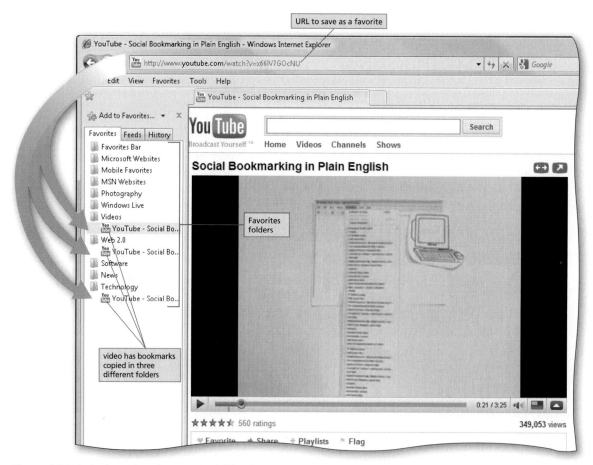

Figure 4-30 Assigning a favorite to many folders in Internet Explorer.

If you were to bookmark this video using Internet Explorer, you might place the bookmark in the Technology folder of your Favorites collection. Because the video also relates to Web 2.0, you also might want to place a copy of the bookmark in the Web 2.0 folder. Finally, because you have a Videos folder, you could place a third bookmark there. To accomplish this, you would have to manually create a new bookmark for the same video and place it in each of these folders.

Sharing and Tagging Bookmarks with Delicious

Created by Joshua Schachter in 2003, Delicious introduced the idea of making bookmarks available online and using tags to describe them. You have to create an account and be logged in to Delicious to access your bookmarks, as shown in Figure 4-31, but you can do so from any browser on any computer with Internet access.

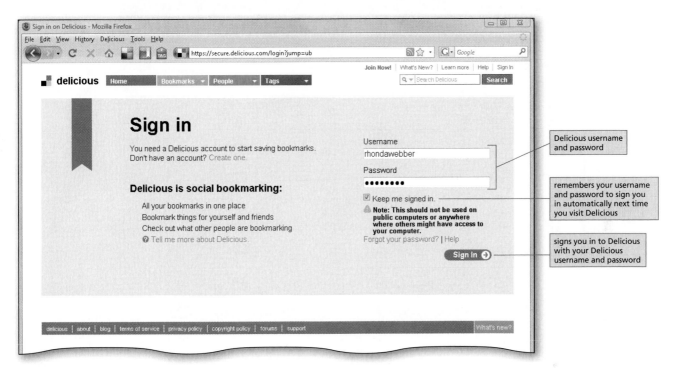

Figure 4-31 Signing in to Delicious.

When you log in to Delicious, you can elect to have the site remember your last login so that you do not have to log in every time you access Delicious. This is a convenient feature if you are the only person using your computer. You should not use this feature if you are accessing Delicious on a public computer, such as in a computer lab or Internet café, or if you share your computer with other people.

Once your bookmarks are stored online, you can share your bookmarks and see what Web sites other users with similar interests are visiting. Delicious allows you to view all of the tags used to describe a particular bookmark and to also find related Web sites that share the same tags. Delicious also measures the popularity of a particular Web page based on the number of users who bookmark it. Figure 4-32 on the next page displays the Popular Bookmarks tab on the Delicious home page.

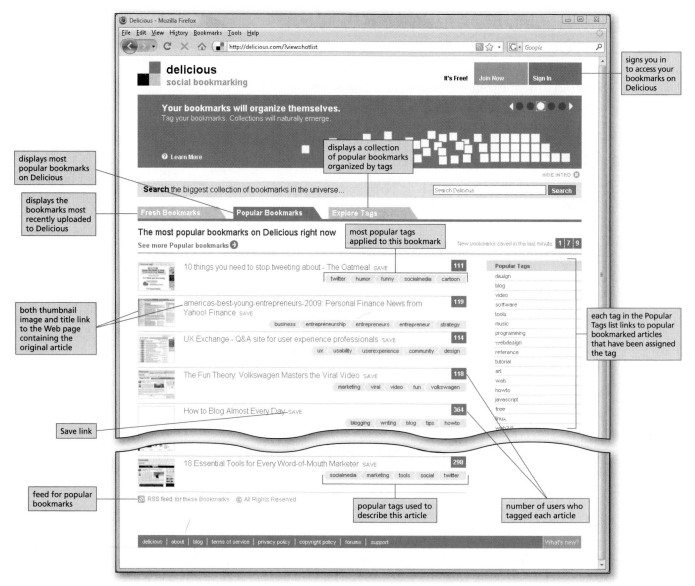

Figure 4-32 The Delicious home page.

Other tabs include the Fresh Bookmarks tab, which shows some of the most recently shared bookmarks from users of Delicious, and the Explore Tags tab, which displays a collection of popular bookmarks organized by the tags used to describe them.

Each bookmark displays a thumbnail image of the Web site or item being bookmarked and the title of the item, both of which link to the original item. Each bookmark also includes the number of people who bookmarked this item and the most popular tags used to describe it. Unlike bookmarks stored from your browser, each bookmarked site in Delicious can be described by one or more tags. The Popular Bookmarks tab also displays a list of popular tags and offers a feed for popular bookmarks.

"There's no such thing as a perfect categorization . . . I'm not trying to categorize the Web but helping people find stuff later."

Joshua Schachter, creator of Delicious

Interacting with Delicious

The easiest way to store bookmarks to Delicious is by installing the browser toolbar buttons for your Web browser. Delicious will prompt you to do so when you create your account and log in for the first time. The browser toolbar buttons link to your bookmarks page in Delicious, save a new bookmark to Delicious, and display a sidebar panel in your browser containing your Delicious tags. Figure 4-33 shows the browser toolbar buttons and sidebar panel for Firefox; these buttons may appear slightly differently in other browsers for which this add-on is available.

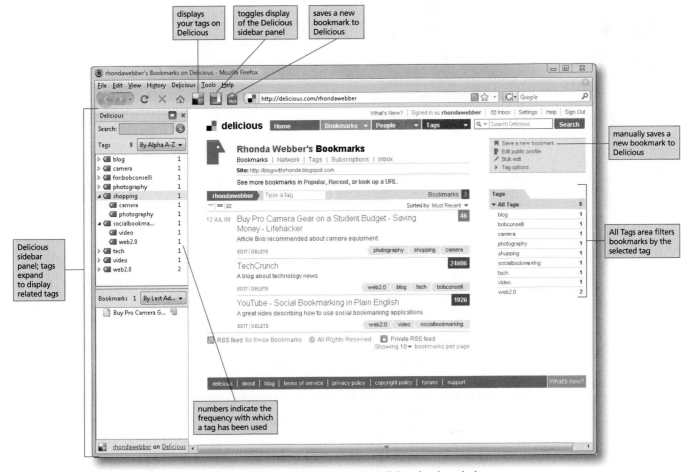

Figure 4-33 Firefox Browser shows Delicious toolbar buttons and a user's Delicious bookmarks home page.

The Delicious browser panel displays a list of your tags and the frequency with which each is used. You may expand a tag to see related tags. You may also filter your bookmarks by selecting one of the tags in the All Tags area of your bookmarks page.

SAVING A BOOKMARK To bookmark a Web site using the browser toolbar buttons, navigate to the site you would like to bookmark, and then click the Save a Bookmark button (depicted by the tag icon in your browser's toolbar) to display the Save a Bookmark page, shown in Figure 4-34.

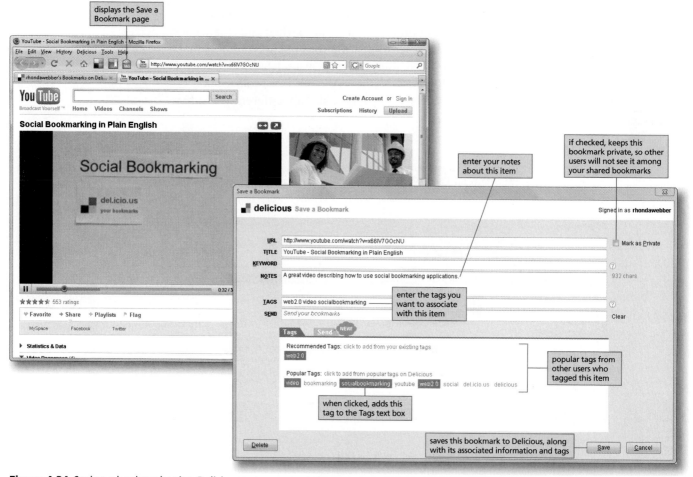

Figure 4-34 Saving a bookmark using Delicious.

When you bookmark a Web site with Delicious, you can tag it with one or several descriptive keywords. On the Save a Bookmark page, you can enter your own tags in the Tags text box or select from among popular and recommended tags from other users who bookmarked the same item. If you do not have the browser buttons installed, you can click the Save a new bookmark link to manually save a bookmark by entering its URL and any tags.

When viewing a bookmark posted by other Delicious users, you can save their bookmark in your collection by clicking the Save link. This is an effective way to recall useful resources posted by other users. Figure 4-35 displays a sample of the tags and bookmarks from the Explore Tags tab.

Figure 4-35 A sample of tags and bookmarks.

Three bookmarks accompany each tag, and a link is provided to find additional bookmarks identified with the same tag. You also can search for bookmarks by entering a tag into the search box. You can save some of these bookmarks in your own collection by clicking the Save link. The Popular Bookmarks page, shown in Figure 4-36, filters popular bookmarks to display only those with the specified tag.

Figure 4-36 The Popular Bookmarks page filtered by the tag "museum."

You can also click on related tags to find other bookmarks that may be of interest. Each number is a hyperlink to the Everyone's Bookmarks page that displays a list of all of the users who saved a particular bookmark, when they saved it, and the tags they that used, organized in reverse chronological order, as shown in Figure 4-37.

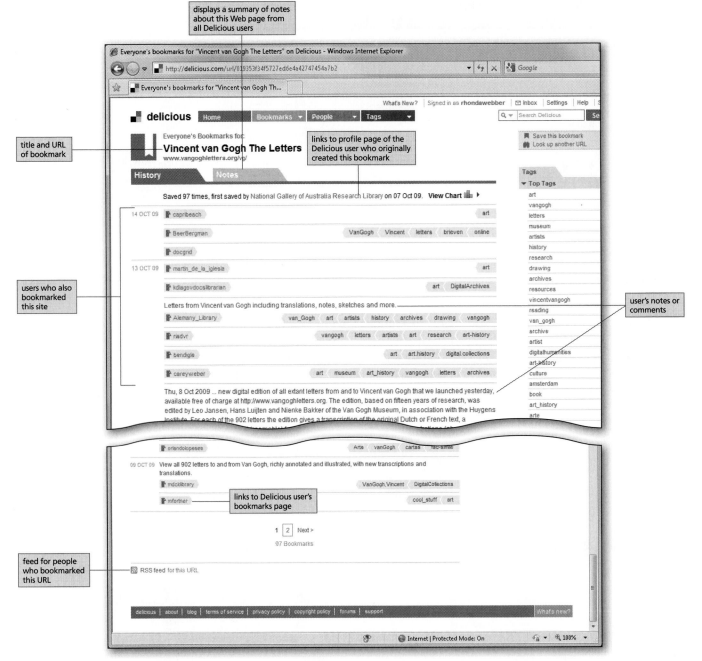

Figure 4-37 The Everyone's Bookmarks Page displays information about all users who saved the same bookmark.

The Everyone's Bookmarks page also displays the user who first saved this bookmark. Every username links to the profile page of the user who saved this bookmark. The Notes tab on the Everyone's Bookmarks page displays a summary of all of the comments added by users when bookmarking an article. One benefit of reviewing the Everyone's Bookmarks page is that it provides access to other Delicious users who may have interests similar to yours. From this page, you can explore other users' Bookmarks pages to possibly identify more items of interest.

SEARCHING FOR BOOKMARKS   A tag-based search using Delicious offers different results than entering keywords or phrases into a search engine such as Google or Yahoo! Search engines find relevant items that match a keyword or phrase that appears within the article or Web page, whereas the results of a search based on user-specified tags in Delicious are Web sites, blog posts, and other articles recommended by people who read, comment on, and bookmark them. This additional metadata, combined with the number of people who tagged a particular page, may be useful to readers who are trying to decide whether or not a resource may be useful to them, before reading the entire article. As with many Web 2.0 applications that rely on the wisdom of crowds, the number of people that tag a particular resource is a probable indication of its relevance.

To search for bookmarks on Delicious, enter a tag as a search term. Delicious will find bookmarks identified with that tag. As you enter additional tags, Delicious will refine the results to display only those articles that have been assigned all of the search tags you entered. Figure 4-38 displays the results of a tag search using Delicious.

Step 1
Enter search term to filter bookmarks.

Step 2
Enter additional tags to refine the results even further.

Figure 4-38 Performing a tag-based search.

The user begins by entering the tag "netbook" in the Tag search box on the Explore Everyone's Tags page available from the Explore Tags tab. When the user types a second tag, "asus," Delicious filters all of the results to show only those bookmarks that were tagged with both "netbook" and "asus." Typing a third tag such as "battery" would refine the results even further to show only those items that discuss the battery life of Asus netbook computers. Adding tags to a search is an incremental way to identify only those bookmarks that match your specific interests.

Advanced Features of Delicious

Delicious offers additional features that enable users to interact with tagged data. Users may subscribe to RSS feeds to be notified of new bookmarks posted with specific tags. Users may also use widgets to display their tags or links on their blogs.

SYNDICATING BOOKMARKS USING RSS   Delicious offers several RSS feeds to which users can subscribe to be notified of new bookmarks of interest. The feed icon, usually located in the lower-left corner of a Delicious page, indicates the feed available on that page. Available feeds include all popular bookmarks on Delicious identified with a particular tag, the most popular bookmarks now, and the bookmarks from a specific Delicious user.

When members of a group all use a common tag to bookmark interesting Web pages or blog posts, this collaborative organization process dynamically creates a shared resource list for everyone in the group. Figure 4-39 shows several bookmarks from students enrolled in a college course, all tagged with "bentleycs299." By subscribing to this

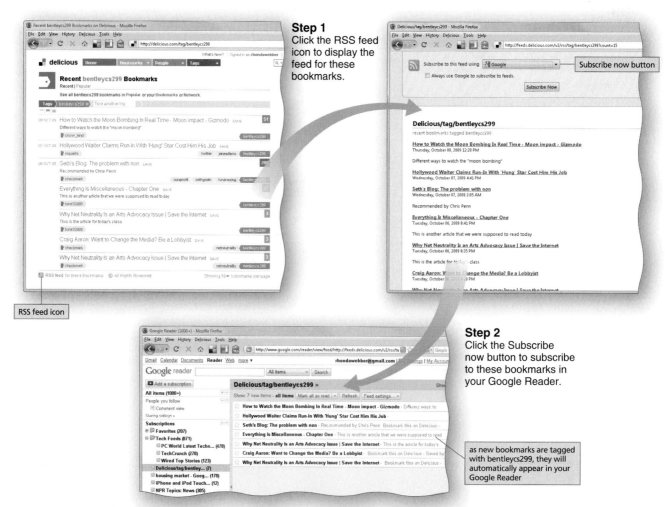

Figure 4-39 Syndicating Bookmarks with RSS.

feed in a feed reader, students will be notified automatically when one of their classmates shares a new bookmark on Delicious.

SHARING BOOKMARKS WITH OTHER USERS If you see a Web page or blog post that you want to share with someone else, you could send an e-mail message to that person, including the URL and title of the article in your message. However, if you know your friend's Delicious username, you can share the bookmark directly through Delicious by adding the tag "for:username", where "username" is your friend's username on Delicious. For example, tagging an article "for:bobconselli" sends a bookmark to Bob Conselli's Delicious inbox. Figure 4-40 displays Bob Conselli's inbox, where Rhonda Webber has shared a bookmark to the TechCrunch blog.

Figure 4-40 Sharing a bookmark with another Delicious user.

After reviewing the bookmarks in your inbox, you can save them in your bookmark collection or remove them from your inbox. You can also click on the link containing the name of the person sharing the bookmark with you to view all of his or her bookmarks.

TAG AND LINKROLLS Delicious provides tools that allow you to share your bookmarks and tags on your blog and, thus, provide updated content to your readers about what you are reading online. A **linkroll** displays the most recently added bookmarks on your blog or Web site. When you create a linkroll in Delicious, a preview of the linkroll is displayed on the same page that generates the HTML code for your blog, as shown in Figure 4-41 on the next page.

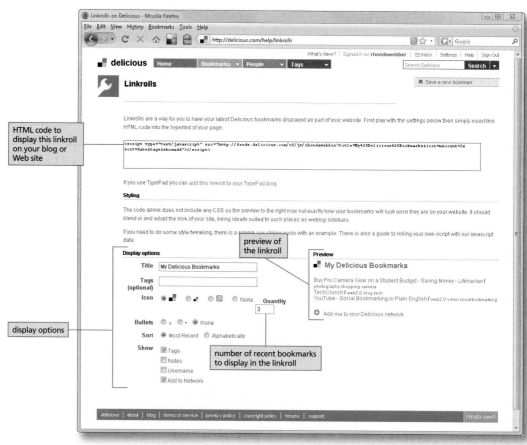

Figure 4-41 Creating a Delicious linkroll.

A **tagroll,** previewed in Figure 4-42 along with the HTML code, displays your tags as a tag cloud. Because your more frequently used tags are displayed in a larger size than your less frequently used tags, a tagroll provides your readers with a snapshot of your interests.

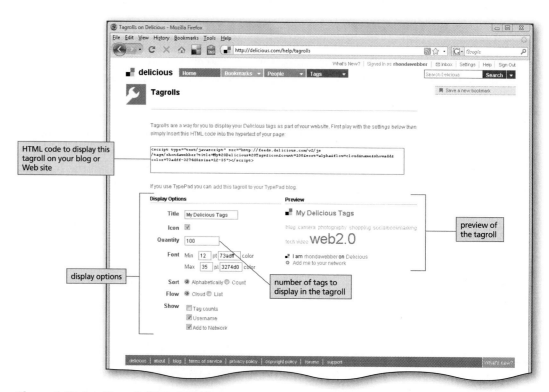

Figure 4-42 Creating a Delicious tagroll.

To display a linkroll or tagroll on your blog, copy and paste the HTML code for the linkroll or tagroll from the Delicious Web site into the HTML editor for a blog post or the HTML sidebar gadget on your blog. Figure 4-43 displays a blog post containing a linkroll of Delicious bookmarks and a sidebar gadget displaying a tagroll of Delicious tags.

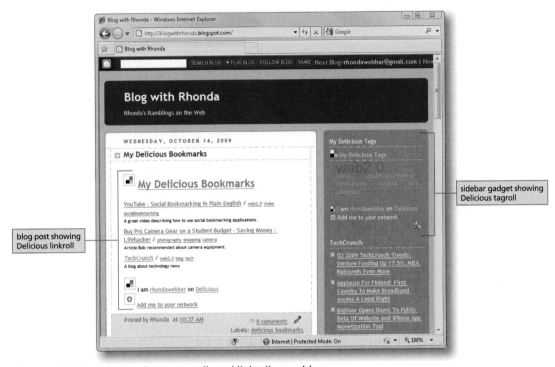

Figure 4-43 Displaying Delicious tagrolls and linkrolls on a blog.

ENCOURAGING USERS TO TAG YOUR CONTENT ON DELICIOUS   Many Web sites facilitate the process by which users share their blog content on Delicious and other social media sites. When readers share your content on their blogs, Web sites, or social bookmarking services, your content gains additional exposure. AddThis, shown in Figure 4-44, provides a bookmark-sharing tool that enables readers to quickly share your blog posts using several social bookmarking and networking services.

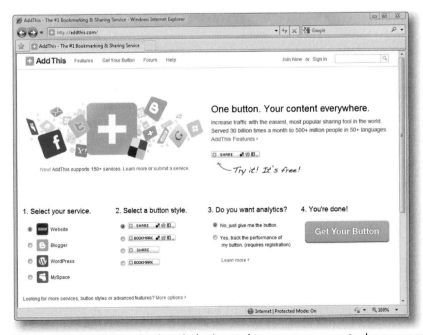

Figure 4-44 AddThis is a bookmark-sharing tool to encourage users to share your content.

A blogger can install the AddThis gadget by including HTML code provided by AddThis after each blog post. The AddThis gadget displays as a plus sign icon. Figure 4-45 shows the process of interacting with the AddThis gadget, as installed on the Fox Sports Web site, to directly bookmark a sports news story.

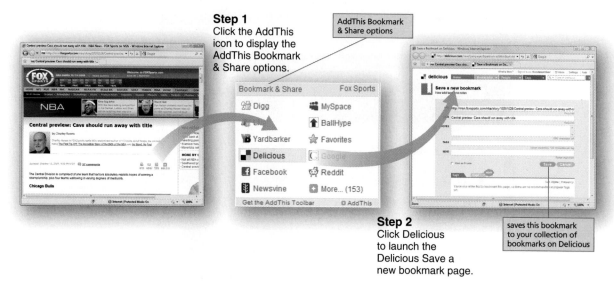

Step 1
Click the AddThis icon to display the AddThis Bookmark & Share options.

AddThis Bookmark & Share options

Step 2
Click Delicious to launch the Delicious Save a new bookmark page.

saves this bookmark to your collection of bookmarks on Delicious

Figure 4-45 Using the AddThis bookmarking tool to bookmark content from the Fox Sports Web site on Delicious.

After reading the sports article, you can use the AddThis bookmark-sharing tool to add the bookmark to your collection of Delicious bookmarks. When you hover over the AddThis icon with the mouse, the icon expands to show Bookmark & Share options. You can select the desired social-bookmarking service with which to share this bookmark. By selecting Delicious, the browser displays the Delicious Save a new bookmark page, from which you can enter notes and tags and save the bookmark. If you are not currently logged in to Delicious, you will have to log in before you can save the bookmark.

Summary

Tagging allows individuals to use keywords to describe digital information, such as photos, music, or Web site bookmarks. Tagging is a collaborative process that takes advantage of the wisdom of crowds to create folksonomies that are nonhierarchical, informal, and meaningful.

Several Web sites allow users to organize digital content using tags. On Flickr, users store and share digital photos on the Web, organizing their photos by assigning tags that categorize, describe, or locate them. Delicious enables the sharing of bookmarks on the Web, rather than storing bookmarks on one's own computer. Users may share their bookmarks with others or view other bookmarks that use similar tags. A tag-based search on Delicious may uncover different results than a search using a traditional search engine, because bookmarks on Delicious are manually entered by users who have taken the time to read the article, rather than by a search engine that simply matches keywords.

Both Flickr and Delicious promote the use of tags to describe and organize content in ways that are personally relevant. When aggregated with tags from other users, tagging provides a classification that reflects an online community's understanding of Web content.

Think

Submit responses to these questions as directed by your instructor.

1. Why use more than one label or tag to describe the same piece of information?

2. Give an example of a hierarchical way to organize digital information and a nonhierarchical way to organize digital information. What is a benefit and drawback of each method?

3. Why is Creative Commons licensing an important development for sharing digital information? Would you allow others to use your photos? What licenses would you apply?

4. What are two features of the freemium business model? Have you seen other Web sites that use this model?

5. Name three ways that social bookmarking is a social process, enabling you to learn about or connect with other people from their bookmarks.

6. How do collaborative tagging sites such as Flickr and Delicious improve as more people use them?

Watch

Watch the video for Chapter 4 on the Online Companion at scsite.com/web2. Be prepared to answer or discuss the questions posted on the Online Companion as directed by your instructor.

Try

Visit the Online Companion at scsite.com/web2 and follow the steps as you complete the tutorials for this chapter.

Tutorial 4-1 Using Flickr
In this tutorial, you will learn to upload, organize, and search for photos on Flickr.

Tutorial 4-2 Using Delicious
In this tutorial, you will use the Delicious Web site to save and search for bookmarks online.

Blog

Complete these exercises on the blog that you created for this class.

1. Follow the instructions for embedding a video on your blog, as shown in Chapter 2, but instead of embedding the video code, embed the HTML code to display one of your Flickr images. Write a blog post in which you compare two different approaches for displaying an image on a blog, first by uploading an image directly to Blogger and second by embedding an image stored on Flickr. What is the biggest advantage of each approach?

2. Add a Flickr badge to your blog. The Flickr badge is available under the Tools link in the Help row at the bottom of your photostream page. Follow steps similar to those in Chapter 2 to add an HTML/Javascript gadget to your blog's sidebar, and paste in the HTML code that Flickr generates.

3. Add a gadget to your blog to display photos from a Flickr-hosted RSS feed. On the Add a Gadget page, enter Flickr Feed as the search term, and select a gadget of your choice to display. You will need to know the URL for the Flickr Web feed of the picture that you want to display. Copy the URL from Flickr, and paste it in as part of the gadget's settings.

4. Add a linkroll and a tagroll showing your recent Delicious bookmarks and tags to your blog as a post or in the sidebar.

5. Edit your previous blog posts on Blogger to add labels to them. Give two different labels to one of your posts. Use the same label on two different posts.

6. Add the Labels gadget to your blog's sidebar. Verify that the labels you assigned in the previous exercise appear.

7. Write a blog post in which you state your opinion on whether Flickr does enough to promote the use of Creative Commons licensing. Why do you think people change their settings to allow their photos to be shared? Would you?

8. Write a blog post comparing the use of a social-bookmarking site such as Delicious with a search engine such as Google to find relevant information on a popular topic. Search for the same term using both, and compare the results. How many of the results are the same on the first page of search results from each application? Which set of results do you find more reliable? Which are more useful? Which are more current? Take screenshots of the results from each Web site, and post them to your blog along with a discussion of your findings. Assign appropriate labels to your blog post.

These activities encourage you to explore Web 2.0 sites and applications on your own. Submit your responses as directed by your instructor.

1. Select a photo archive from The Commons section of the Flickr Web site. Explore the photos and add a tag or a comment to those already in place for the image you select.

2. Subscribe to any feed of photos from Flickr.

3. Subscribe to a feed of bookmarks on a topic of interest using Delicious.

4. Exchange e-mail messages with a friend and assign tags to your messages in Gmail.

5. Create an account on Last.fm and search for or tag some of your favorite music or artists.

6. Use Delicious for two weeks to tag articles of interest as you browse the Web.

7. Find a current article about Web 2.0 of interest to you, and tag it with the tag SCWeb20. Then, look on Delicious for other items that are tagged with SCWeb20 to see articles that other readers of this book recommend.

8. Install the Delicious browser buttons for the browser, other than Firefox, that you use most frequently.

9. Digg is a Web site that allows users to vote (or digg) news stories, similar to tagging Web sites on Delicious. The site relies on the "wisdom of crowds" to determine the most popular content. The more people that digg a particular resource, the higher on the list it appears. Near each article is the number of diggs or votes that it received. Explore the site; create an account on Digg, and use it for a week. Compare the top news stories on Digg with those on a traditional news media Web site. Write a blog post summarizing your experience with the quality of the articles that make up the top of the list. Does the wisdom of crowds work? Do you find the content aggregated from the wisdom of crowds to be interesting or useful?

If your instructor set up a class wiki, complete these exercises.

1. Create a list of Web sites that you encounter that make use of tags to find information. Add hyperlinks to these Web sites in a page on your class wiki.

2. Add your Flickr photostream URL to a page on your class wiki.

5 | Connecting People

Overview

For as long as there has been an Internet, people have been using it to connect with each other. Web 2.0 has created new opportunities for, and new methods of, connecting with others who share similar social, personal, or professional interests.

Social media applications inform, educate, and entertain people through shared blog posts, bookmarks, images, music, videos, podcasts, and other online media. A **social networking application** allows users to create profiles for sharing information about themselves and to designate as friends or contacts users with whom they share a common interest. Both social media and social networking applications connect people who share common goals and interests. The ability to quickly upload and share information and images, the capability to communicate via e-mail or instant messaging, and the availability of social networking applications on both Web browsers and mobile phones all contribute to the increased use and popularity of social networks. Networks such as Facebook, LinkedIn, MySpace, and Twitter, shown in Figure 5-1 on the next page, allow users to discover and maintain personal and professional relationships with each other.

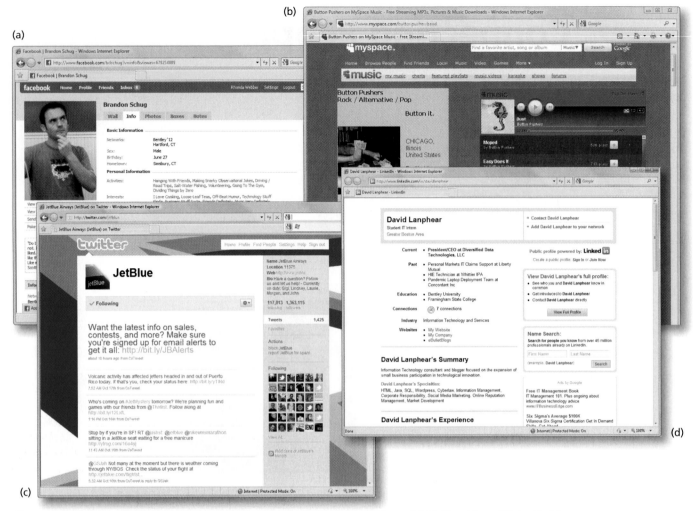

Figure 5-1 Popular social networking applications include Facebook (a), MySpace (b), Twitter (c), and LinkedIn (d).

Facebook started as a tool for college students to connect with each other and has expanded to allow anyone to locate and communicate with friends. LinkedIn is a network for professional social networking; users share their resumes and ask business acquaintances to write letters of recommendation on their behalf. MySpace is a social network often used by musical bands, comedians, filmmakers, and other artists to promote themselves. Many MySpace users submit audio and video files of their performances as a way to gain publicity. On Twitter, users maintain a **microblog**, in which each post contains, at most, 140 characters. Twitter began by inviting people to answer the question "What are you doing?" but has grown into a tool for individuals and organizations to share information, ideas, URLs to blog posts or other interesting online resources, and calls to action with the people in their network.

Many businesses also use social networks to connect internally with their employees and externally with their customers. They create channels of communication that allow employees to collaborate with other employees and encourage customers to provide feedback about products or services.

Common Features of Social Networking Applications

Social networking sites let people get to know each other online. In addition to sharing and updating personal and professional information, many users of social networking sites keep their status messages up to date. A **status message** displays a current location, activities, or thoughts so that friends and contacts will know what a user is doing. Friends may also comment on a user's status message. All social networking applications share similar features: the ability to create a profile, the ability to designate other members as friends or contacts, and the ability to identify a friend's friends. You can ask someone with whom you share an interest to be a **friend** (the term used by personal networks such as Facebook and Twitter) or a **contact** (the term used by the LinkedIn professional network). Your collection of friends forms your social network. On most social networks, a person must confirm your friend request in order for you to join his or her network. Because both parties must agree to be friends, this helps to create trust among all members of a social network. By looking at a list of your friends' friends, you can identify friends who you share in common. Though a larger social network is generally more useful than a smaller one because of the additional potential connections, it also is important that the people who you connect with add value to your network.

Before using a social networking application, you must register with the site and create a profile. Your **profile** contains personal information, including name, e-mail address, gender, age, location, and a photograph, as shown in the Facebook and LinkedIn profiles in Figure 5-2.

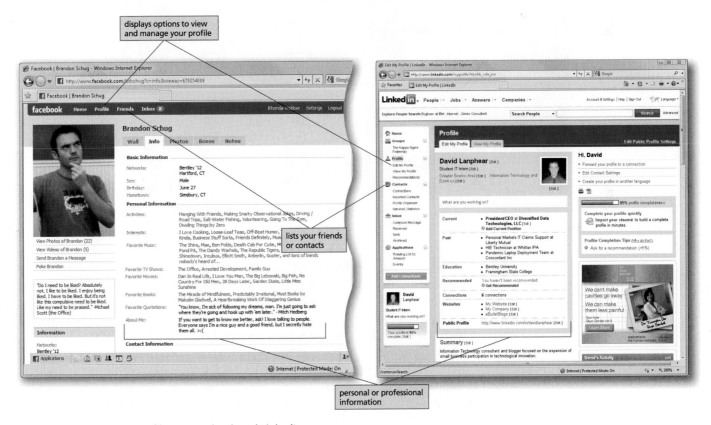

Figure 5-2 Comparing profiles on Facebook and LinkedIn.

Personal information on a Facebook profile includes gender, birthday, hometown, interests, and favorites. Professional information on a LinkedIn profile includes current and past employment, education, and a summary of professional skills. Both sites allow you to list your friends or contacts. On LinkedIn, adding a recommendation to the profile pages of people who you know enhances the value of the profile to potential employers.

On MySpace, shown in Figure 5-3 on the next page, profiles of bands may include information about the type of music they play, samples of their music as recorded audio files, information about the members of the band, and details about upcoming concerts.

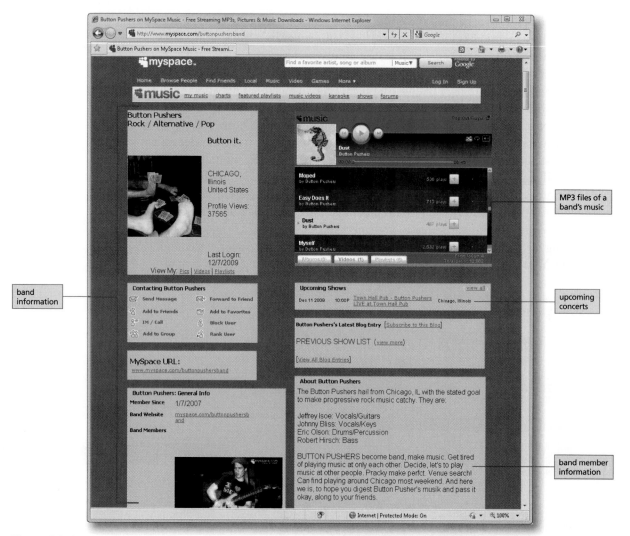

Figure 5-3 On MySpace, a profile includes information about a band and samples of its music.

The power of social networking comes when networks of friends and contacts overlap. Your friends also have networks to which they belong; you can often browse their friends and invite them to become friends of yours or connect with those people directly. Immediate friends of your friends are known as your **second-level contacts**. They and their friends are your **extended contacts**. Your extended contacts give you even greater access to people in many places. Extended contacts may be especially important when using social networks for job seeking or to find people with specific knowledge or skills that could be helpful to you. By completing your profile and participating regularly online in blogs and social networks, you place yourself in a good position to be found by others looking for people with your skills.

Social networking sites, such as Facebook and LinkedIn, facilitate the process of finding people who you already know, as shown in Figure 5-4.

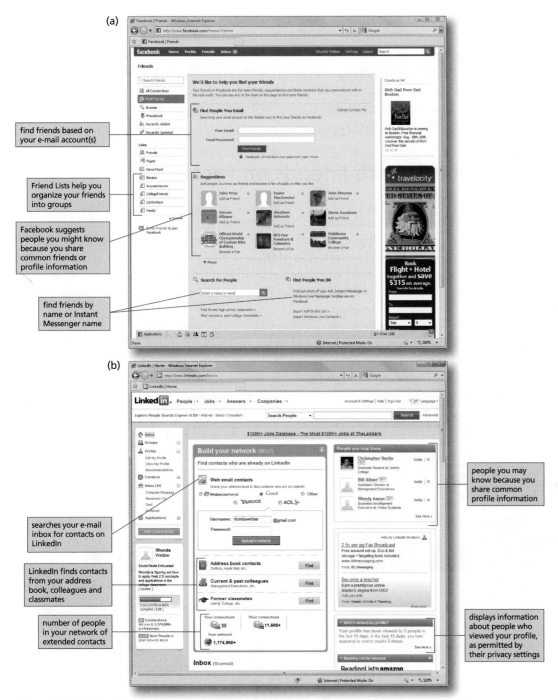

Figure 5-4 Finding friends on Facebook (a) and building your social network on LinkedIn (b).

Allowing a social networking site access to your e-mail address book is one way to find people who you already know are registered on that site. Each site will search its user database to find registered users whose e-mail addresses match those in your address book. The site will notify you about which of your contacts are also members and invite you to connect with them on the social networking site. Both Facebook and LinkedIn also suggest people whom you might know because you share common friends or profile information, such as the same educational institution or employer. You can often search for people based on their screen names, real names, e-mail addresses, or Instant Messenger names. On Facebook, you can also search for groups of people, such as members of a high school or college class, members of an organization, employees of a company, and people with common interests. On LinkedIn you can search for contacts, classmates, and colleagues. You can also look for people who have particular jobs or who work at companies of interest.

As people discover you through your use of social networks, they may send requests asking you to join their networks. Social networking sites themselves may also make recommendations of members who you might know through common friends or overlapping education or employment histories. If you know these people, you might choose to invite them to join your social network. You should only accept requests from people whom you know, people who come recommended to you, or people whose profiles indicate that they would add value to your network.

Connecting with Friends on Facebook

Mark Zuckerberg started Facebook in 2004 as a network for students at Harvard University to connect with each other. The site got its name from the paper booklet of students' photographs distributed to students at Zuckerberg's high school so that they could find each other. Within a few weeks of the site going live at Harvard, other colleges in the Boston area requested to participate, and within a few months, Facebook added 30 more colleges to its network. Facebook quickly grew from a network for college students to a network open to everyone.

In 2009, it was estimated that there were as many Facebook users between the ages of 35 and 49 as there were between the ages of 18 and 34. In December 2009, Mark Zuckerberg reported on the Facebook blog, shown in Figure 5-5(a), that more than 350 million people had signed up for Facebook. Figure 5-5(b) contains a table from Wikipedia showing the population of the 10 largest countries in the world. If Facebook were a country, its population would be larger than the population of the United States. The number of Facebook users has more than doubled in 2009, as shown in Figure 5-5(c).

(a)

(b)

Rank	Country / Territory	Population
1	China[5]	1,334,640,000
2	India	1,173,730,000
3	United States	308,139,000
4	Indonesia	231,369,500
5	Brazil	192,175,000
6	Pakistan	168,186,000
7	Bangladesh	162,221,000
8	Nigeria	154,729,000
9	Russia	141,909,279
10	Japan	127,560,000

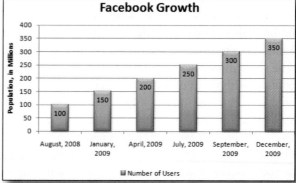

(c)

Figure 5-5 Facebook by the numbers: Facebook reaches 350 million users in December 2009 (a); the number of Facebook users compared to world populations by country (b); and the growth of Facebook users during 2009 (c).

"Think about what people are doing on Facebook today. They're keeping up with their friends and family, but they're also building an image and identity for themselves, which in a sense is their brand. They're connecting with the audience that they want to connect to. It's almost a disadvantage if you're not on [Facebook] now. . . . Everyone's trying to . . . communicate, build a reputation, build relationships with people, and just have more information out there."

Mark Zuckerberg, founder of Facebook

Connecting with Facebook

Your profile on Facebook contains a variety of pages and tabs where you can share information with your friends. For example, the Info tab of your Facebook profile, shown in Figure 5-6, displays personal information that you want to share with friends, classmates, or coworkers on Facebook.

Figure 5-6 A Facebook Profile page contains a user's personal information.

A Facebook profile contains biographical and contact information, as well as information about favorite activities, interests, networks, and other items. Facebook uses this data to connect you to other members whose profiles contain similar information.

Facebook's **Wall** tab, shown in Figure 5-7, displays a blog-style page on which you can update your status messages.

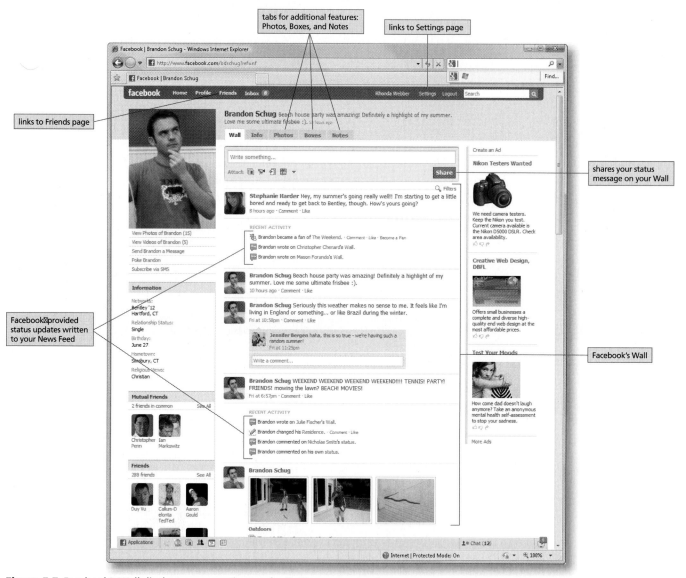

Figure 5-7 Facebook's Wall displays your greetings and activities on Facebook.

You or your friends can write comments, greetings, or other messages on your Wall. A Facebook Wall also displays a log of your activities, such as becoming friends with new people or writing a message on a friend's Wall. Posts on your Facebook Wall are stored online indefinitely and form a record of your life activities for all of your friends to see.

Other tabs shown in Figure 5-7 include the Photos tab, the Boxes tab, and the Notes tab. The Photos tab shows pictures that you wish to share on your profile or photos in which you were tagged, which have been uploaded by other Facebook members. The Boxes tab shows the applications that you have associated with your Facebook profile. The Facebook Notes tab may be configured to import and display content from a blog. As you post new articles on your blog, they will automatically appear on your Notes tab.

Your **News Feed** is a log of several actions that you might take on the site, such as adding a comment, changing your relationship status, adding a friend, posting on a friend's Wall, commenting on a photo, or removing an item from your profile. As you update your profile with new information, Facebook will add a record of the activity to your News Feed, which is displayed on your Wall.

Facebook's Friends page, linked from the top navigation bar, displays a list of your current friends, helps you to find new ones, as shown in Figure 5-4(a) on page 173, and offers recommendations about people who you might know.

Unlike search engines, whose goal is to provide external links to needed information as quickly as possible, Facebook's approach is to integrate as much information as possible into the site so that users will stay there longer. The more time that a user spends on Facebook, or any social networking site, the more attractive it may be for advertisers to place ads on the site.

Extending Facebook with Applications

One key to Facebook's popularity is the thousands of applications that are available to Facebook users. The Facebook Application Directory page, shown in Figure 5-8, displays several applications that you can include as part of your profile. Partnering with third-party developers increases Facebook's value to its users, as more applications are available for users to interact with through Facebook.

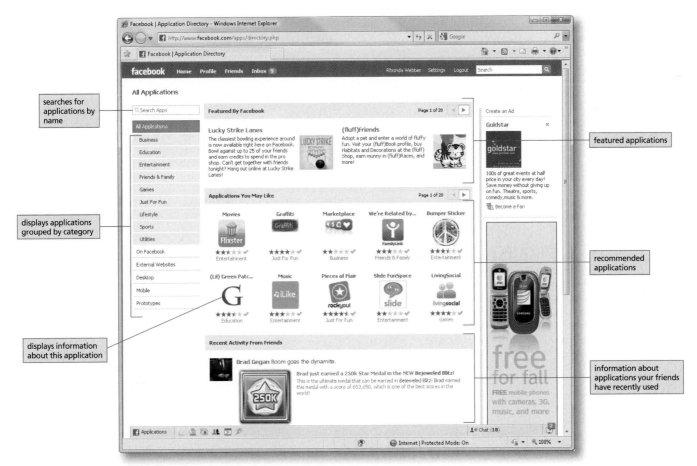

Figure 5-8 You can browse applications to add to your profile on Facebook's Application Directory page.

The Applications Directory page displays featured applications, applications organized by category, recommended applications that you may like, and information about applications that your friends have recently used. Many applications show you which of your friends are also using them. Because you and your friends can share information about which applications you interact with on the Applications Directory page and as entries in your News Feed, Facebook applications can become popular very quickly. When you add an application to your profile, it displays in the Boxes tab, shown in Figure 5-9.

Figure 5-9 The Boxes tab displays applications added to your profile.

The Facebook Causes application displays organizations or causes that you wish to support. The New England Patriots Fans application connects you with other Patriots fans and notifies you of upcoming games. The Applications menu in the toolbar displays all of your installed applications and allows you to organize and manage them. A chat feature, accessed by clicking the Chat button in the toolbar, displays a list of your friends who are currently online with whom you can exchange instant messages.

Third-party companies, organizations, or developers who are not affiliated with Facebook develop many of the Facebook applications, shown in Figure 5-10. Some applications are interactive games, such as Farmville, which users can play with their friends. Flixter and iLike are popular applications that allow members to read about and provide reviews of movies and music. SuperPoke adds features to Facebook's standard Poke feature, allowing users to say hello to their friends with humorous or meaningful greetings. Third-party applications may also include external content, such as Twitter posts and RSS feeds.

Figure 5-10 A sample of popular Facebook applications.

Because Facebook is designed to accommodate applications developed by third parties, it has become a platform for all of a user's social networking activities, including multiplayer games, e-mail messages, and instant messaging.

Privacy Concerns

Social networks have a **privacy policy** that describes how they will use your personal information. Figure 5-11 shows Facebook's Privacy Policy page.

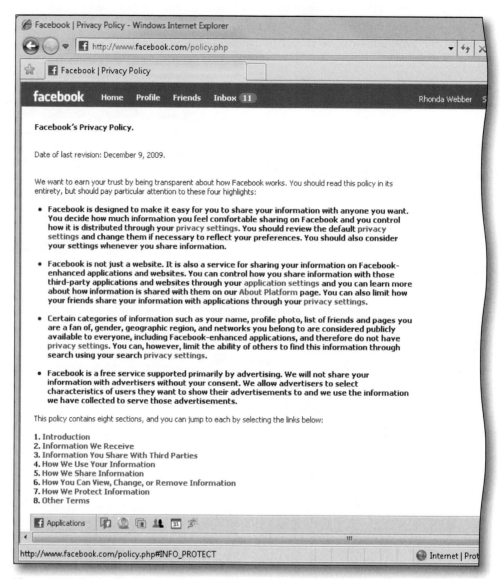

Figure 5-11 Facebook's Privacy Policy page describes how Facebook could share your information.

The Privacy Policy is a legal document that describes how Facebook may share information from your profile with other Facebook members, third-party applications, and advertisers, and use it for internal market research. Although Facebook and other social networking sites provide recommendations for default privacy settings, the responsibility lies with users to establish appropriate privacy settings for their personal information. By leaving your information open, anyone, whether on Facebook or not, may have access to information found in your profile. By restricting search engines and third-party applications from accessing your profile information, you can limit the information that they present to others about you.

Even if you delete information or files from your Facebook profile, or deactivate your account, earlier copies of those files may be stored in backups on Facebook's servers. If you deactivate your account, Facebook will not delete your information. Even though other users will not be able to see it, Facebook will retain your profile information so that it will be available should you decide to activate your account again at a future time.

Facebook's Privacy Settings page, shown in Figure 5-12 contains links to pages where you can specify privacy settings for your personal information. It is accessed from the Settings menu.

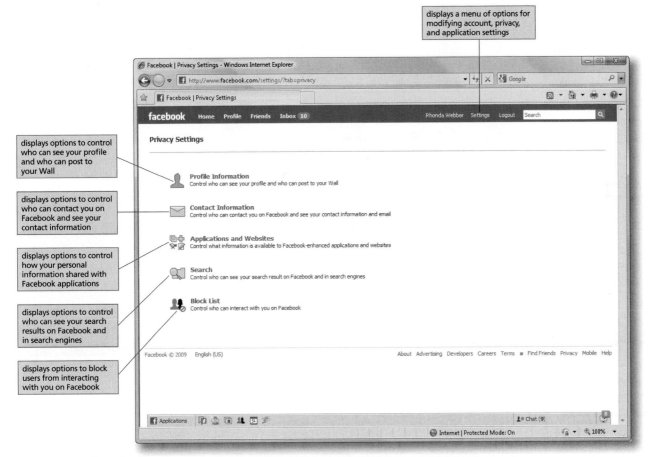

displays a menu of options for modifying account, privacy, and application settings

displays options to control who can see your profile and who can post to your Wall

displays options to control who can contact you on Facebook and see your contact information

displays options to control how your personal information shared with Facebook applications

displays options to control who can see your search results on Facebook and in search engines

displays options to block users from interacting with you on Facebook

Figure 5-12 Privacy Settings page in Facebook.

The Privacy Settings page contains links to pages where you can decide who can see information from your profile page, how other users can find you, which of your activities will be visible to other users, and how Facebook applications and search engines can use information from your profile.

Facebook allows you to select which friends or third-party applications can see each piece of information associated with your Facebook account. Figure 5-13 shows the pages available from the Privacy Settings page.

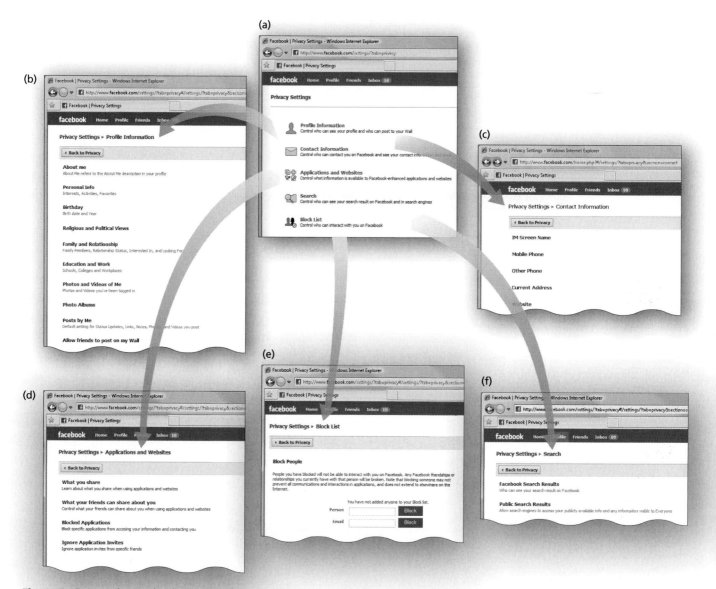

Figure 5-13 From the Facebook Privacy Settings page (a), you can specify privacy settings for your profile information (b), contact information (c), third-party applications (d), search results (e), and blocked users (f).

Your profile information includes your interests, activities, birthday, religious and political views, family and relationship information, education and work experience, photos and videos. Your contact information includes ways others can contact you, such as by Instant Messenger, phone, on the Web, or in person. You can block users from accessing information about you on Facebook. When you do, any Facebook ties you have with that person will be broken, however blocked users may still be able to find out about you by examining search results from other Web sites. You may also specify who can see your Facebook information in search results within Facebook or on the Web.

Facebook applications may gather information from your profile that is available to your friends and use that information as part of applications or product advertisements. For example, an application that sends birthday cards may use your date of birth and your list of friends in order to invite your friends to send you a birthday greeting. The Friends Quiz application, shown in Figure 5-14, creates a quiz by randomly choosing a profile item from four of your friends' profiles and asks you to guess the friend to which the profile item applies.

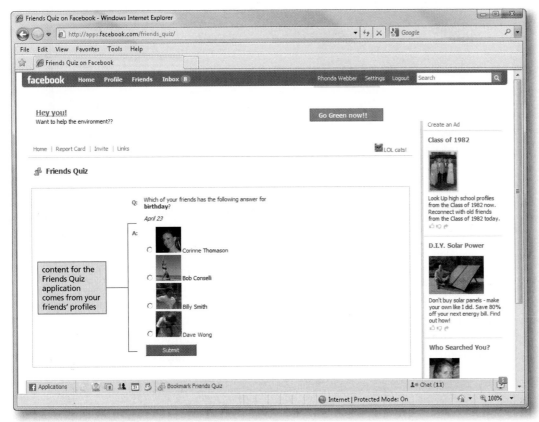

Figure 5-14 The Friends Quiz is an application that uses your profile information and that of your friends.

When you add an application to your Facebook page, Facebook lists your friends who also have added the application, and records your activity in the application in your News Feed. It is up to you to specify appropriate privacy settings if you do not want your data to be incorporated into or accessed by third-party applications. The Privacy Settings Applications and Websites page, shown Figure 5-13(d), contains links to pages that allow you to specify how applications may interact with your profile information. The What you share page describes the personal information that you share when visiting Applications and Websites, as shown in Figure 5-15(a) on the next page. The What your friends can share about you page specifies which personal items from your profile that Facebook applications can access, as shown in Figure 5-15(b).

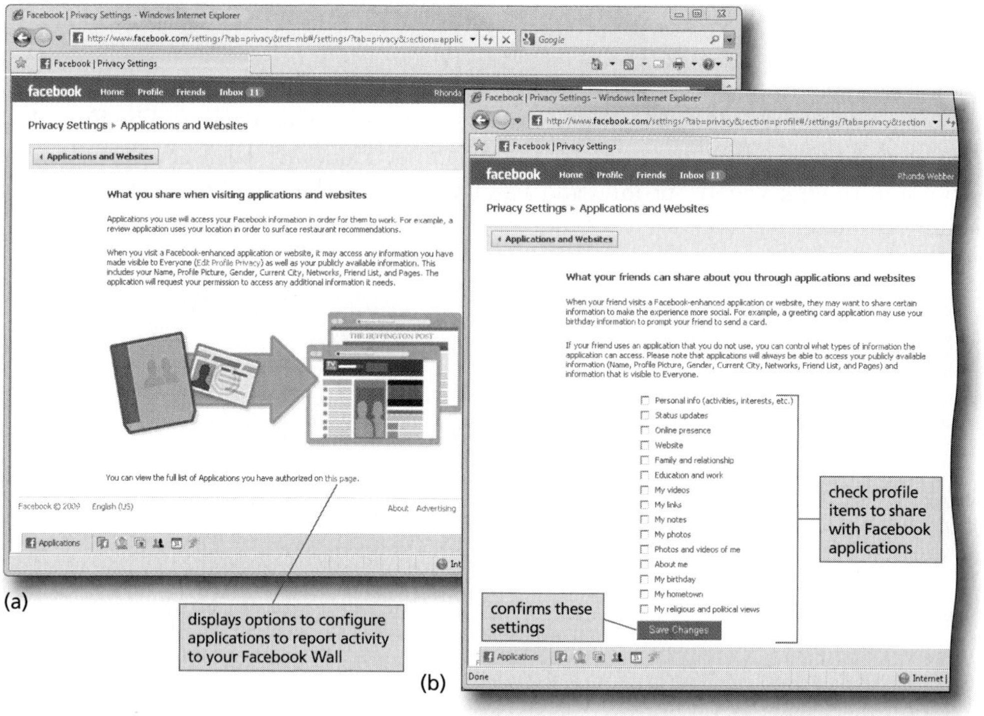

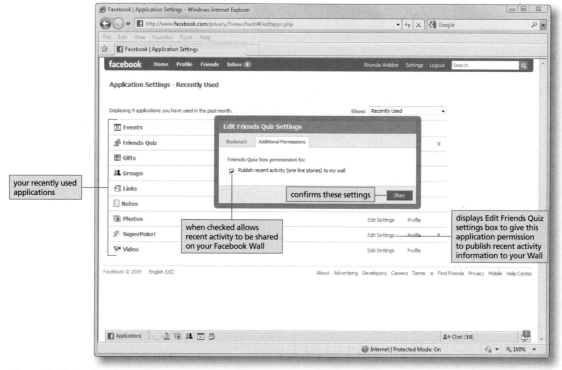

Figure 5-15 Configuring privacy settings for sharing profile information with Facebook applications.

On the Applications and Websites settings page you can specify which items from your personal profile, such as your profile picture, interests, education, or work history, to make available to Facebook applications. The Application Settings - Recently Used page, accessible from the What you share page, allows you to modify the settings of individual applications. Modifications specifically include whether or not you permit the application to write a record of your recent activity to your Facebook Wall, as shown in Figure 5-16.

Figure 5-16 Configuring privacy settings for applications.

As real-time search becomes a common feature of most search engines, search results on your name may contain your most recent updates to Facebook, Twitter, and other social networks, unless you explicitly turn off this feature.

By checking the Allow indexing checkbox in Figure 5-17, you give Facebook permission to share information from your profile with search engines such as Google or Bing. Facebook will make your publicly available information and any information you have set as visible to everyone available for search engines to include in search results for searches on your name. If an image of you stored on Facebook appears as part of a Google image result, and you would rather that it did not, you can remove the image from Facebook. Search engines only show those items to which you give them access.

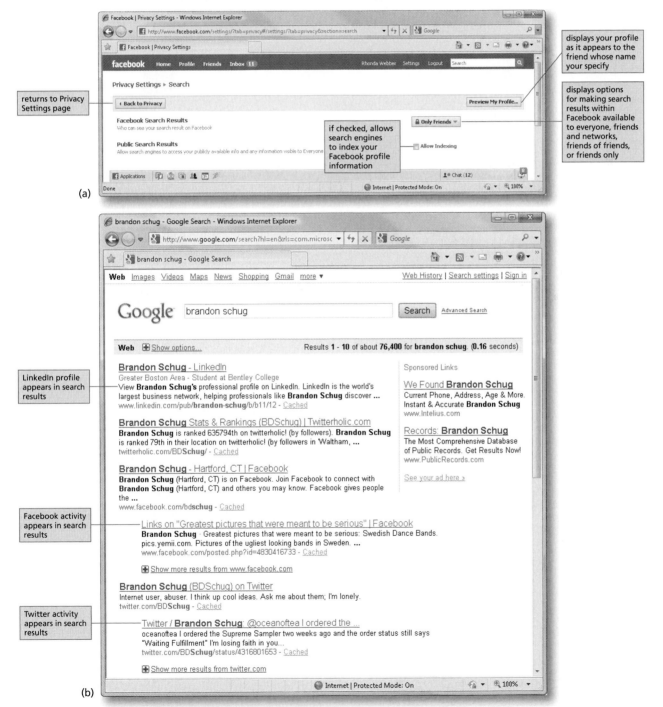

Figure 5-17 Configuring privacy settings for sharing profile information with search engines (a), and viewing search results that include information from social networking activities (b).

An effective way to both organize your friends and control which items from your profile are available to different groups is to create a Friend List. Friend Lists group your friends based on your relationships with them, as shown in Figure 5-18.

Figure 5-18 Creating Friend Lists is a way to organize your Facebook friends.

By default, the Friend List provided by Facebook includes all of your friends. You might, however, create a list named CollegeFriends to include friends from your college and a CoWorkers list to group the people with whom you work. Other lists might include a Family list of family members on Facebook and an Acquaintances list for friends of friends or other people you don't know very well. Friend Lists are like tags you assign to organize your friends: one friend might be a member of more than one friend list. The Friend List page provides options for creating new Friend Lists, adding and removing friends from lists to which you assigned them, and deleting unneeded lists.

If your friends are organized into Friend Lists, you can assign specific privacy policies to each list. Doing so gives access to only those parts of your profile that you want members of each list to see. For example, you might want to make your mobile phone number available only to your college friends who you actually know. Figure 5-19 describes the process to assign these settings.

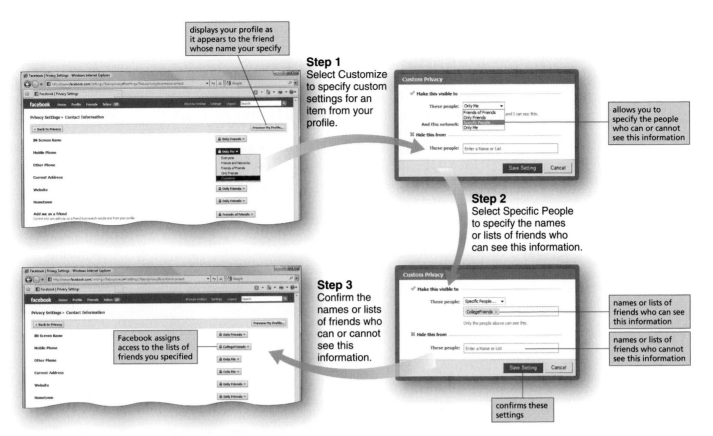

Figure 5-19 Assigning privacy policies based on members of a Friend List.

You can designate the friends or lists of friends who you would like to allow or remove access to see each section of your profile. After assigning permissions, you can enter the name of a friend to preview how your profile will appear when your friend views it.

You also can control who can view the information that appears in your News Feed or Wall. Each time you update your profile on Facebook or interact with an application, an entry may be recorded in your News Feed unless you chose not to include that activity. Some applications may report your recent activity as well. Facebook will never reveal certain information about your activities to other members, such as if you view their profiles or when you add or remove someone from a Friend List.

Because friends, family, colleagues, and present and future employers can potentially have access to your information on social networking sites, be cautious about the information that you post. Postings on social networks may last forever. Whereas disabling or closing an account is relatively easy, it is virtually impossible to remove your information from archives on the social networking site or a search engine's database.

Business and Professional Networking with LinkedIn

LinkedIn connects people with professional colleagues. Reid Hoffman started LinkedIn with five of his friends in 2003. They invited 350 contacts to join the site, and within a month, it grew to 4,500 members. By 2009, there were more than 33 million members on LinkedIn. As the company grew, in order to compete in the social networking arena, it opened its platform to third-party applications such as Reading List, with which you can share or recommend books on Amazon. Members of the site may also receive requests from other contacts regarding employment or consulting opportunities or inquiries related to their jobs or expertise.

Your LinkedIn profile, shown in Figure 5-20, lists your current and previous work experience, your education, your Web site or blog, recommendations, interests, honors and awards, and other personal or contact information that you wish to share.

Figure 5-20 A LinkedIn Profile displays professional information.

The professional network that you build on LinkedIn can be helpful when you are seeking employment. Your LinkedIn network can help you find professionals who can introduce you to people employed at companies where you might like to work or people working in or hiring individuals for positions that are similar to those that interest you. Because your contacts recommend them, you already have a connection. To search for a job, click the Jobs link on the top navigation bar, enter your search terms in the keyword text box, select your country and zip code, and then click search. When you search the employment database on LinkedIn, the job search results, shown in Figure 5-21, often contain jobs posted by people who are in your extended network.

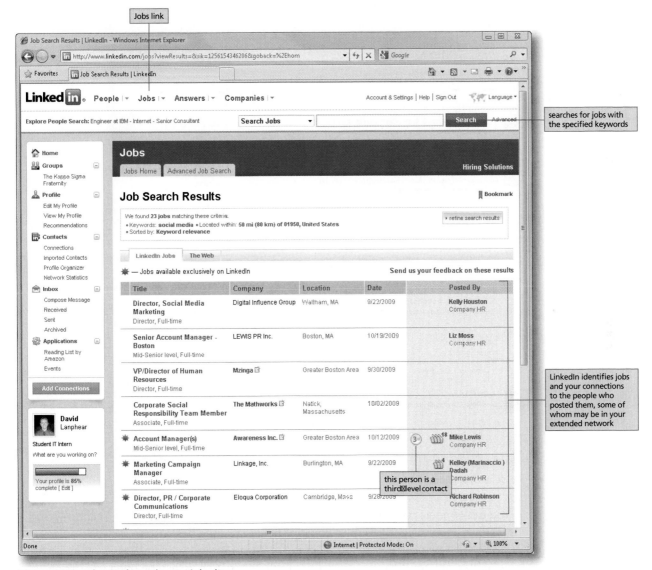

Figure 5-21 Job search results on LinkedIn.

For each job listing found, LinkedIn displays the person who posted the job and your first-level contacts who know that person. This may give you an inside connection to the company so that you can request an introduction to find out more information before applying for the job. Advanced job search options allow you to specify the location, experience level, job function, industry, and company, in addition to a job title or keywords.

The appearance of a "2nd" or "3rd" logo near a person's name indicates that that person is a second- or third-level connection or someone who is a contact of one or more people in your network. LinkedIn identifies the people in your network who know the people that you want to meet so that you can ask your contacts to help make the introduction.

LinkedIn's people search capability also helps you to identify people who share the same professional interests, who work for companies that you might like to work for, or who have jobs that you might like to learn more about. Figure 5-22 displays the results of a search on LinkedIn of people in a user's extended network who are involved in social media.

Figure 5-22 Finding people with common professional interests on LinkedIn.

You can connect with people of interest by adding them to your network, requesting an introduction, or using InMail to contact them via LinkedIn's e-mail service. LinkedIn is not only used by people who are seeking employment. Many members of LinkedIn are already employed but list themselves on the site because they may be open to hearing about new job opportunities, they want to professionally network with others in similar positions at other companies, or they want to keep in touch with coworkers from their current or former positions.

Many companies use LinkedIn as a recruiting tool for finding prospective employees. LinkedIn offers an effective way to review an applicant's credentials and reviews prior to a job interview because you can search across many dimensions. LinkedIn provides Webcasts, a blog, and other online resources to help companies learn how to use LinkedIn to reach out to potential job candidates, as shown in Figure 5-23. Customer testimonials allow companies to share their stories about using LinkedIn to find successful hires.

online resources for using LinkedIn as a recruiting tool

customer testimonials

Figure 5-23 Companies may use LinkedIn as a recruiting tool.

LinkedIn's Answers section, shown in Figure 5-24, is an online forum for asking and answering questions posed by members.

ask or answer questions to get help or demonstrate your knowledge

experts have provided the best answers to questions in this category

categories for answers

Figure 5-24 LinkedIn Answers is a forum for connecting with other members and promoting yourself as an expert on a topic.

By answering questions, you can demonstrate your expertise on a particular topic. In addition to helping those who asked the questions, future employers can get a sense of your writing style and knowledge by looking on LinkedIn to see any answers that you contributed to questions. You can rate the quality of the answers that you read. Members whose answers are rated highly appear on LinkedIn's list of experts.

Most social networking sites do not charge users a fee to create profiles or use the basic functions of the site. Because social networks are the most effective when a large number of people participate in them, sites like Facebook and MySpace rely on advertising rather than user fees as a source of revenue. In contrast, LinkedIn uses the freemium model. LinkedIn provides basic functionality for free but charges users a fee for additional services. These premium services include the ability to send out more than five introductions at a time and the ability to contact other members directly by sending InMails, which use LinkedIn's internal e-mail application. Figure 5-25 compares some of the premium features available to users who upgrade their account type from Personal to Business, Business Plus, or Pro.

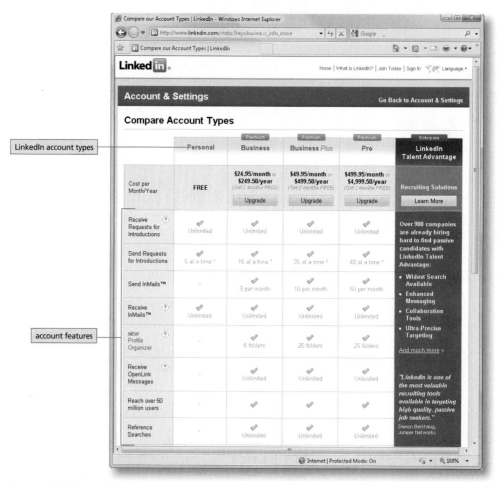

Figure 5-25 Comparison of LinkedIn account types.

Connecting People with Special Interests

Social networking sites like Facebook and LinkedIn typically are used to connect people with their friends, families, or coworkers. Special-purpose social networks connect targeted groups of people with similar interests or situations, enabling them to share information with each other regardless of whether or not they know each other in real life or will ever meet in person. Social networks that reach out to special interest groups, such as people who enjoy similar activities or support the same charitable causes or organizations, bring people together because they share common goals.

Several online tools enable the creation of social networking sites and online communities. One way to connect targeted groups of people is to add social networking capabilities to a blog or Web site. These capabilities allow people who visit the blog or Web site to connect with each other and create a community. Nonprofit organizations use social networking tools such as Facebook's Causes application or Network For Good as a way to raise both awareness and funds for their organizations. Individuals and businesses who wish to create their own social networks to meet people online who share similar specialized interests may use an online service such as Ning for creating new social networks.

Adding Social Networking Features to your Blog or Web Site

Bloggers and Web site owners can build an online community around their Web sites by adding social networking features using third-party applications. Friend Connect is a service from Google that bloggers and Web site owners can use to provide social networking features on their sites. With Friend Connect, users may sign up as a member of a blog or Web site and then may see the profiles of other site members. Friend Connect uses your Google profile and login information to access the social network.

Friend Connect can be enabled in a blog or Web site by adding a gadget to a blog's sidebar or by embedding HTML code supplied by Google. Using Friend Connect, a blog or Web site can offer functionality to let members connect with each other. Whenever you join a site with Friend Connect, your Friend Connect profile will include a list of blogs or Web sites that you have joined. Other members who view your profile may see this information. Go2Web20, an index of Web 2.0 applications, uses Friend Connect to create communities on their site. Figure 5-26 shows the members page of the Go2Web20. Clicking any one of the profile icons displays that member's profile, favorite links, and sites that they have joined.

Figure 5-26 Members join Go2Web20 using Friend Connect.

Google Friend Connect allows members to join a site with an existing Google, AIM, or Yahoo ID, as shown in Figure 5-27, without having to create another new account for each site that a member wishes to join.

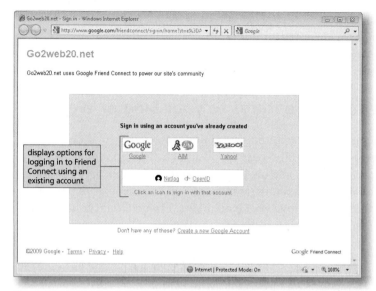

Figure 5-27 Signing in to Go2Web20 using Google Friend Connect.

Because every blog or Web site that you join using Friend Connect is linked to your Google ID, they also appear on your reading list on your Blogger blog's Dashboard page, shown in Figure 5-28.

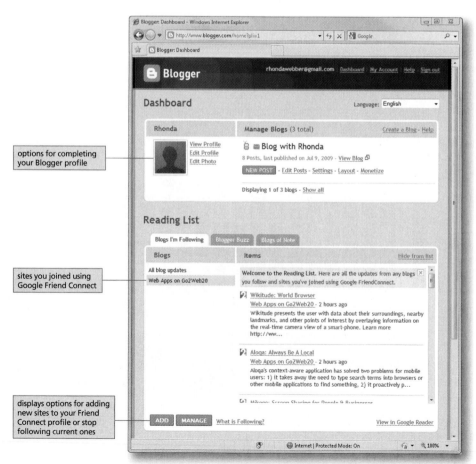

Figure 5-28 Sites that you joined with Google Friend Connect.

Other Friend Connect members who view your profile will see the blog and Web sites of which you are a member. This type of endorsement can increase the visibility and overall traffic to a blog or Web site.

Special Purpose Social Networks

The Web has become the home of many niche social networks that allow users to connect with each other for very specific purposes. The following are just a few examples of these targeted social networks. Meetup is a social network that enables people who live near each other to gather in person and engage in common activities. PatientsLikeMe is a social network for people to provide support and information for each other as they live with life-changing illnesses. Slideshare is a social network for people to share their PowerPoint presentations with others. These examples illustrate the range and diversity of social networks.

MEETUP   Using Meetup, people can find nearby activity partners who share common interests. Since Meetup was started in 2002, approximately 4 million people in 130 countries have joined the site, which averages more than 80,000 meetings each month. Meetup groups, shown in Figure 5-29, range from the Anchorage Adventurers Meetup Group, for people from Alaska who share outdoor interests, to the Baltimore Guitarist Group, for people from the Baltimore area who enjoy playing guitar together. Meetup uses the connecting power of the Internet to allow anyone to organize a group of people in their local community to connect with each other in person for a shared purpose.

Figure 5-29 Meetup Groups bring people together to share activities of common interest.

The Meetup home page displays listings of happenings around the world. Meetup members can also create their own groups to find local people who share their particular interests. A search capability allows users to find nearby Meetup Groups on topics of interest.

"Let's use the Internet to get people off the Internet."

From the Meetup Manifesto

To use Meetup, users first create a profile, and then they can either browse the site for groups that they would like to join or create their own Meetup Group. Many Meetup Groups hold activities in public spaces to safely bring members together. Figure 5-30 shows the locations of all of the Dining Out Meetups Groups, where people around the world who share an interest in trying various cuisines have gathered.

Figure 5-30 Dining Out Meetup Groups are located all over the world.

PATIENTSLIKEME On the PatientsLikeMe Web site, patients with life-changing conditions reach out to others in similar situations to discuss their symptoms, treatments, and experiences and to provide words of comfort and support. The PatientsLikeMe site, shown in Figure 5-31, has created an online community of doctors, patients, and supporting organizations who can give patients the information that they need as they live with their illnesses.

community pages for patients with life&changing conditions

share your profile information, find, or connect with other patients

Figure 5-31 PatientsLikeMe is a social network for people sharing life-challenging illnesses.

James and Ben Heywood founded PatientsLikeMe in 2004. Their brother Stephen was suffering with ALS (Lou Gherig's disease), for which there is no known cure, and the Heywood family used the global reach of the Internet to find people and ideas that would improve their brother's quality of life. Gradually, the site expanded to include other diseases and ailments and formed partnerships with pharmaceutical companies, medical professionals, and support organizations, many of whom have taken interest in PatientsLikeMe because of the vast amount of data that its members have generated.

PatientsLikeMe members may use the site to seek support from others who share their conditions as their disease progresses. They may also contribute their own health profiles, experiences, and information so that, when combined with that of thousands of PatientsLikeMe users, their information can be a valuable resource to other patients and medical professionals. Patient data can also be used to inform future research and ultimately improve medical care. Figure 5-32 displays the ALS/Motor Neuron Disease community page.

Figure 5-32 The online community for ALS/motor neuron disease on PatientsLikeMe.

SLIDESHARE SlideShare is an online community and repository for people to share PowerPoint presentations and other documents. Some people might use SlideShare to store their presentations online so that they can be accessed from any computer with an Internet connection, whereas others might post presentations online and send a hyperlink, instead of the presentation itself, to attendees. Finally, because presentations are shared, many people use SlideShare as a source of information to browse for presentations on topics of interest. When a presentation is stored online, it can be embedded on another Web site.

After you create an account on SlideShare, you can upload a presentation. SlideShare converts a PowerPoint file to Adobe Flash, which allows the presentation to play from within any Web browser that has the Flash plug-in installed, as shown in Figure 5-33. You can also establish privacy settings, including who can view or download the presentation.

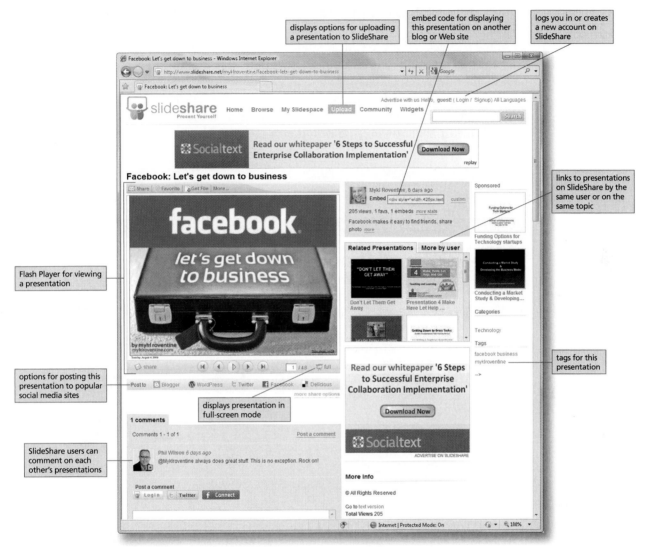

displays options for uploading a presentation to SlideShare

embed code for displaying this presentation on another blog or Web site

logs you in or creates a new account on SlideShare

links to presentations on SlideShare by the same user or on the same topic

Flash Player for viewing a presentation

options for posting this presentation to popular social media sites

displays presentation in full-screen mode

SlideShare users can comment on each other's presentations

tags for this presentation

Figure 5-33 Viewing a presentation on SlideShare.

SlideShare provides the necessary embed code to embed the presentation into a blog or Web site or share it on other social media sites. Users can tag presentations to make them easier to find, comment on each other's presentations, and search for presentations on topics of interest. Some presenters display their presentations stored on SlideShare in full-screen mode when giving their presentations to an audience.

Nonprofit Organizations and Social Networking

Social activists and nonprofit organizations have found the value in social networking as a tool for increasing awareness about and raising funds for their causes. Organizations that are trying to reach people of a particular demographic can create a presence on a social network that appeals to that particular group. For example, an organization that is reaching out to musicians might create a presence on MySpace, whereas Facebook may be better suited to reaching out to college students. Organizations may use Twitter to send out brief announcements about upcoming activities or may use Flickr and YouTube to post photos and videos, respectively, from their events.

Facebook's Causes application, shown in Figure 5-34, provides members who support a cause, such as an organization or a call for action, with the tools to share information and multimedia about their cause with their Facebook friends.

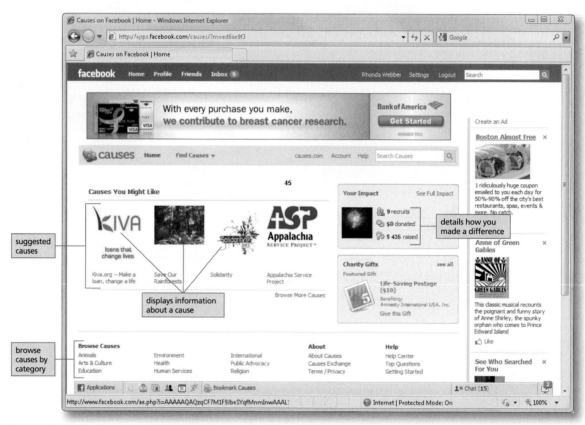

Figure 5-34 The Causes application page recommends causes that you might support.

The Causes application page displays popular causes on Facebook. Members may browse for causes by category, view each cause's own page, or create new causes for a specific organization. The Causes application allows Facebook users to support the charity of their choice and to help recruit volunteers and donors. The application also keeps track of the number of donors or volunteers, the amount of a member's donations, and the amount of money that a member raised to support his or her causes. Because the Causes application is listed as part of a Facebook profile, friends can see each other's causes and choose to join them as well. Figure 5-35 displays the page for the Global Warming cause.

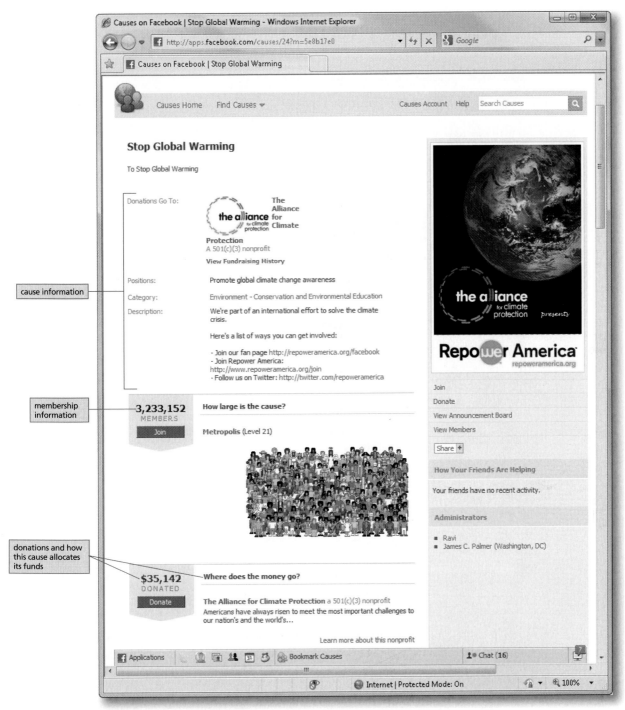

Figure 5-35 Exploring a popular cause on Facebook.

Individual members of nonprofit organizations also can use their profiles on social networks to help raise awareness. For example, volunteers might link to an organization's Web site from their LinkedIn profiles, where they list their service to the organization as relevant work experience. These activities use social networking tools to raise awareness about nonprofit organizations.

Charitable organizations also may register themselves with a social networking site for charities, such as Network for Good, shown in Figure 5-36.

Figure 5-36 Network for Good links supporters with nonprofit organizations.

Users can join Network for Good to search for charities that they wish to support and to make donations online. For each donation received, Network for Good charges a percentage for providing the service of enabling donors to give to charitable organizations online and for processing the associated credit card transaction.

Organizations rely on their supporters to reach out to new donors. Though Facebook Causes and Network for Good provide the tools and the Web infrastructure for publicizing a charitable organization and its activities, the challenge is building up an organization's social network. Regularly updating content on Facebook or on an organization's blog can extend an organization's reach and be a useful tool for recruiting donors and volunteers.

Creating Niche Social Networks with Ning

Ning is a Web-based application that allows its members to create custom social networks or online communities for niche markets. Ning provides the technology infrastructure for supporting member profiles, uploading photos and videos, and conversing with other members via discussion forums or instant messaging. To publicize activity on the social networks, Ning also offers blogs, wikis, event calendars, and RSS feeds. Since it was launched in 2007, Ning has had more than 6 million frequent visitors and more than 240,000 active social networks.

You can create a social network on Ning in three steps. First, provide information about a network, such as its name and description. Next, select the social networking features that you wish to add your social network's Web site, such as displaying members, events, and photos. Finally, customize how the site will appear in a Web browser by choosing the fonts, colors, and design. Figure 5-37 displays the features on a social networking site built using the Ning platform and shows how the site will appear in a Web browser.

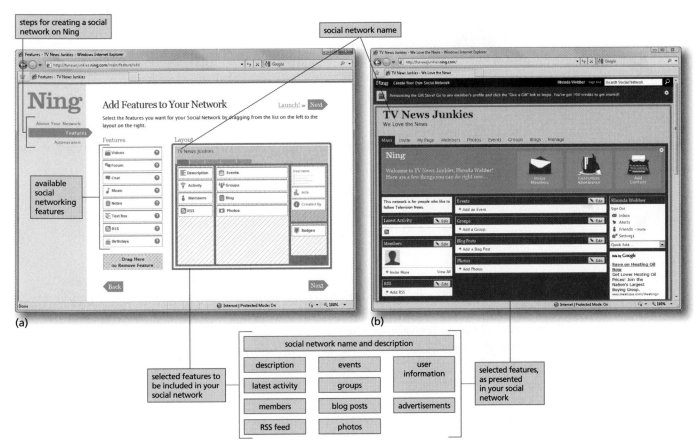

Figure 5-37 Configuring a social network created using the Ning platform (a) and displaying enabled features of a Ning social network page (b).

When creating a social network on Ning, you must provide a name and a short description. Figure 5-37(a) on the previous page illustrates several features that you might want to display on your social network's page, including the network's latest activity, a list of members, RSS feeds, events, groups, blogs, and photos. In addition to creating events and posting photographs, Ning provides a blog associated with the social network so that its creator might share thoughts and ideas with its members. The Groups feature allows members to organize themselves with a social network according to special interests. You can drag desired features from the list on the left to their place in the layout diagram on the right. Figure 5-37(b) shows what the completed social network page looks like on Ning.

After creating the social network, you can use Ning tools to invite members from your other networks or contact lists to join your social network, modify its appearance, or add new content. Ning supports the ability to use custom logos and styles so that an organization's social networking site created with Ning can have a look and feel similar to their existing blog or Web site. Ning also maintains a directory of all social networks created using Ning so that users can find and join them.

"[Ning] is focused on providing the [means for] people to create new social networks around their interests and passions. We think that's a very critical element of organization. The Facebook phenomenon connects you to people you already know, and Twitter is amazing for news and real-time events. What we see with people who gravitate to Ning is meeting new people with similar interests."

Gina Bianchini, cofounder of Ning with Marc Andreessen, inventor of the Mosiac Web browser

Ning is used for a variety of social networks, as shown in Figure 5-38. Burnt Marshmallows is a social network for people who like to go camping. Movie Fans is a social network in which members can discuss videos from Netflix, an online video rental service. The site is customized to have a look and feel similar to the Netflix corporate site, although Movie Fans is not affiliated with Netflix. Movie Fans navigation contains links to the Netflix site, which further gives the appearance of being integrated with Netflix. The United Way built their social networking site, Live United, using the Ning platform. Live United provides a way for volunteers of the nonprofit organization to connect with each other about ways that they have made a difference in their home communities.

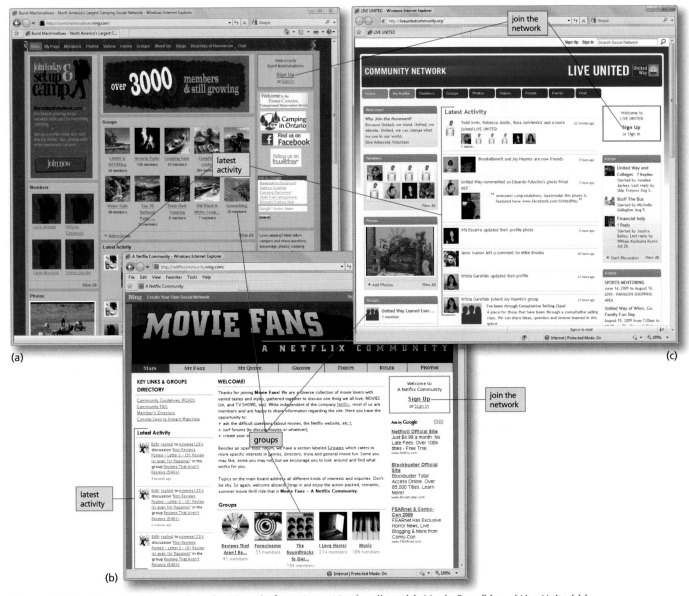

Figure 5-38 Social networks created on the Ning platform: Burnt Marshmallows (a), MoviesFans (b), and Live United (c).

Although all three of the networks' Web sites in Figure 5-38 have a highly customized appearance, they all include several of the same social networking features. For example, all three include the capabilities to display groups and the network's latest activity, along with the option to join the network.

The Long Tail

One of the reasons that Amazon is successful as an online retailer is the fact that its online shelf space is virtually unlimited. The same is true of songs for sale at the iTunes Store and videos available from the Netflix online rental service. Their collections are larger than what you would find in a physical store because their stores exist online.

At physical retailers, shelf space is at a premium, so stores only keep the most popular books, albums or movies in stock. When stores are virtual, they can offer not only the most popular titles but also many more obscure titles.

Economist and *Wired Magazine* editor Chris Anderson called this phenomenon the **Long Tail**. The Long Tail refers to the shape of the graph shown in Figure 5-39.

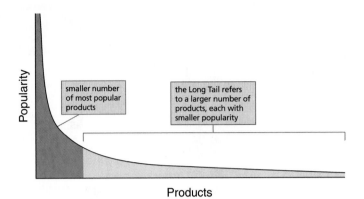

Figure **5-39** The Long Tail is a Web 2.0 model that accommodates both mainstream and niche markets.

The area beneath the left portion of the curve represents the more popular items that meet the needs of larger numbers of people. These are the items that you are likely to find in your local bookstore, music store, or video store. The area beneath the right portion of the curve represents the Long Tail. These are the niche market items with a smaller following, which you can only order online. Retailers would not allocate shelf space for these items because of their low sales volume.

On the Internet, because information is digital rather than physical, shelf space is unlimited, and as the cost of online storage continues to rapidly decrease, retailers can reach more people who have an interest in specialized items. The Long Tail refers to the ability to reach a larger number of people with a large number of narrowly targeted items, even though each single item may appeal to a much smaller number of people than its more mainstream counterparts.

The concept of the Long Tail can be applied to the social networking world. Many people join Facebook, MySpace, and LinkedIn because of the likelihood that their friends and colleagues are also members of those social networks. These networks would fall under the left portion of the curve in Figure 5-39. Specialized networks, such as those for sharing similar life-changing situations, camping interests, and movie reviews, make up social networking's Long Tail. These networks will attract fewer people than a more general social network, yet those who join them find greater value in them precisely because of their narrow appeal. Ning and Google Friend Connect are two tools that facilitate the process of creating such specialized networks. Advertisers also are interested in niche networks because ads placed on them are more likely to reach their target customers.

"Sure, the traffic today is still mostly going to Facebook and MySpace. But as they struggle to target ads based on the faint signals of consumer behavior in a generic social network, the smart money is going to the niche sites, where laser-focused content and community makes targeting easy. The Long Tail of social networks isn't just more satisfying if your community is actually about something, it's richer, too."

Chris Anderson, author of *The Long Tail: Why the Future of Business Is Selling Less of More*

Twitter

Biz Stone and Evan Williams started Twitter as a way for people in their office to keep in touch with each other by exchanging short messages about what they were doing. They limited the size of each message to 140 characters so that people could send and receive messages using text messaging on their cell phones. Twitter has experienced rapid growth despite modest beginnings, as shown in a blog post on TechCrunch in Figure 5-40, and is now used by technology and social media enthusiasts, journalists, celebrities, politicians, and others.

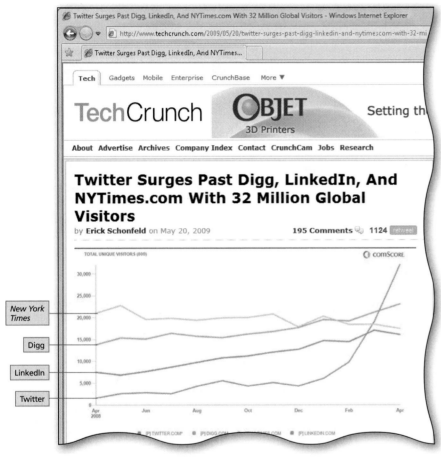

Figure 5-40 Twitter has experienced rapid growth.

As shown in Figure 5-40, the number of unique visitors to Twitter surpassed that of the *New York Times*, Digg, and LinkedIn during 2009.

Twitter is an online application for creating a social network in which you interact by sending and receiving short messages from two groups of people: people from whom you receive messages, known as your following, and people who receive messages from you, known as your followers. Every time that you send a message, or **tweet**, on Twitter, the tweet is broadcast to every one of your followers. Every time that one of the people who you are following sends a tweet, you will receive it, as will all of their other followers. Users can access Twitter through their cell phones, desktop applications, or other Web sites.

Messages on Twitter can spread virally. If one of your followers forwards a message that you sent, or **retweets** your message, all of his or her followers will receive it as well. Retweeting drastically expands the reach of any message that you send. Searching Twitter has become a useful way to get a pulse on what people in the Twitterverse (slang for everybody on Twitter) are collectively talking about.

"In the case of Twitter, it's not quite obvious why to use it, but eventually it will be."

Evan Williams, cofounder of Twitter

Using Twitter

Twitter suggests that your tweet respond to the question, "What are you doing?", although many people also use Twitter to share what they are thinking about, blog posts that they have written, or other interesting resources that they find online. Your most recent tweet appears beneath the text box in which you enter a tweet on the Twitter Web site, as shown in Figure 5-41. After entering a tweet, click the update button to post it on the Twitter network.

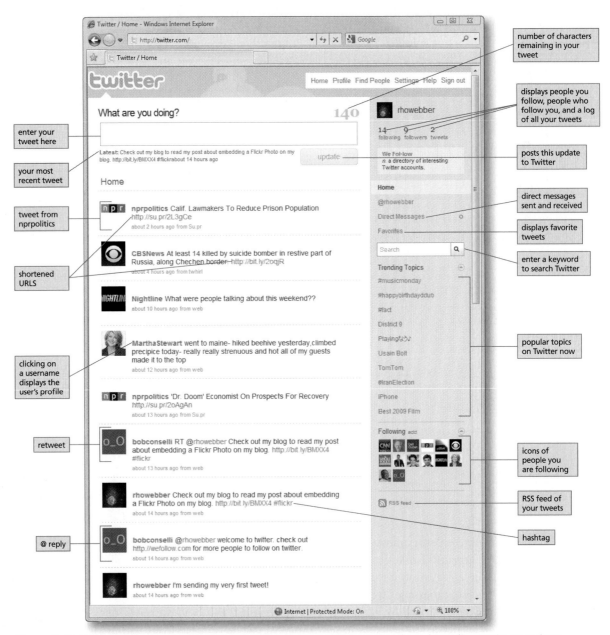

Figure 5-41 Your Twitter page displays your recent tweets, your Twitter network, and trending topics on Twitter.

Because each tweet must be 140 characters or less, many tweets make use of shortened URLs that redirect a user to a Web site whose original URL contains many more characters. Shortened URLs permit users to include hyperlinks in their tweets.

You can view the profile page of any user who you follow on Twitter by clicking his or her profile name or icon. Twitter also publishes your Twitter stream, which is your collection of most recent tweets, as an RSS feed to which you or other Twitter users may subscribe.

The Trending Topics section on a Twitter page describes popular current topics across the entire Twitterverse. Each topic listed is a hyperlink to a Twitter search results page that contains recent tweets associated with that topic.

You can send a tweet in four basic ways: to every one of your followers, as a reply to someone (who may or may not be following you), as a retweet of a tweet that you received from someone else, and as a direct, or private, message to another Twitter user. Direct messages also appear in the recipient's e-mail inbox. Table 5-1 summarizes the syntax for each of these.

Table 5-1 Twitter Commands and Conventions

@username	Sends a copy of the tweet to the specified username (in addition to all of your other followers) regardless of whether you are following this user.
d username	Sends a direct (private) message to the recipient both in Twitter and to the recipient's e-mail account. You must be following the person to whom you want to send a direct message. Only the author and the recipient of a direct message can view it.
RT	Short for retweet. Forwards someone else's tweet to your followers. RT is typically followed by @username to reference the original poster.
#hashtag	Hashtags describe a tweet with a keyword. Hashtags are used to find related posts when searching Twitter.

To assist in categorizing tweets, a convention has evolved to include a **hashtag**, which is the hash symbol or number sign (#), followed by a descriptive tag in tweets related to specific topics or events. One of the first widespread uses of hashtags on Twitter came in 2007 when the hashtag "#sandiegofire" was used to organize tweets about this disaster. An example of one of the #sandiegofire tweets is shown in Figure 5-42. By searching for posts with this hashtag, people were able to get help and updated information from those on the scene via Twitter.

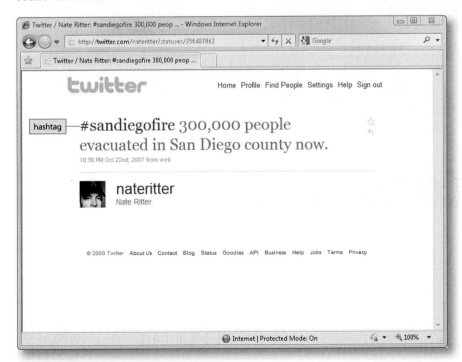

Figure 5-42 Tweets about the San Diego fire were easily grouped through the use of the hashtag #sandiegofire.

As with tags on Flickr or Delicious, hashtags on Twitter add additional context and metadata to your tweets. Hashtags bring order to a series of tweets, whether posted from an event or in response to current news, which makes conversations on Twitter easier to follow. Anyone can follow a conversation marked with hashtags by entering the desired hashtag on a Twitter search page, regardless of whether he or she uses Twitter.

In addition to using the Twitter Web site to send their tweets, many people interact with Twitter through a client application that runs on a personal computer or cell phone, shown in Figure 5-43. Client applications notify users of new tweets and often provide additional features not found on the Twitter Web site. The ability to post messages and photos to Twitter from an Internet-enabled cell phone has enabled people to tweet about what they are doing or thinking from virtually anywhere.

Figure 5-43 Twitter clients include TweetDeck (a), Twhirl (b), and Twitterific (c).

TweetDeck, shown in Figure 5-43(a), is a popular Twitter client application that organizes tweets into columns based on who sent them, the type of tweet, or the results of a search for a keyword or hashtag. TweetDeck's columns in Figure 5-43(a) display tweets from all of a user's followers, those that mention the user, any direct messages, and recent tweets containing the #flickr hashtag. Twhirl, shown in Figure 5-43(b), is one of several Twitter clients that integrate URL-shortening and photo-posting services into their applications. Twitterific, shown in Figure 5-43(c), is a Twitter application for the iPhone that uses the location from the iPhone's global positioning system (GPS) to search for tweets from other nearby Twitter users. As the number of local organizations posting their events on Twitter increases, displaying tweets from people nearby becomes a new way to connect with people in your community.

Finding and Following People on Twitter

The ability to search Twitter opens many possibilities to find and follow people who are interested in or are tweeting about topics that interest you. WeFollow, shown in Figure 5-44, is one of several directories of Twitter users.

searches for people on Twitter by tag

displays a form so you can add yourself to WeFollow

displays a user's Twitter profile

Figure 5-44 WeFollow is a directory of Twitter users.

So that others may find you more easily, you can add yourself to WeFollow using appropriate tags to describe yourself and the topics that you are most likely to tweet about. Following your friends' followers is another way to expand your Twitter network. It is perfectly acceptable Twitter etiquette to follow people whose profiles or tweets you find interesting, even if you do not know them personally. A personal note introducing yourself to someone whom you choose to follow helps to strengthen the connection between both parties.

One of the best ways to have people follow you on Twitter is to take a meaningful part in many conversations. By tweeting messages that are of value to your followers, people who follow you will be more likely to retweet your messages to their followers. Some of those people who find your tweets to be of interest may choose to follow you themselves. If you maintain a blog, sending tweets to announce a new blog post and providing the permalink to it will help to draw traffic to your blog.

Once your network reaches a critical mass, it can be a beneficial source of information. The wisdom of crowds principle suggests that in a large group, many people know more than any single person about a particular topic, so asking a question of your Twitterverse is likely to result in finding someone who may know the answer.

Twitter Applications

Developers have made possible thousands of specialized applications that repurpose Twitter data to provide additional functionality that is not found on the Twitter Web site. These applications can track top Twitter users, analyze user tweet statistics, plot tweets on maps, manage lists of followers, and embed user Tweets in blogs. Samples of these applications are shown in Figure 5-45.

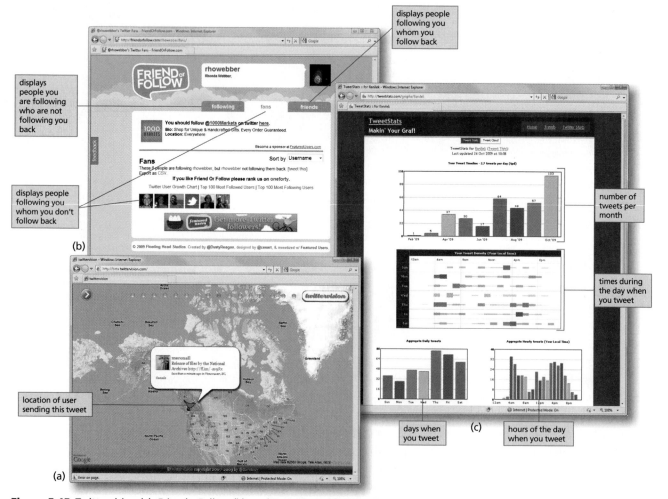

Figure 5-45 Twittervision (a), FriendorFollow (b), and TweetStats (c) are Web applications that reuse Twitter data.

Twittervision is one of the first applications to plot random tweets from Twitter's public timeline on a map. FriendorFollow identifies which of your Twitter followers you are not following back and enables you to follow them. TweetStats analyzes how often you tweet, including your average numbers of daily and hourly tweets.

SIDEBAR | Twitter and Popular Culture

Twitter has become a source for connecting with celebrities and reading about breaking news stories as they unfold.

In June 2009, after the Iranian election, the Iranian government cracked down on Web communication by shutting down text messaging, Facebook, YouTube, and news services. Posts on Twitter tagged with #iranelection became a lifeline for supporting democratic expression and getting information to the outside world. The use of social media as a news source made the front page of the New York Times, as shown in Figure 5-46.

Note that news and information reported on Twitter (or Wikipedia or anywhere else on the World Wide Web) is as reliable as the person who posts it. Twitter has taken steps to verify accounts belonging to high-profile individuals, such as politicians and celebrities, in order to confirm that they really are associated with the person whose identity is suggested by the account name.

Figure 5-46 Twitter became a source of information during the Iran elections of 2009.

URL Shorteners

Twitter is an effective tool for sharing the URLs of a new blog post that you wrote or of an interesting article or resource that you found on the Web. However, the permalink to a blog post or the URL for an article or Web site may be too long to include in a tweet while leaving a sufficient number of characters to write a brief introduction. In this case, a URL shortener service such as Bit.ly or TinyURL, shown in Figure 5-47, can help. **URL shorteners** are Web applications that encode a long URL in order to create a shorter, equivalent URL often with 18 to 25 characters. Shortened URLs contain http:// followed by the shortening service's domain name, and often a four- to six-character key that uniquely identifies the original URL.

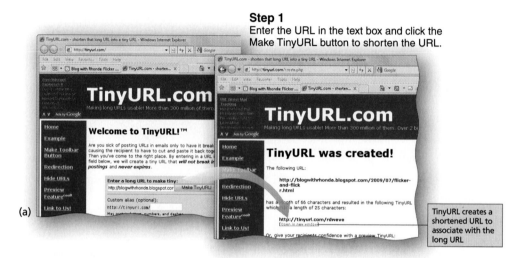

Step 1
Enter the URL in the text box and click the Make TinyURL button to shorten the URL.

(a)

TinyURL creates a shortened URL to associate with the long URL

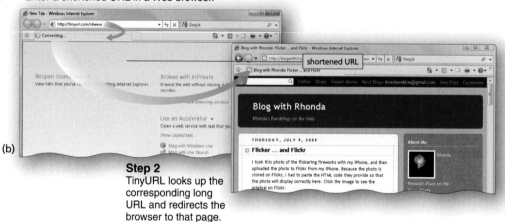

Step 1
Enter a shortened URL in a Web browser.

(b)

shortened URL

Step 2
TinyURL looks up the corresponding long URL and redirects the browser to that page.

Figure 5-47 Creating a shortened URL with TinyURL (a) and accessing a Web page using the shortened URL (b).

When a user enters the shortened URL in the browser, the shortening service looks up the key in its database, finds the corresponding original long URL, and redirects the user's browser to that location. This appears to the user as if the shortened URL takes the visitor to the desired location automatically.

Because accessing a Web site via its shortened URL requires a visit to an intermediate Web server (where the URL-shortening service resides), the URL-shortening service may track the number of clicks and other statistics about the shortened URL's usage. This information allows those who add shortened URLs to their tweets to view the number of people who click through to the recommended sites.

Twitter clients such as Twhirl and TweetDeck offer URL-shortening features directly in their applications. The Twitter Web site does as well. Before posting tweets, Twitter automatically converts long URLs found in messages submitted via the Twitter Web site into shortened URLs.

Shortened URLs also are useful to replace long hyperlinks in e-mail messages. The URLs accompanying online maps, permalinks to blog posts, or items for sale by online retailers often contain more than 100 characters. Some e-mail programs cannot handle URLs that span more than one line and may break them onto two or more lines, rendering the hyperlink unable to be clicked in an e-mail message.

A danger of using URL-shortening services is that, like all free Web-based services, the companies that host them might go out of business, resulting in broken URLs. URL shorteners are a useful short-term solution to provide easy access to Web resources but should not be relied upon indefinitely.

Shortened URLs are also useful for posting links to images within tweets. Twitpic is one of several similar services that facilitate posting images on Twitter. Posting images on Twitter is especially popular when tweeting from a cell phone that has a built-in camera. Images of breaking news stories have been posted on Twitter in this way, as shown in Figure 5-48.

Figure 5-48 Posting an image of a breaking news story using Twitpic.

Many Twitter clients and phone applications include image-posting capabilities. Whether a user uploads an image from a computer or takes a photo using a cell phone, the processing is the same, as shown in Figure 5-49.

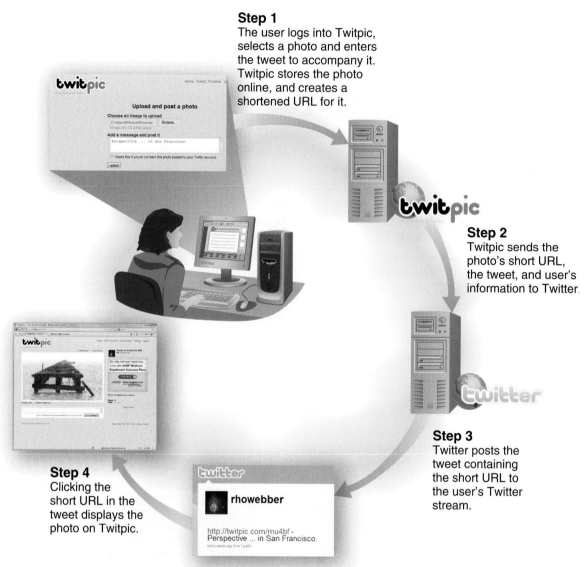

Step 1
The user logs into Twitpic, selects a photo and enters the tweet to accompany it. Twitpic stores the photo online, and creates a shortened URL for it.

Step 2
Twitpic sends the photo's short URL, the tweet, and user's information to Twitter.

Step 3
Twitter posts the tweet containing the short URL to the user's Twitter stream.

Step 4
Clicking the short URL in the tweet displays the photo on Twitpic.

Figure 5-49 Using Twitpic to add a photo to a tweet.

A user uploads a photo to Twitpic. Twitpic stores the image and generates a short URL to access it. Twitpic sends the image's short URL and the user's tweet to Twitter on the user's behalf. When the shortened URL is clicked in a tweet, Twitpic displays the uploaded image.

Business Uses of Social Networking

The social Web, a term referring to the combination of social networking and social media applications, can be defined by conversations between people and organizations over many channels of Web-based communication. Online interactions take place in or on blogs, social networks, videos, images, and text messages, as suggested by the Conversation Prism in Figure 5-50. Created by social media thought leader Brian Solis, the intent of this diagram is to show the vast choices available in social media and their applications

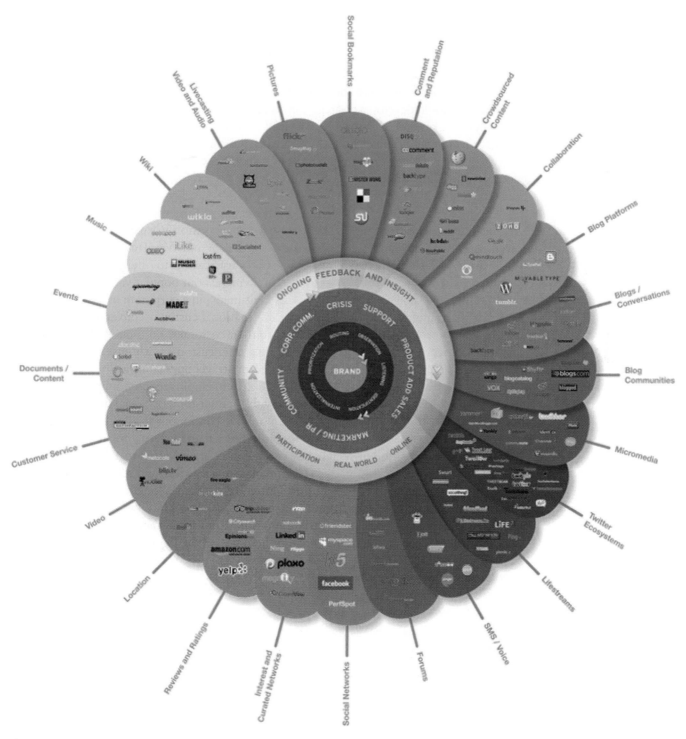

Figure 5-50 The Conversation Prism.

to business. With so many social media alternatives available, companies need to identify those that best apply to their business, industry, or brand in order to locate the conversations that are the most relevant to them.

At the center of the Conversation Prism is the word "brand," suggesting that building a brand is the most important goal of a company's Web presence. Building and reinforcing a brand identity extends to the use of social media tools as well. The innermost ring of the Conversation Prism encourages companies to make use of the social Web by discovering and listening to the various online communities where people talk about the company's brand and products. The middle ring identifies the different parts of an organization (Marketing and Public Relations, Community Outreach, Corporate Communications, Support, Product Sales) in which social media may be used to build relationships and respond to customers. Various social networks and social media providers that appear in the colored petals serve as ongoing sources of information for businesses to monitor and sometimes participate in to reach their customers.

Companies looking to use social media and social networking to raise awareness about their brands should develop a strategy for doing so. A first step might be to search for relevant keywords on both large and niche social networks (not only Facebook and Twitter) and see what conversations people are having about their company and their competitors. Doing so will give a sense of the networks on which a company should have a social presence, because competitors are there also or because they want to attract customers from the membership of a particular network. Developing a strategy may help a company build its social network and find friends who become actual customers.

Smaller companies can also make use of the Conversation Prism. For example, a travel company might monitor sites such as TripAdvisor and WikiTravel to see what people are saying about their services. They might use Twitter to offer special deals to customers. The company could post images and video about popular vacation destinations on Flickr and YouTube and then embed this multimedia in a corporate marketing blog. They could bring in external content about international currency conversion rates from an RSS feed to provide an additional service to their customers on their Web site. Finally, creating a presence on Facebook might help to attract customers who use word of mouth and the recommendations of friends when selecting travel opportunities.

Many companies are using social networks to help employees communicate with each other within the organization or to connect with their customers. Social networking platforms offer a means by which companies can provide continuous feedback and support to customers by creating online communities both internal and external to an organization. A presence on many different social networks helps an organization to promote itself and its brand through the use of blogs, video, rankings, music, wikis, and social networks.

Twitter can be a great source of information for companies looking to see what their customers are saying about them and their products, as shown in Figure 5-51. Companies such as Pizza Hut (a chain of pizza restaurants) and Comcast (a cable, Internet, and phone service provider) can use information about them posted on Twitter to improve their customer service and build their social networks.

(a)

PizzaHut tweets help respond to customer inquiries and promote the PizzaHut brand

Comcast tweets help customers troubleshoot technical problems and provide customer service

(b)

Figure 5-51 Companies such as Pizza Hut (a) and Comcast (b) use Twitter to communicate with their customers.

Pizza Hut uses Twitter to promote its brand and offer special incentives, service, and support to customers. Comcast uses Twitter to provide technical support and service to its customers and to reply to their inquiries.

Fan Pages on Facebook

Facebook users can become fans of products, and companies often use feedback from customers to guide future product offerings. Companies and organizations may advertise their brands by creating Fan pages on Facebook. **Fan pages** are marketing tools with which companies can share information, promote products, and offer specials deals or coupons to customers. Figure 5-52 on the next page displays the Fan page for Pop-Tarts toaster pastries.

Figure 5-52 The Pop-Tarts Fan page on Facebook.

Customers can share comments, suggestions, and product reviews on the Wall section of a company or product's Fan page. Because the companies and products of which you are a fan are listed on your Facebook page, your friends may be encouraged to try them or become fans as well. Becoming a fan of a company or product opens a channel of communication between you and the company.

Corporate Social Networks

Companies can create customized social networking sites focused around building relationships with a company's employees and its customers. This can be especially important for companies with a global presence. For example, IBM's internal social network, Blue Pages, shown in Figure 5-53, allows employees to list their skills and interests in their business profiles.

Figure 5-53 Blue Pages is IBM's internal social network for employees to connect with each other.

A Blue Pages profile contains an employee's contact information and an area where an employee can update a status message regarding current projects. The site integrates internal organizational data, such as a reporting chain that includes the name of an employee's supervisor and his or her supervisors and links to their profile pages, as well as an employee's professional information, as posted on LinkedIn. The profile page also displays the tags that the employee uses to describe internal corporate resources and links to internal Web pages that the employee has bookmarked.

IBM employees use the Blue Pages network to connect with others who share professional interests, such as software development or healthcare and life sciences. These virtual communities provide employees an opportunity to connect with colleagues throughout the company with whom they may not directly work.

Employees can also use Blue Pages to quickly find other employees who have a desired skill set or expertise in a particular area or to find work opportunities on projects of interest within the company. Search results can be refined based on location or degrees of separation within a person's social network. This encourages collaborative projects that involve employees who need not be physically located in the same place. Blue Pages relies on both prepopulated organizational data (such as name and job history, which are part of a person's employment record) and user-entered personal and professional information.

Many organizations and businesses also encourage employees to create blogs that are only available internally. Employee blogs are forums to share the employee's personal expertise or interests; teams may share a blog to write about current projects and lessons learned; management may use a corporate blog as a way to share organizational information with employees and solicit feedback. Because blogs are linked to an employee's professional profile within the company's social networking platform, they can become a valuable source of information and knowledge sharing within larger organizations.

Starbucks, an international chain of coffee shops, launched My Starbucks Idea in 2008 to solicit feedback from customers about its products and services. My Starbucks Idea, shown in Figure 5-54, takes the traditional suggestion box that might be found at a store location and moves it online, allowing registered users to offer suggestions and propose new ideas.

Figure 5-54 My Starbucks Idea is a virtual suggestion box.

My Starbucks Idea combines the ranking feature of Digg with the commenting feature of blogs so that customers may rank or comment on ideas posted by other Starbucks customers. The most popular suggestions appear at the top of the list of ideas in each category. This feedback, combined with an online survey on the My Starbucks Idea Web site, gives Starbucks a sense of their customers' opinions about what the company is doing well and how the company might improve.

Social Customer Relationship Management

Customer Relationship Management (CRM) describes a set of tools and processes that companies employ to manage customers throughout the company-customer relationship, including finding potential new customers, converting those potential customers to actual customers, gathering information about sales, and providing customer support after the purchase of a company's product or service. CRM systems are software applications that companies use to manage the process of attracting new customers and maintaining relationships with existing ones.

CRM systems, illustrated in Figure 5-55, track a customer's contact information; product orders; dates when purchases were made, shipped, and received; service or support calls; and marketing campaigns to which that customer responded. This data is made available throughout the company. Using the information captured by a CRM system, companies are better able to support their customers.

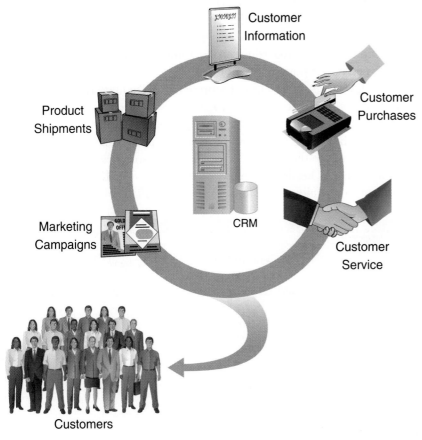

Figure 5-55 A CRM system centrally stores all aspects of interactions with current and prospective customers.

Traditional CRM systems must be installed, configured, and maintained on servers located within a company's data center. In contrast, in Web-based CRM systems, both the CRM application software and a company's customer data are stored on the server of the CRM service provider. Customers can connect to the service by logging in to the application that runs within a Web browser. Under this model, the CRM service provider hosts and manages the application, and customers pay for a license to use the software for a given period of time.

When a software application and the data that it interacts with are located on the Web, data from other online sources also can be integrated. **Social CRM** is an extension of traditional CRM systems that allows organizations to monitor the conversations on various social networks for keywords related to their products in order to provide improved customer support. Traditional CRMs and social CRMs differ in the types of customer information that they capture. Traditional CRM systems focus on campaigns that generate customer leads and ultimately new customers. Social CRM relies on harnessing user-generated content from Web-based social networks to enable companies to build relationships with their customers through online conversations.

While traditional CRM systems are logging a company's conversations with customers made by phone, mail, e-mail messages, or online chat via a company's Web site, customers and potential customers are talking about their experiences with a company's product all of the time on Twitter, Facebook, YouTube, and other social networks. Whenever someone blogs, tweets, tags an article, or posts a video or product review online, the transaction results in a new piece of data about the company. Social CRM applications monitor content from social networks and social media sites in order to find out what customers are saying about a company or its products. Social CRM applications may analyze that information to find trends regarding product inquiries or issues and to respond to requests from current or potential customers.

Social CRM systems allow a company's support representatives to identify conversations that people are having about their products in order to provide solutions. A support representative might use a social CRM system to monitor conversations on Twitter or Facebook about the company's products by searching for keywords, such as product names. For example, Figure 5-56 shows a screen from the Salesforce Service Cloud software that monitors Twitter posts related to a company's headset product with model number KC770. Salesforce. com is one of the pioneering companies in providing Web-based CRM software services.

Figure 5-56 Salesforce.com social CRM software monitors Twitter posts about a company's products.

The Salesforce Service Cloud software provides real-time search results containing tweets about this product. A customer support representative who sees these tweets may select those that seem the most urgent to monitor or follow up on. By clicking the Monitor button, the support representative can create a record for this case in the CRM system and then log the customer's name and note that the issue was discovered via a post on Twitter. After researching a potential solution, the representative could contact the customer on Twitter to share the solution and follow up to confirm that the solution worked. Recording the entire interaction in the CRM system documents the issue so that if other customers have the same issue, support representatives can find a solution that worked and pass it along.

Summary

Social networks provide tools for connecting people personally and professionally. Facebook and LinkedIn are two popular social networks that also serve as platforms for integrating other social media applications. Niche social networks and tools to create them, such as Ning, enable people with specific interests to share information, activities, or support services with each other. Twitter has emerged as a microblog for sharing updates about personal activities, interesting Internet resources, and breaking news stories.

Businesses can use social networks within their organizations as a tool for gathering and managing organizational knowledge and promoting employees and their projects. Internal social networks allow employees to connect with each other to find new job opportunities and identify knowledge experts within a company. Externally, business-oriented social networks connect organizations with their customers and those customers with each other. Social CRM software assists in finding, tracking, and responding to issues that arise from social networking sites such as Facebook and Twitter.

Think

Submit responses to these questions as directed by your instructor.

1. What social networking elements can be found in Flickr and Delicious, Web 2.0 sites introduced in Chapter 4?

2. How does the Facebook Friends Quiz application access the information from your Facebook friends?

3. What purpose does Ning fill that social networks such as MySpace or Facebook do not?

4. Suppose you created your own social network on Ning. Describe three different ways that you might publicize it, so people would join.

5. How is Facebook Causes an example of the Long Tail model described in this chapter?

6. Name two ways that Twitter gives access to the World Live Web as described in Chapter 2.

7. Starbucks has both a Fan page on Facebook and its own independent enterprise social networking site (My Starbucks Idea). What are two advantages of each approach to using social networking as a marketing tool to connect with customers?

Watch

Watch the video for Chapter 5 on the Online Companion at scsite.com/web2. Be prepared to answer or discuss the questions posted on the Online Companion as directed by your instructor.

Try

Visit the Online Companion at scsite.com/web2 and follow the steps as you complete the tutorials for this chapter.

Tutorial 5-1 Using Google Friend Connect
In this tutorial, you will add Google Friend Connect to your blog and then add and manage friends on your Google Friend Connect network.

Tutorial 5-2 Using Twitter
In this tutorial, you will set up an account on Twitter, find and follow people, and send tweets to your followers.

Blog

Complete these exercises on the blog that you created for this class.

1. Carefully read the Terms of Service and privacy policy for a social network on which you have an account. What does it say about how they will use your information? What will they do if there is a breach in security on their site? Write a blog post summarizing your findings.

2. Create an account on SlideShare and upload a PowerPoint presentation to your account. Alternately, search SlideShare for a presentation that someone else created about social networking applications, and embed it in a new post on your Blogger blog.

Explore

These activities encourage you to explore Web 2.0 sites and applications on your own. Submit your responses as directed by your instructor.

1. Use a search engine to see what information about yourself is available when performing a search on your name. If there are search results, what are the sources of that information? Are you surprised at what was found? If there are no search results with your name, why do you suppose that is?

2. Alexa and Compete are Web-based tools that track the usage and number of visitors to various Web sites. Select one of them and use it to create a chart showing the number of unique visitors during the past year on the four social networks shown in Figure 5-1. How has the growth of these social networks changed? Why do you suppose that is?

3. Create an account and a profile on Facebook if you do not already have one. Search for and invite some of your real-life friends or relatives to become friends with you on Facebook. Write on a friend's Wall. Add a Facebook application to your Facebook account.

4. If you have a Facebook account, examine your privacy settings. Review the following questions, and if necessary, select new privacy settings that make you comfortable with the access that others have to your information.

   a. Who can see your basic profile information?

   b. Who can post to your Wall?

   c. Is your Facebook profile available for a search engine to find?

   d. Which of your recent activities on Facebook do you want to appear in your News Feed or on your Wall for friends to see?

   e. Will you allow third-party applications or networks the right to use your Facebook information in ads shown to your friends if Facebook policy changes to allow this?

   f. What information will you allow other users to see about you via the Facebook platform?

5. Post a tweet on Twitter that describes, in your own words and in 140 characters or less, the difference between social media and social networking. Use a hashtag provided by your instructor so you can then search for all of the tweets from your classmates on this topic to compare your answers.

6. Install a Twitter client such as Twhirl or TweetDeck and configure it for your Twitter account. How is using a Twitter client different than using the Twitter Web site?

7. Add yourself to WeFollow. Use WeFollow to find 10 people who work for companies or in professions of interest to you and follow them on Twitter.

8. If you have an Internet-capable cell phone, install a Twitter application on your phone. Compare its user interface and features with those found in a Twitter client application or Twitter's Web interface.

9. Add an RSS gadget to your blog and configure it to display the RSS feed of all of your Twitter feeds.

10. Create an account and a profile on LinkedIn if you do not already have one. Post your education and work experience. Ask three people to join your network. Ask someone for a recommendation or write a recommendation for a friend. Search for the profiles of family members or friends who you know, and invite them to join your network on LinkedIn.

11. Search on LinkedIn for the profiles of any one of the founders of the social networks mentioned in this chapter. Do you have any connections to them? Look at their profiles as a model for the type of information you might place on your own profile.

12. Create a social network on Ning for a student organization in which you are involved. How will you publicize it?

Collaborate

If your instructor set up a class wiki, complete these exercises.

1. Working in a small group, create a short presentation that explores one of the social media sites shown in The Conversation Prism in Figure 5-50. Use the wiki page to sign up for groups. Share your finished presentation on SlideShare and embed or post a link to the shared presentation on the wiki page.

2. Use the class wiki to create a Twitter directory for the people in your class. Work with your instructor to structure it like the WeFollow directory. Enter your name and Twitter name or Twitter URL so that your classmates can easily find you on Twitter. Follow several classmates on Twitter and ask them to follow you as well.

6 | Linking Data

Overview

Web 2.0 has become characterized by applications that connect people and technologies that link data. The Internet has become a platform for creating, storing, and delivering both applications and data, making access to one's information possible from any Internet-connected device. New opportunities for using the Web emerge when applications and data live on the Internet and users can access them from almost anywhere. As Figure 6-1 suggests, Web-based tools for collaboration, software infrastructures for building complex Web applications, and technologies for sharing information are products of the Web 2.0 era. These developments lay the groundwork for an emerging Web where machine intelligence, meaningful search, and a personalized user experience will guide the next wave of Web applications.

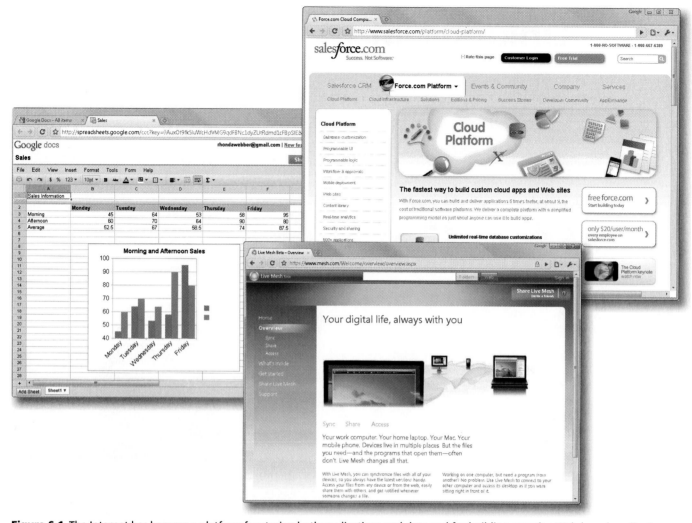

Figure 6-1 The Internet has become a platform for storing both applications and data and for building complex Web-based applications.

Computing in the Cloud

Cloud computing describes how applications are stored and deployed on a network of Internet servers. The Cloud represents the Internet, as its frequent use in many computer network diagrams often suggests. Users of a Cloud computing service interact with and manage data and applications stored on servers located in a remote data center accessible via the Internet. Cloud computing service providers offer server space and processing on an as-needed, on-demand basis. Computing resources may be allocated dynamically as applications require additional bandwidth or processing power. Customers pay as they go for the computing storage and resources that they actually use in a given period of time.

Rather than storing data or installing applications on a user's own computer or on a company's own server, data is stored and applications are run on servers operated by companies such as Google, Amazon, Microsoft, and Salesforce. From the user's perspective, as shown in Figure 6-2, the location of the application and the data that it accesses are not important. The fact that they are available in the Cloud is what matters.

Figure 6-2 Users may access e-mail services, blogs, bookmarks, data, and other applications in the Cloud.

Cloud computing includes three main areas of service: Infrastructure as a Service, Platform as a Service, and Software as a Service.

- **Infrastructure as a Service (IaaS)** is the delivery of a networked computing infrastructure over the Internet. This infrastructure includes high-end servers with increased storage and processing power, Internet connectivity, a secure environment for housing equipment, and online tools to remotely manage and monitor performance. IaaS provides infrastructure for storing files in the Cloud so that users can access them from anywhere and for managing virtual servers using software tools.

- **Platform as a Service (PaaS)** is the delivery of a computing platform over the Internet. Developers can create and deploy large-scale business Web applications using development tools that are hosted within the Cloud. PaaS provides the tools for storing, running, and monitoring the performance of social networking, business, and computing applications over the Internet.

- **Software as a Service (SaaS)** is the delivery of software applications over the Internet. Software applications are stored and deployed from servers on the Internet. SaaS provides the ability for business applications such as Salesforce Social CRM, discussed in Chapter 5, and consumer applications such as Google Docs, an online office suite for collaboratively creating documents, spreadsheets, and presentations, to run over the Internet.

As Internet access becomes ubiquitous and applications continue to shift from the desktop to the Web, Cloud computing suggests that it is more cost-effective to place computational and storage needs on a centralized system and provide users access to those systems with small, inexpensive devices like netbooks, smartphones, and even video game systems. Figure 6-3 summarizes several features of Cloud computing that are discussed in this section.

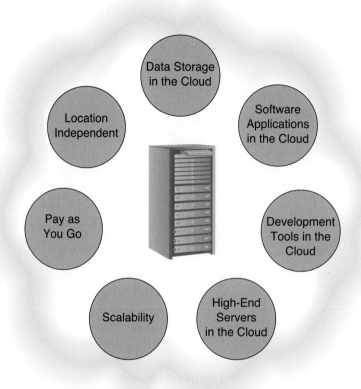

Figure 6-3 Features of Cloud computing.

Infrastructure as a Service: Computing in the Cloud

Infrastructure as a Service offers computing resources on demand to individuals and organizations that need them. Resources include storage of data as well as allocation of additional computing power for running applications that require intense processing or that receive thousands of visitors.

CONSUMER INFRASTRUCTURE IN THE CLOUD One popular application of a Cloud computing infrastructure for consumers is the ability to store photos, music, documents, and other files in the Cloud so that they are available on many devices, as shown in Figure 6-2. Some Cloud storage applications automatically back up and synchronize these files, whereas others serve as holding places for documents, photos, and music that users upload to the Cloud.

Documents and other files stored in the Cloud are available from any computer with an Internet connection. By storing files in the Cloud, users no longer have to make copies of their files to take with them as they use different computers; instead, the files can all be accessed using a Web browser. Cloud storage provides a centralized location for storing files so that the most recent version will always be available, regardless of the device from which it is accessed. Several Cloud storage providers are shown in Figure 6-4.

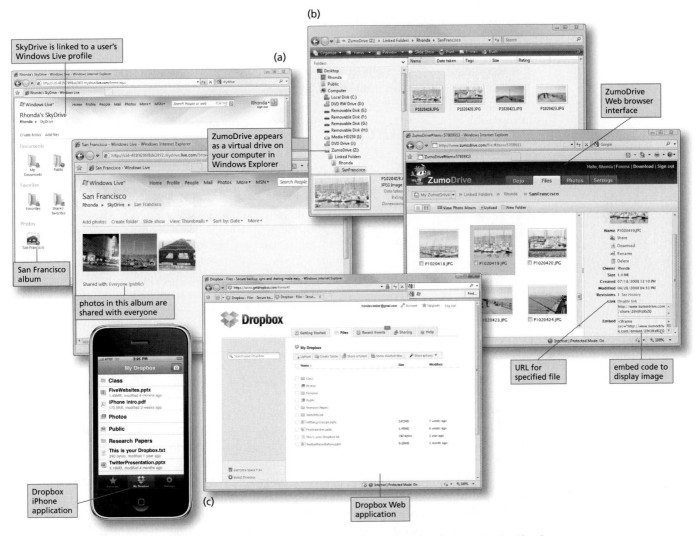

Figure 6-4 Windows SkyDrive (a), ZumoDrive (b), and Dropbox (c) are three examples of storage in the Cloud.

Skydrive is an example of storage in the public Cloud. In the **public Cloud**, a service provider makes online storage and resources available to the public over the Internet. Dropbox and ZumoDrive both make use of storage in the hybrid Cloud. In the **hybrid Cloud**, files and resources are stored on a user's computer or an organization's internal network, as well as on a service provider's servers in the Cloud. In contrast, a **private Cloud** refers to corporate hosting services on an organization's internal or proprietary network. Many Cloud storage providers follow a freemium business model, offering a reasonable but limited amount of Cloud storage for free and charging fees for additional storage space. Table 6-1 summarizes key features of the Cloud storage providers shown in Figure 6-4.

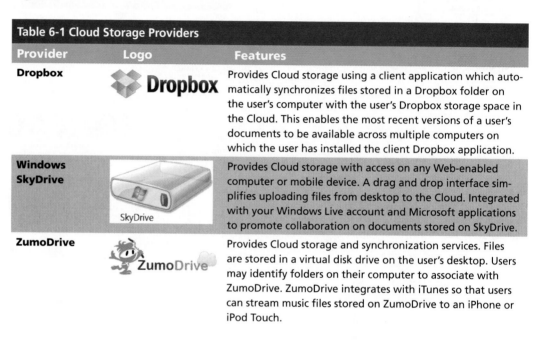

Table 6-1 Cloud Storage Providers		
Provider	Logo	Features
Dropbox	Dropbox	Provides Cloud storage using a client application which automatically synchronizes files stored in a Dropbox folder on the user's computer with the user's Dropbox storage space in the Cloud. This enables the most recent versions of a user's documents to be available across multiple computers on which the user has installed the client Dropbox application.
Windows SkyDrive	SkyDrive	Provides Cloud storage with access on any Web-enabled computer or mobile device. A drag and drop interface simplifies uploading files from desktop to the Cloud. Integrated with your Windows Live account and Microsoft applications to promote collaboration on documents stored on SkyDrive.
ZumoDrive	ZumoDrive	Provides Cloud storage and synchronization services. Files are stored in a virtual disk drive on the user's desktop. Users may identify folders on their computer to associate with ZumoDrive. ZumoDrive integrates with iTunes so that users can stream music files stored on ZumoDrive to an iPhone or iPod Touch.

Cloud storage is especially useful for users of netbook computers and Internet-enabled cell phones, as these devices have limited internal storage capacities. Cloud storage is also a useful alternative instead of attaching large documents, images, or presentations to e-mail messages. Because files are stored in the Cloud, each file has its own URL. You may share a file's URL in an e-mail message or an instant message, save it as a bookmark on Delicious, or post it online in order to make it available for others to access or download.

In addition to storing files in the Cloud, many consumers benefit from Infrastructure as a Service by accessing computing capabilities and applications available through virtual computing platforms. A **virtual computer** is a Web application that provides computing capabilities similar to those offered by a physical computer. It is hosted on a server running in a remote data center and accessed over the Internet by visiting a Web page in a browser. G.ho.st is a company that provides a virtual computer and operating system services within the Cloud, as shown in Figure 6-5.

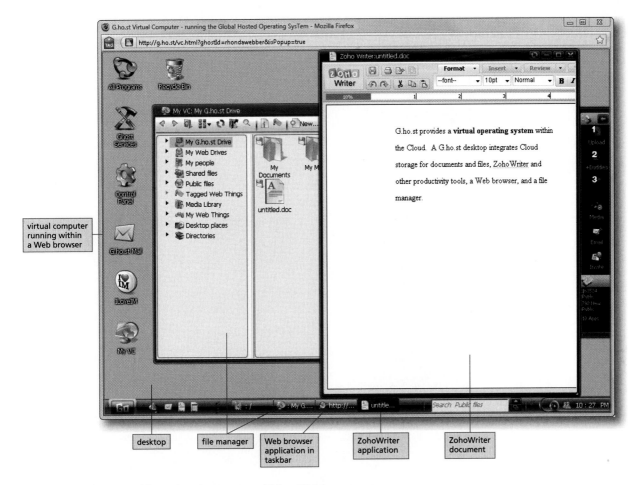

Figure 6-5 G.ho.st provides a virtual computer within a Web browser.

The G.ho.st (Global Hosted Operating System) virtual computer includes many features found in a physical computer, including a desktop, file storage, and applications. The files and applications are stored in the Cloud. A G.ho.st desktop integrates Cloud storage for documents and files, ZohoWriter and other productivity tools, a Web browser, and a file manager. There is no need to install software or transfer files. Whenever you log in to G.ho.st, your files and applications are always available.

BUSINESS INFRASTRUCTURE IN THE CLOUD   Businesses are interested in Infrastructure as a Service because it allows them the ability to scale their applications without having to procure additional hardware resources. Instead, businesses rent space and computing power from an IaaS provider. The IaaS provider operates data centers that contain high-end servers, each with multiple processors and terabytes of storage. Through a process known as **virtualization**, one host machine may be configured to operate as if it were several smaller, special-purpose servers. A **virtual server** is one of several servers that may be configured on a host machine. Since one physical server may host several virtual servers, virtualization consolidates the need for many physical devices, as shown in Figure 6-6 on the next page. Using virtual servers provides a more efficient and effective use of processing and storage resources that might otherwise be underutilized. Virtualization allows businesses to have their own servers in the Cloud without having to manage any hardware or share a server with other companies.

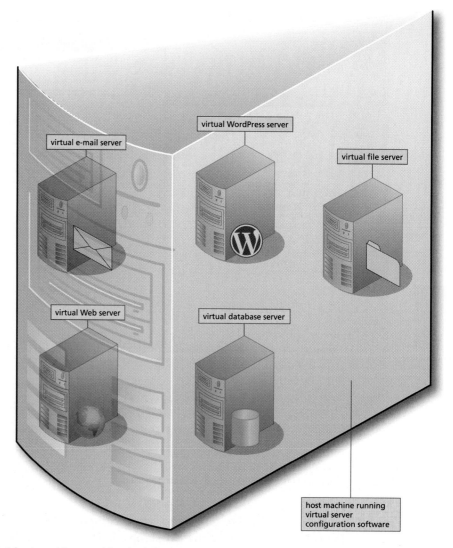

virtual e-mail server

virtual WordPress server

virtual file server

virtual Web server

virtual database server

host machine running
virtual server
configuration software

Figure 6-6 A host machine provides the infrastructure to run several virtual servers.

Each virtual server may support a particular business function such as deploying Web pages and applications, storing files, hosting e-mail applications or blogs, and storing internal corporate data. Virtual servers may also be used as a sandbox, or testing environment, for developing or evaluating new Web applications. By using a virtual server as a sandbox, it is possible to test an application or configuration change before deploying it, without impacting previously installed software on existing servers.

Although each virtual server appears to be an actual server, in reality it is a server that has been emulated using software tools. Virtual Server management software allows system administrators to create and configure new virtual servers as if they were actual physical servers located on site. Virtual servers are administered remotely using virtual server management software such as Microsoft Virtual Server 2005, shown in Figure 6-7.

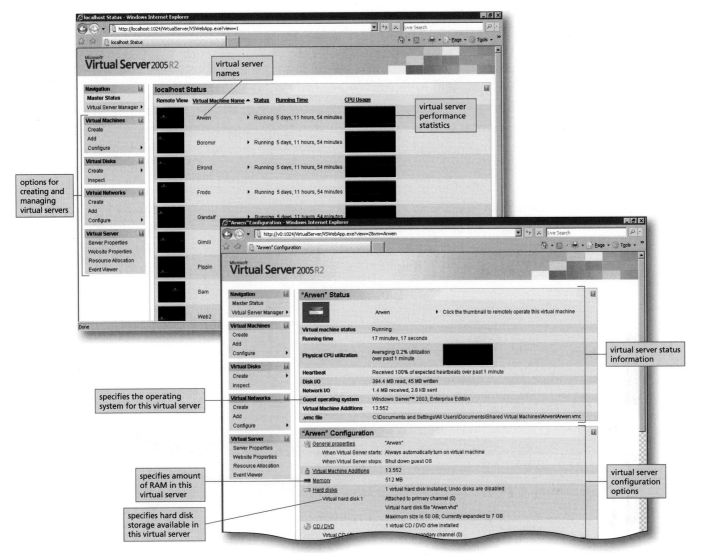

Figure 6-7 Virtual server management software is used to create and configure virtual servers.

Even though one physical server may host several virtual servers for different Web sites or applications, each owner of a virtual server has full control over it. Unlike a physical server, where storage, memory, and processing capabilities are limited by installed hardware, these capabilities may be reconfigured dynamically on a virtual server.

| Amazon Implements Virtualization

Each month between 2008 and 2009, Amazon averaged between 55 and 65 million unique visitors to their Web site, with the exception of November and December. During those months, the site reached 75 million unique visitors due to holiday-related purchases, as shown in Figure 6-8.

Amazon had to scale their application to handle 10 million additional visitors very quickly during the holiday season. The acquisition of new hardware and setup of server platforms can be costly, with delivery times of days if not weeks. After the holiday season, these resources would not be used. Virtualization allows existing applications to be scaled across existing computing resources as needed.

Amazon turned the lessons that they learned about scalability and virtualization into a business opportunity. By providing Infrastructure as a Service to other companies, Amazon allows small businesses that cannot afford their own network computing infrastructure to purchase computing power and storage from Amazon's virtualized resources. Amazon used their own Infrastructure as a Service to scale their own enterprise and, from that experience, learned that they can offer this service to other companies with similar needs.

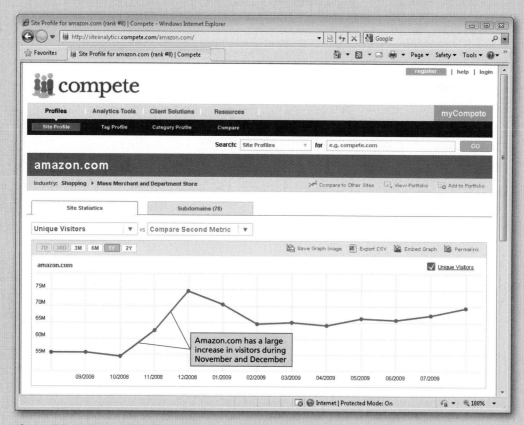

Figure 6-8 Amazon's Web site receives more visitors in November and December.

Platform as a Service: Application Development in the Cloud

In order to create software applications, companies have to purchase, maintain, and configure software, servers, databases, network access, and development tools. Platform as a Service (PaaS), shown in Figure 6-9, provides browser-based tools to develop and deploy Web applications, without having to purchase, install, or maintain any hardware or software.

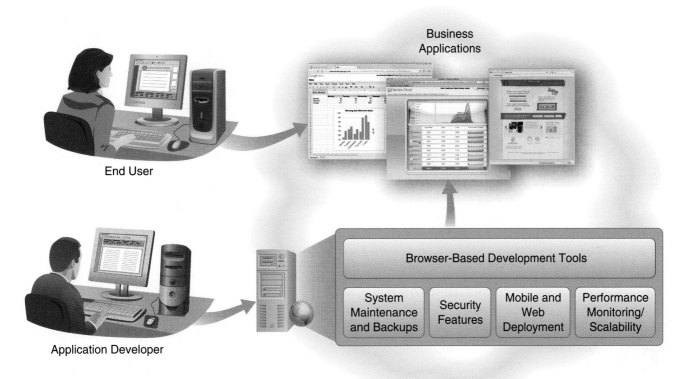

Figure 6-9 Features of Platform as a Service.

Many PaaS providers offer browser-based development tools that can be used by developers to design and build applications that are then deployed on the Web or to mobile devices. Once an application is deployed, performance tools monitor the application as it runs, capturing statistics that include the number of visitors, page load times, and other performance indicators. The PaaS provider monitors an application's performance and facilitates scalability by providing additional computing resources and data storage. A Platform as a Service provider will also perform regular system maintenance tasks, such as backups and software updates, and offer security features so that only authorized users can access data and applications.

Platform as a Service is an attractive option for companies because PaaS vendors offer pay-as-you-go plans. Customers are only charged for the computing services that they actually use. Windows Azure Platform, Amazon Elastic Compute Cloud (Amazon EC2), Force.com Platform from Salesforce, and Google App Engine are four PaaS products that offer development tools, technologies, and computing and storage resources to companies who wish to design and deploy applications in the Cloud. Table 6-2 on the next page summarizes the services of these Platform as a Service providers.

Table 6-2 Platform as a Service Providers

Provider	Logo	Description
Windows Azure		A Cloud operating system for developing and managing Web applications hosted on servers at Microsoft data centers. Integrated with Microsoft's software development tools.
Amazon Elastic Compute Cloud (EC2)		Provides resources to increase or decrease memory and processing power as needed in order to run Web applications over Amazon's computing environment.
Google App Engine		Enables the development of automatically scaled Web applications running on the same systems used for Google applications. Integrated with Google services including maps, calendar, and documents.
Force.com		Provides tools for developing and deploying Web-based business applications that run on the Salesforce.com platform.

Each PaaS provider offers developers the storage, processing, and bandwidth necessary to deploy, manage, and host scalable Internet applications. The Cloud provides additional processing capacity on a remote server. Service agreements between PaaS providers and their customers describe the levels of service that each provider makes available to its customers, including system availability, system performance, storage capabilities, and the ability to recover data.

Starbucks Uses Platform as a Service

Starbucks used Salesforce CRM when developing My Starbucks Idea, their customer feedback and social network discussed in Chapter 5. Salesforce also provides a development platform known as Force.com for software developers to create, deploy, and manage Web applications. Salesforce CRM powers Starbucks' Pledge5 Web site, shown in Figure 6-10, which encourages customers to take part in community service.

Because the Pledge5 site was going to be promoted on national television, it needed to be able to handle the hundreds of thousands of anticipated users who would visit after viewing the program. Force.com provided a scalable infrastructure, connectivity to Facebook, and Web site management tools necessary to rapidly build and deploy this application.

Starbucks uses Salesforce CRM to build, deploy, and manage their Pledge5 site

Figure 6-10 Starbucks' Pledge5 Web site is built using the Salesforce application platform.

Software as a Service: Applications in the Cloud

Web 2.0 is characterized by applications with which users interact in the browser. These applications are delivered to customers over the Internet. The Web adds connectivity to many traditionally desktop-hosted applications, often enabling documents to be shared and facilitating collaboration between users. Large companies such as Amazon, Google, and Facebook rely on the Internet to make their business and consumer applications available to customers. These companies offer Software as a Service (SaaS), which provides Internet-based applications that are typically hosted in a centralized data center and available through a Web browser, as shown in Figure 6-11.

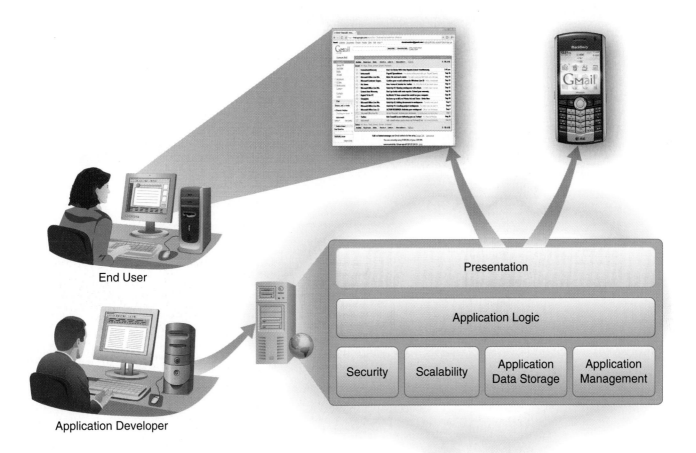

Figure 6-11 Features of Software as a Service.

Software as a Service is a model for delivering software applications and tools from a Web server to a Web browser or Internet-enabled device at any time. SaaS applications are hosted in the Cloud. The application developer provides the necessary logic and steps for the application to function, as well as instructions for presenting the application within a Web browser, mobile phone, or other device. The SaaS provider stores the user data and manages the security, scalability, and performance of the application.

SaaS providers manage their applications from central servers accessed remotely from a Web browser. Software updates can take place frequently and with little interruption to the user. As a result, when a user accesses a Web application, the browser always loads the latest version. The collection of servers, called a **server farm**, is housed in a computing data center facility, and may host several applications. Many small to medium sized companies find that making use of SaaS solutions is an attractive option because they do not have to purchase or maintain any computer hardware.

CONSUMER APPLICATIONS IN THE CLOUD Cloud computing makes it possible for companies to offer Web-based versions of popular personal computer applications such as e-mail services, document editing, photo editing, and instant messaging. Applications that were once limited to desktop use become more valuable when they can leverage the capabilities of the Internet. For example, both Gmail and Microsoft Office Outlook Web Access provide access to e-mail messages from within the browser, as shown in Figure 6-12.

Figure 6-12 Gmail (a) and Outlook Web Access (b) offer access to e-mail applications in the Cloud.

Gmail is an entirely Web-based e-mail service, whereas Microsoft Office Outlook Web Access is the online counterpart to the Microsoft Office Outlook desktop application. Gmail also provides links to a user's accounts on other Google-provided software applications that run within the Cloud, including Google Docs, Google Reader, and Google Sites.

Users who would previously create or edit documents using applications installed on their personal computers and share these files with others via e-mail messages, may now take advantage of applications that run in the Cloud to create and share documents. ZohoWriter, Google Docs, and Microsoft Office Live, shown in Figure 6-13, provide online document, spreadsheet, and presentation editing, and storage, collaboration, and sharing capabilities.

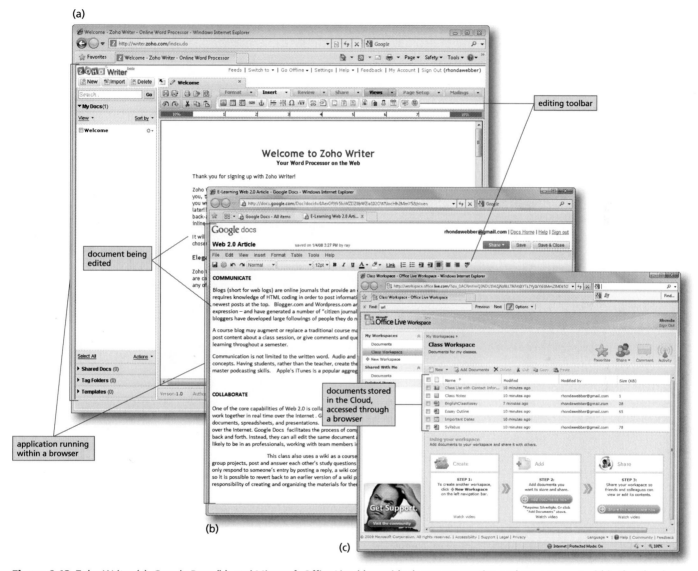

Figure 6-13 Zoho Writer (a), Google Docs (b), and Microsoft Office Live (c) provide document creation and management within the Cloud.

Users may upload, create, and store documents online to facilitate sharing with others. Each application offers many of the same tools that you would find in the equivalent desktop word processing and spreadsheet applications. Whereas applications like Microsoft Office require substantial disk space and processing power for editing and storing a user's documents, their online counterparts only require the processing power needed to run a Web browser. For consumers, this dramatically reduces the requirements of a client computer connected to the Cloud. Many netbook systems are capable of Cloud computing and can be acquired for a fraction of the cost of business-class laptops.

Sumo Paint provides photo-editing software capabilities within a Web browser that are comparable to those found in desktop applications. Because Sumo Paint resides on the Web, users can choose to upload a photo from a personal computer or to import a photo stored on the Web by providing its URL. Users may save photos to their Sumo Paint accounts in order to share them with friends. In Figure 6-14, a photo stored on Flickr is opened in Sumo Paint for editing.

Figure 6-14 Sumo Paint may be used to edit photos stored in the Cloud.

BUSINESS APPLICATIONS IN THE CLOUD   In addition to consumer SaaS applications, many business applications are offered as software services in the Cloud. Software as a Service often has a pay-as-you-go licensing model, in which customers do not own the software but pay a fee for its use. The Salesforce Service Cloud, presented in Chapter 5, is a business application that runs in the Cloud. As shown in Figure 6-15, the Salesforce Service Cloud monitors conversations about a company's products that take place in Internet discussion forums, blogs, Google searches, and social networks.

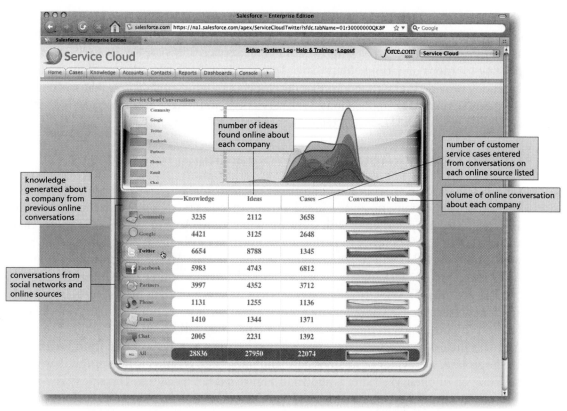

Figure 6-15 The Salesforce Service Cloud is a social CRM application available as Software as a Service.

As customers search the Internet, rather than turn to a company's customer support center, to find answers to their problems, the Salesforce Service Cloud tries to capture the wisdom of the crowds to provide service to customers in the same forums or social networks in which they posed their questions.

Salesforce leverages the fact that it is a SaaS application in order to connect to all of these sources on the Web and share knowledge with business partners. Salesforce users interact with this application through their Web browsers. Salesforce hosts, manages, and deploys the application from the Cloud so that users do not have to purchase or manage hardware or software. In addition to the Service Cloud, Salesforce offers customers the ability to select and subscribe to various modules, such as payment processing, sales forecasting, or customer management, and include them within their individual CRM environment.

Understanding Distributed Web Applications

Complex software applications make use of collections of reusable software modules that implement common tasks or special-purpose capabilities. Software developers rely on application programming interfaces to incorporate capabilities of external application modules in their own applications. An **application programming interface**, or **API**, is a software module that enables software applications to interact with each other. An application hosted on one server may send a request over the Internet to a service running on another server to perform a specialized task and return its outcome. Many companies provide APIs that are accessible over the Internet so that software developers can make use of their business data as part of Web applications. **Web services** are APIs that Web applications can request to run over the Internet.

Web services offer specific information, such as news and sports headlines, stock quotes, and weather forecasts. Other Web services provide transactional services, such as credit card processing, tracking United Parcel Service (UPS) or FedEx packages, and plotting locations on Google Maps. Social networking sites such as Flickr, Twitter, and Facebook provide Web services so that developers can build applications that make use of their data. Unlike Web applications, Web services do not have a user interface. Like RSS feeds, they provide XML-formatted data to other applications.

Understanding Application Programming Interfaces

An API specifies the programming interfaces required for software applications to interact with other applications, much as a user interface specifies menus, screen layouts, and other aspects of how people interact with software applications. An API specifies the values that an application needs in order to perform a transaction or obtain desired information, as well as the values that will result from performing the task. An application that calls an API to accomplish a task does not need to know the details of how the API works.

For example, Travelocity sells travel services online, including flights, car rentals, and hotel reservations. The company provides weather information on their Web site for travelers interested in the forecast for the cities they will be visiting. Rather than maintain their own weather data, Travelocity subscribes to a Web service from Weather Underground, a provider of weather data, and integrates Weather Underground's weather information on their Web site, as shown in Figure 6-16. This allows Travelocity to focus on its core business, travel, while providing value-added information to its customers.

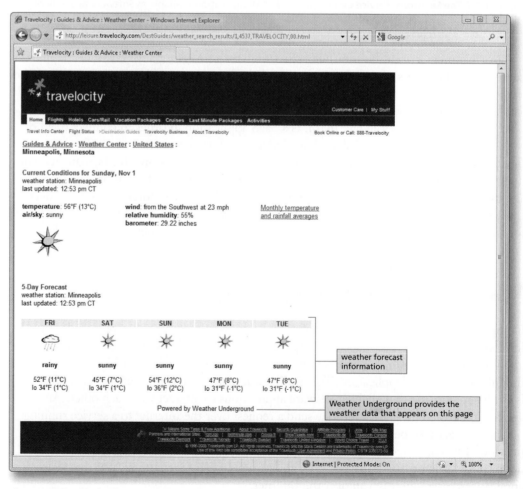

Figure 6-16 Travelocity displays weather information provided by Weather Underground.

Travelocity is powered by a Web application that obtains travel information from its own database and calls upon Weather Underground to provide weather information for the user's specified location. Figure 6-17 shows the process that is involved for Travelocity to obtain the Weather Underground weather information. The Travelocity application must invoke the Weather Underground Web service over the Internet through its API.

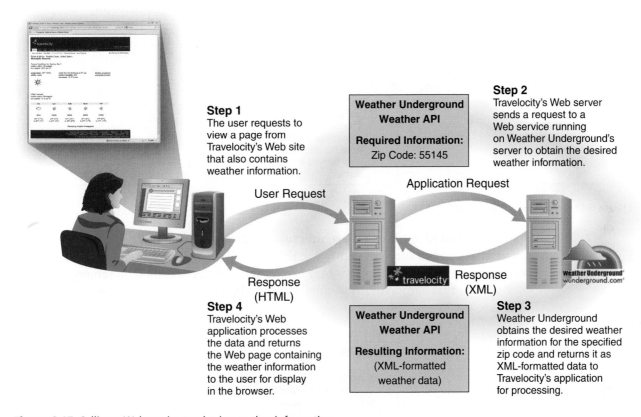

Step 1
The user requests to view a page from Travelocity's Web site that also contains weather information.

Weather Underground Weather API
Required Information:
Zip Code: 55145

Step 2
Travelocity's Web server sends a request to a Web service running on Weather Underground's server to obtain the desired weather information.

User Request

Application Request

Response (HTML)

Response (XML)

Step 4
Travelocity's Web application processes the data and returns the Web page containing the weather information to the user for display in the browser.

Weather Underground Weather API
Resulting Information:
(XML-formatted weather data)

Step 3
Weather Underground obtains the desired weather information for the specified zip code and returns it as XML-formatted data to Travelocity's application for processing.

Figure 6-17 Calling a Web service to obtain weather information.

Travelocity's application requests data from Weather Underground by calling its Web service through its API. Travelocity's application specifies the zip code for the desired city. Weather Underground's servers fulfill the request for weather information from Travelocity and return the requested weather information to the Travelocity application as XML-formatted data. Travelocity's Web application processes the data and returns the Web page as HTML containing the weather information for display in the browser.

The Structure of Distributed Applications

The Internet makes it possible for both people and Web applications to communicate and share information with each other. Many Web applications also take advantage of the Internet's connectivity to access Web services to provide specialized information or content. A model of three-tiered architecture for Web applications was introduced in Chapter 2. To review, three-tiered architecture, shown in Figure 6-18 on the next page, includes a presentation tier, which is responsible for all aspects of displaying information to the user. The presentation tier communicates with the middle tier, which performs the application's logic and obtains data from a database tier.

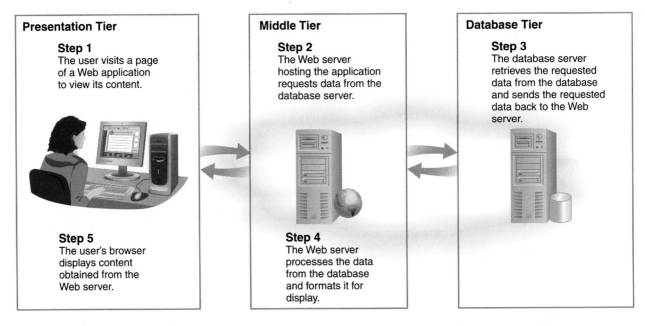

Figure 6-18 Three-tiered architecture.

A **distributed application architecture**, sometimes called multi-tiered application architecture, adds a **services tier** to the three-tiered architecture diagram, so that servers running Web applications may invoke Web services running on remote servers over the Internet automatically. A model of distributed application architecture is shown in Figure 6-19.

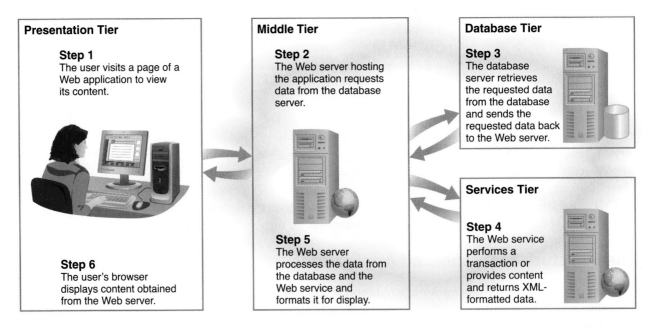

Figure 6-19 Distributed application architecture.

In distributed application architecture, the presentation tier continues to handle the display of information to the user. The middle tier, or business logic tier, handles the interchange of information, and the database tier provides data from associated databases. The services tier represents Web services residing in the Cloud that an application may access over the Internet. In a distributed application architecture, a Web application and its processing are often distributed among many different devices and servers all connected by the Internet.

An application that makes use of Web services is said to have a **service-oriented architecture (SOA).** An advantage of using Web services to build complex applications is that the applications calling Web services do not need to know anything about how the services work. They just need to know what information each service requires as input and in what format the results will be returned as output. This approach allows the applications to concentrate on their core business logic without having to create or manage content that can be obtained from third-party providers.

Examining Data from Web Services

Web applications invoke a company's Web APIs over the Internet to incorporate that company's data. For example, among the capabilities that Twitter provides in its APIs are operations, or methods, to obtain information about a user's friends and followers. Twitter APIs contain methods to search Twitter, obtain user information, and provide statistics on individual tweets. Twitter documents its APIs on a Web site, shown in Figure 6-20, which is available from the API link on the Twitter home page.

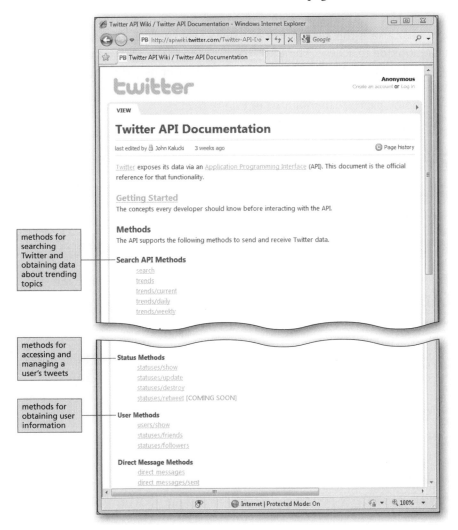

Figure 6-20 Twitter APIs contain methods to search Twitter, obtain user information, and provide statistics on individual tweets.

The Twitter API Documentation contains information about the different methods that Twitter makes available through their APIs for software developers to incorporate in their own applications. These include methods to search Twitter, obtain information about trending topics, and see information about a user, a user's friends, and followers.

(Although the Twitter Web site refers to the people who you follow as your *following*, in the Twitter API, the people who you follow are known as your *friends*.) Each method shown in the Twitter API Documentation queries a Twitter database to obtain the desired information and then provides it in XML format.

You can view the XML-formatted data from some of these methods by entering the URL of the method in your browser. The following URLs, obtained from the Twitter API Documentation, retrieve information about a user's profile, friends, and followers.

- The URL for the users/show method, `http://twitter.com/users/show.xml?screen_name=username`, retrieves information about a user's profile.

- The URL for the statuses/friends method, `http://twitter.com/statuses/friends.xml?screen_name=username`, retrieves information about a Twitter user's friends.

- The URL for the statuses/followers method, `http://twitter.com/statuses/followers.xml?screen_name=username`, retrieves information about a Twitter user's followers.

In each case, `username` is the Twitter screen name of the user whose profile, friends or followers you are looking to access. The URL for the users/show method is entered in a Web browser to display the XML-formatted data about Twitter user rhowebber. The Twitter API returns several data values from a user's profile; those values that commonly appear on a Twitter home page are highlighted in Figure 6-21.

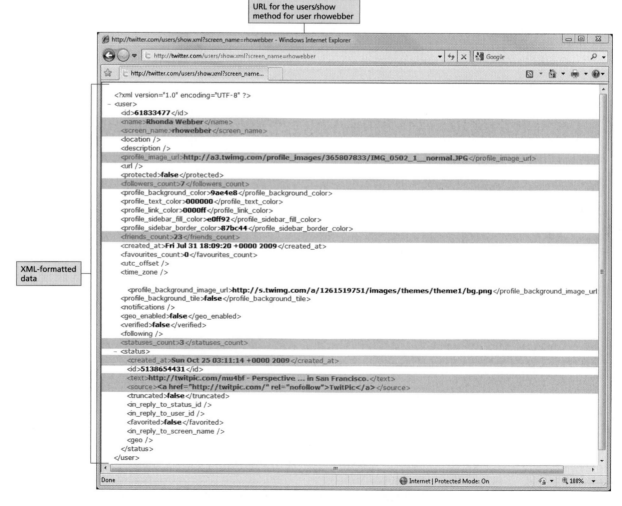

Figure 6-21 Viewing data in a browser using the users/show method of Twitter's API.

The XML tags describe each of the items in a user's profile. Each `<user>` tag contains information about that user, including the user's name, screen name, and friends count. A `<status>` tag contains information about the user's most recent tweet, including its text and the time that it was created. Figure 6-22 displays the structure of the XML tags that the Twitter API uses to describe a user.

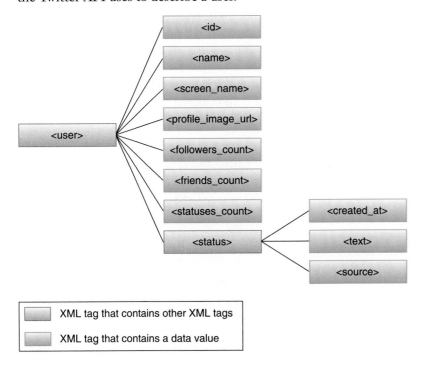

Figure 6-22 The structure of the XML tags that describe a Twitter profile.

As in the XML structure diagrams in Chapter 3, the blue tags contain other tags, and the green tags contain actual data values. In addition to the user's Twitter ID, name, and screen name, the API users/show method provides information about the number of friends, followers, and tweets (shown by the `<statuses_count>` tag) that a user has and the user's most recent tweet. Among the information stored with each tweet is the time and date that it was created, the text of the tweet, and the application that was used to post it on Twitter (shown by the `<source>` tag). Twitter uses the users/show method to display this information on a user's profile page, as shown in Figure 6-23.

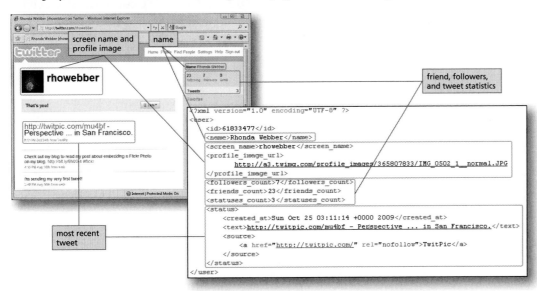

Figure 6-23 A Twitter profile page displays data provided by methods in the Twitter API.

Most casual users do not have a need to view this XML data. Rather, a Web application requests user data from Twitter by calling one of its API methods over the Internet. The application then extracts the values that it needs from the XML. Applications process XML-formatted data by navigating its XML tags in order to create lists of similarly described items.

An **XPath** (short for XML Path) is a list of tags, each separated by a forward slash (/), that describe how to locate specific data items in an XML document. An XPath always begins with the topmost tag in the document and lists all subsequent tags in the hierarchy until the required data items are reached. For example, the XPath that collects the screen names of all Twitter users from the statuses/friends method is `/users/user/screen_name`. The XPath is highlighted by the bold outlined tags in the XML structure diagram shown in Figure 6-24.

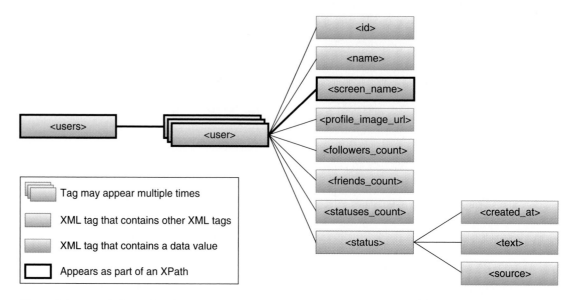

Figure 6-24 An XPath specifies how to navigate through an XML document and collect a list of data items described by all occurrences of that path.

Applications make use of XPath information to extract similar data items from an XML document into a list. For Twitter user rhowebber, given the XML information provided by the statuses/friends API, the XPath `/users/user/screen_name` specifies a list of screen names beginning with bobconselli and PavlikM, as shown in Figure 6-25.

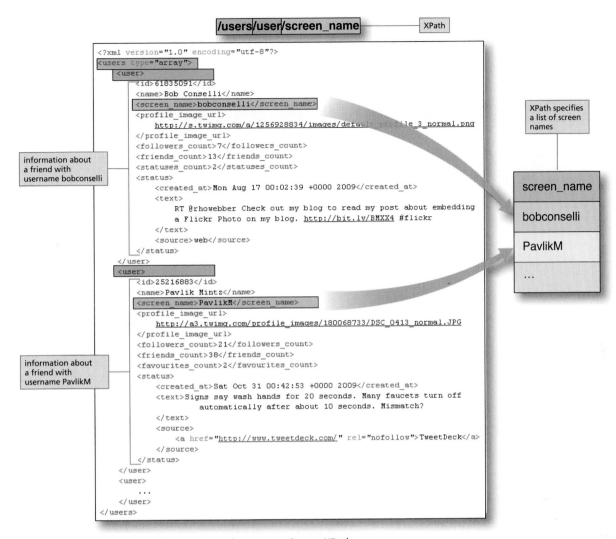

Figure 6-25 Extracting data from an XML document using an XPath.

After obtaining data from an XML document by specifying an XPath expression, a software application can process each item in the list. An XPath provides a way to extract items from an XML document and import them into a list.

Computing in the Cloud with Google Docs

Google Docs is an integrated SaaS suite of Web applications for creating, storing, and sharing documents, spreadsheets, and presentations in the Cloud. Google offers the use of these software tools and the necessary storage for documents created with them as a free service to its customers. Because the documents are stored on the Internet, you can access them from anywhere that you have an Internet connection and share the documents with other users. After logging in to Google Docs with your Google ID, Google Docs displays your Google Docs desktop, shown in Figure 6-26 on the next page.

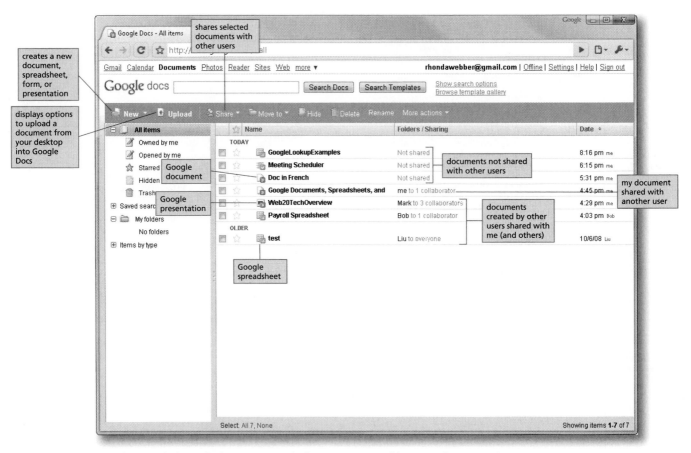

Figure 6-26 The Google Docs desktop displays your Google documents, spreadsheets, and presentations.

You can create a new document, spreadsheet, presentation, folder, or form and organize the document using folders. Google Docs allows you to upload existing documents, spreadsheets, or presentations stored on your desktop in order to edit and share them with other users. These online applications have many of the same features as their Microsoft Office application counterparts. Google Documents, Spreadsheets, and Presentations offer additional features that take advantage of the Internet connectivity that is available when an application runs within the Cloud, such as sharing and collaborating on documents with other users. Shared documents will also appear in the Google Docs desktops of those users with whom you have shared them. Documents that you have not shared will only appear on your desktop. Figure 6-27 displays the process of inviting another user to collaborate on a Google presentation.

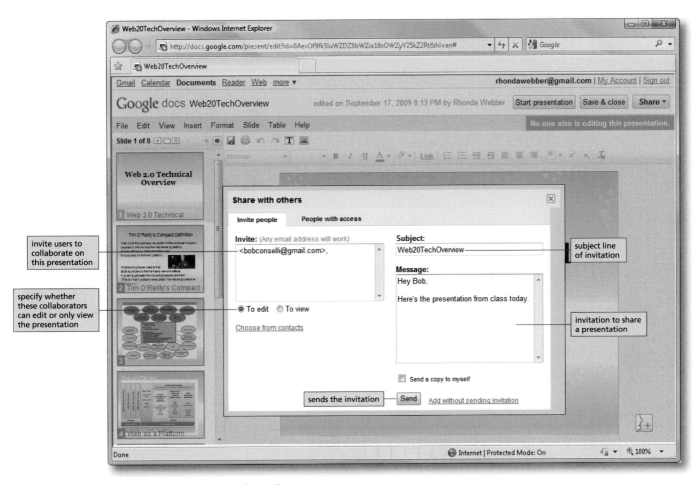

Figure 6-27 Sharing a Google presentation with another user.

Instead of sending a file in an e-mail message to several people to edit and then merging the results or exchanging different versions of a report with teammates or coworkers, Google Docs always makes the most recent version of a document, presentation, or spreadsheet available to those with whom it is shared. After deciding to share a document with other users, Google Docs displays a dialog box where you can enter the e-mail addresses of users with whom you want to share the document. You can allow your collaborators to edit the document or only view it. You can enter a subject and a short message, and then the Google Docs application will send the invitations via an e-mail message. The name of the shared document, spreadsheet, or presentation will appear on the Google Docs desktop the next time the invited users log in.

For real-time collaboration, Google Spreadsheets provides a built-in chat window in which users may chat about a document as they edit it at the same time, as shown in Figure 6-28.

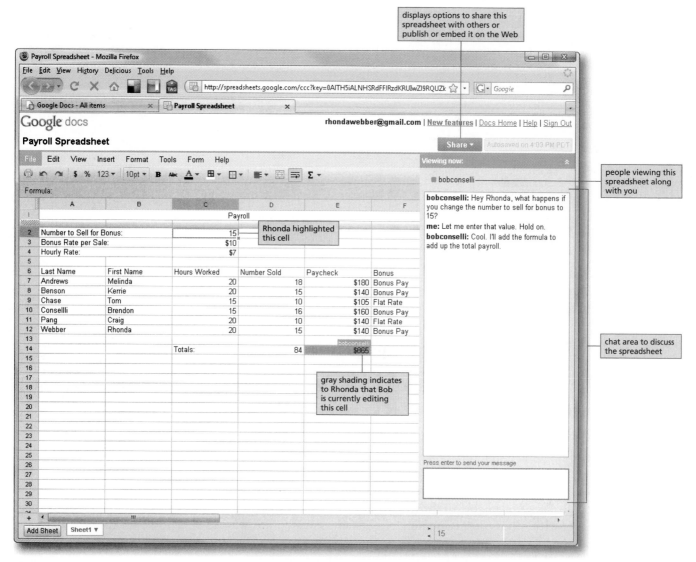

Figure 6-28 Rhonda is collaborating with Bob using the chat window in a Google Spreadsheet.

Another feature that all of the Google Docs applications offer is the ability to directly embed or publish the document, spreadsheet, or presentation on the Web. For example, Google Presentations provides a hyperlink to the presentation and HTML code to embed the presentation within a blog or Web site, as shown in Figure 6-29.

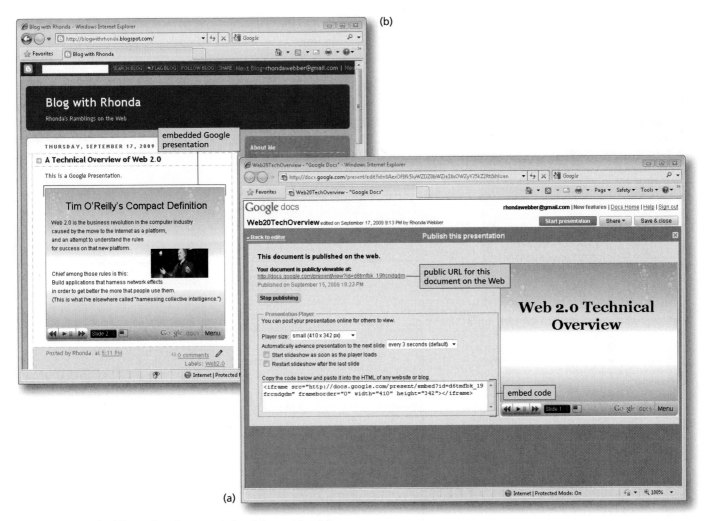

Figure 6-29 Embedding a Google presentation (a) on a blog (b).

Because the presentation is stored in the Cloud, its most current version always appears in a blog post or on a Web site where it is embedded, even if a user edits the presentation after it has been embedded. When creating a presentation using a desktop application such as Microsoft PowerPoint, the process of posting a presentation to the Web is more complex: a user would first save the presentation as HTML, upload the HTML and associated image files to a Web server, and then type the appropriate HTML in a blog post. Alternatively, a user might publish the presentation on a sharing site such as SlideShare and then include the embed code provided by SlideShare in a blog post. In either case, if a modification is made to the original presentation, a user would have to repeat these steps in order for his or her blog to display the most recent version of the presentation.

Another way that Google Docs takes advantage of the fact that it runs in the Cloud is its ability to integrate other Google products. For example, capabilities from Google Translate, Google's online translation application, are implemented within Google Documents so that users may translate documents from one language to another, as shown in Figure 6-30 on the next page.

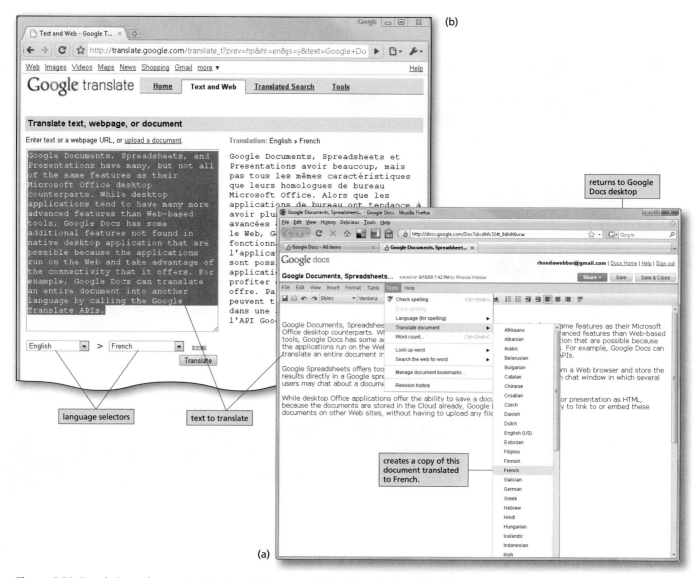

Figure 6-30 Translating a document using Google Documents (a) and Google Translate (b).

On the back end, Google Documents uses the same API as Google Translate to perform the translation from one language to another. Consistent with the way that Web 2.0 applications are built with the intention of creating small functional units that can be combined into different applications, Google built one translation service, which both of these applications share.

Advanced Cloud-Based Features of Google Spreadsheets

Google Spreadsheets takes advantage of its connectivity to the Cloud by allowing users to create simple online surveys with its Google Forms application and to include and manipulate live data from the Web.

Creating Online Surveys with Google Forms

Google Spreadsheets offers an online editor called Google Forms to create forms for surveys, as shown in Figure 6-31. Forms can be distributed by including the URL in an e-mail message to friends or in a tweet to followers on Twitter.

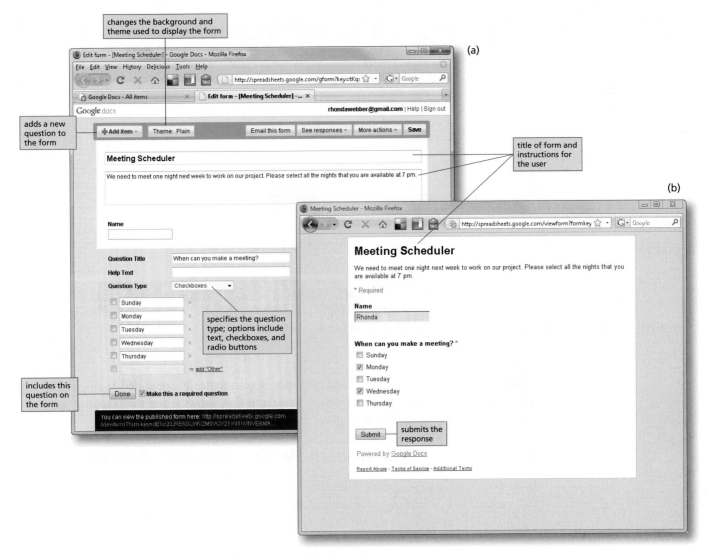

Figure 6-31 Creating (a) and viewing (b) a form created with Google Forms.

Users completing the survey view the form in their Web browsers, as shown in Figure 6-31(b). Google Forms stores the form and any user data submitted through the form in the Cloud as part of the Google spreadsheet. Each user's response is recorded directly in a Google spreadsheet, as shown in Figure 6-32.

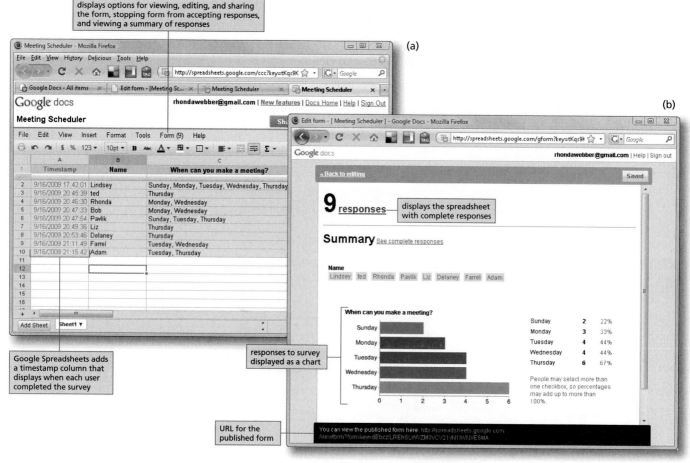

Figure 6-32 Viewing the survey results (a) and the results summary (b) in a Google spreadsheet.

As users complete the form, each response is automatically appended as a new row in the Google spreadsheet, along with a timestamp that shows when the response was received. The results summary displays the responses to the survey as a chart.

Including Live Data from the Web in a Google Spreadsheet

In addition to computational functions that you are familiar with from a desktop spreadsheet program such as Excel, Google Spreadsheets includes Web functions that look up information on the Web and insert the results in spreadsheet cells.

For example, computational functions such as SUM, AVERAGE, MAX, and MIN perform calculations on data. Each of these functions has arguments that specify the data values to which the function should be applied. For example, =SUM(3,5,7) calculates the sum of the numbers 3, 5, and 7, and the function =AVERAGE(B1:B4) calculates the average of the values of cells B1, B2, B3, and B4. Typically, the user must enter the values for which to calculate the sum or average as well as the formulas to do so.

In Google Spreadsheets, Web functions, such as GoogleLookup, access live data on the Web by requiring the user to specify the information for which to search and to then bring the search results into the spreadsheet. Each function calls a Google API in order to access the requested data over the Web and include it in the spreadsheet. Table 6-3 describes some of the functions in Google Spreadsheets that access data from the Web.

Table 6-3 Selected Google Spreadsheet Functions

Function	Example	Description
=GoogleLookup(*item, value*)	=GoogleLookup("Amazon River", "length")	Searches Google to find the length of the Amazon River.
=GoogleFinance(*symbol, attribute*)	=GoogleFinance("GOOG", "price")	Searches Google Finance to find the current price of Google stock.
=GoogleTranslate (*item, fromLanguage, toLanguage*)	=GoogleTranslate ("apple", "en", "fr")	Translates the word apple from English to French. GoogleTranslate makes use of standard two-letter language codes.
=ImportFeed (*url*)	=ImportFeed("http://news.google.com/?output=rss")	Imports content from the Google News Web feed. Optional arguments (not shown) allow you to specify exactly which and how many items to import.
=ImportHTML (*url, ListOrTable, index*)	=ImportHTML("http://en.wikipedia.org/wiki/Demographics_of_the_United_States", "table", 5)	Imports data from a table or list found on a Web page. The example imports the data in the fifth table on the Wikipedia page whose URL is specified.
=ImportXML (*url, XPath*)	=ImportXML("http://twitter.com/statuses/friends.xml?screen_name=rhowebber", "/users/user/screen_name")	Imports the screen names of all of Rhonda Webber's followers on Twitter from the Twitter statuses/friends API

Google provides detailed online documentation about how each of these functions works. You can find the online documentation, shown in Figure 6-33 on the next page, by searching for the name of the function, GoogleLookup, followed by the word documentation in your favorite search engine.

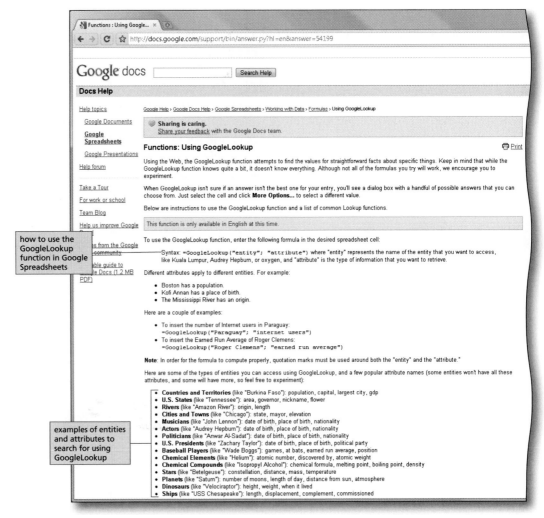

how to use the GoogleLookup function in Google Spreadsheets

examples of entities and attributes to search for using GoogleLookup

Figure 6-33 The GoogleLookup Documentation page contains information about using the GoogleLookup function.

USING GOOGLELOOKUP **GoogleLookup** is a Google Spreadsheet function that searches the Web for information about a particular item. It requires two arguments: the item that you are looking for information about, such as the Amazon River or Paris, and the type of information that you would like Google to find, such its as length or population. Like all spreadsheet formulas, a formula to invoke GoogleLookup must begin with an equal sign (=) followed by the name of the function and its arguments. GoogleLookup will find the desired information by searching the Web and place the results in a cell of the Google spreadsheet. GoogleLookup can find information about a variety of items, as indicated in the online documentation. For example, to look up the length of the Amazon river, you could enter the formula =GoogleLookup("Amazon River", "length") in a cell of the spreadsheet, as shown in Figure 6-34.

(a)

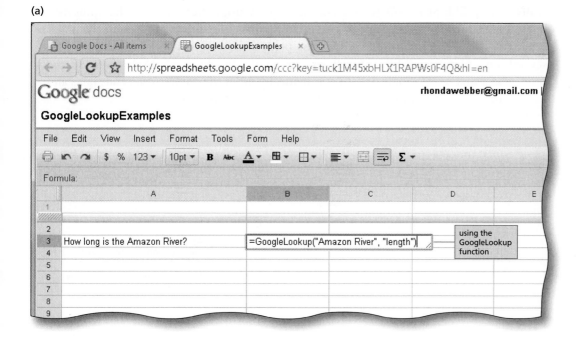

(b)

Figure 6-34 Entering a formula using GoogleLookup (a) and viewing the results (b).

After entering a GoogleLookup formula, Google Spreadsheets momentarily displays the word "Loading" until it evaluates the formula to determine the value to display in that cell. Hovering over the cell displays a dialog box with a hyperlink to the Web site from which GoogleLookup obtained the information.

USING GOOGLE SETS TO AUTO-FILL CELLS **Google Sets** is a tool that finds lists of related values. After entering one or two related values in a spreadsheet, point the mouse at the cell's handle in the lower right corner, press the CTRL key, and drag the cell down several rows. Google will fill each cell with a related value. Figure 6-35 displays a Google spreadsheet that uses Google Sets to automatically fill in the names of several states and uses GoogleLookup to look up the name of each state's Governor.

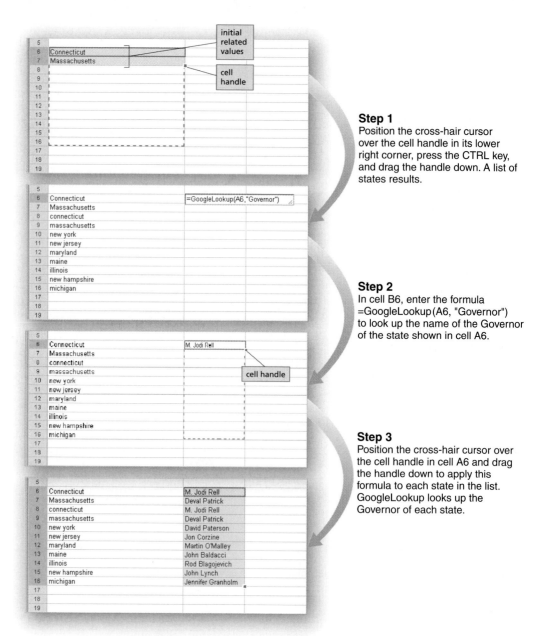

Step 1
Position the cross-hair cursor over the cell handle in its lower right corner, press the CTRL key, and drag the handle down. A list of states results.

Step 2
In cell B6, enter the formula =GoogleLookup(A6, "Governor") to look up the name of the Governor of the state shown in cell A6.

Step 3
Position the cross-hair cursor over the cell handle in cell A6 and drag the handle down to apply this formula to each state in the list. GoogleLookup looks up the Governor of each state.

Figure 6-35 Using Google Sets and GoogleLookup to find multiple values.

USING IMPORTHTML The ImportHTML function imports a table or list from a Web page into a Google spreadsheet. Consider the Wikipedia page shown in Figure 6-36.

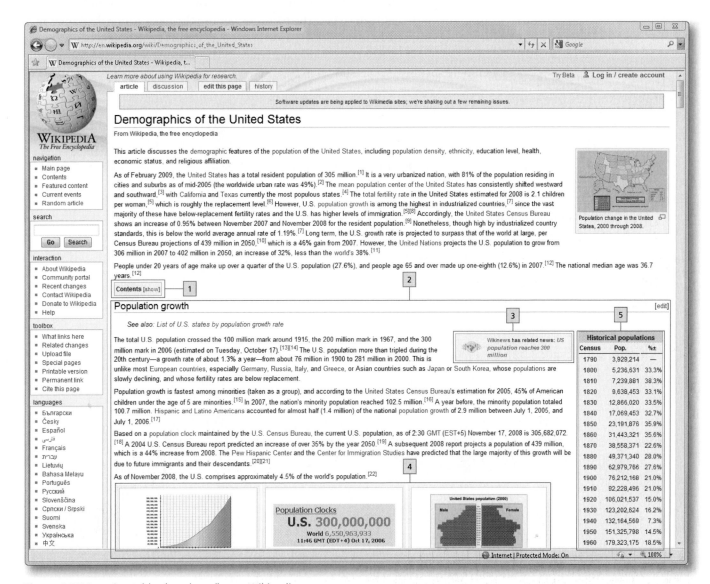

Figure 6-36 Locating tables (numbered) on a Wikipedia page.

To import the data from the Historical Population table on this page, you need to know which table on the page contains this information. Because this page contains multiple tables, you could view the HTML source of the page and count `<table>` tags until you find the one that begins the table containing the desired information, or you could make an educated guess based on the layout of the page to find the correct index value. Each number on the Wikipedia page shown in Figure 6-36 indicates data formatted as an HTML table. In this case, the table containing Historical Population data is the fifth table on the page.

The ImportHTML function has three arguments: the URL for the Web page from which to import HTML, whether the data to import is coming from a table (in which case you would write "table") or a list (in which case you would write "list"), and the index, or position, of the table or list on the page containing the data. Enter the function =ImportHTML("http://en.wikipedia.org/wiki/Demographics_of_the_ United_States", "table", 5) in cell A1 to add the Historical Populations table data to a Google spreadsheet, as shown in Figure 6-37.

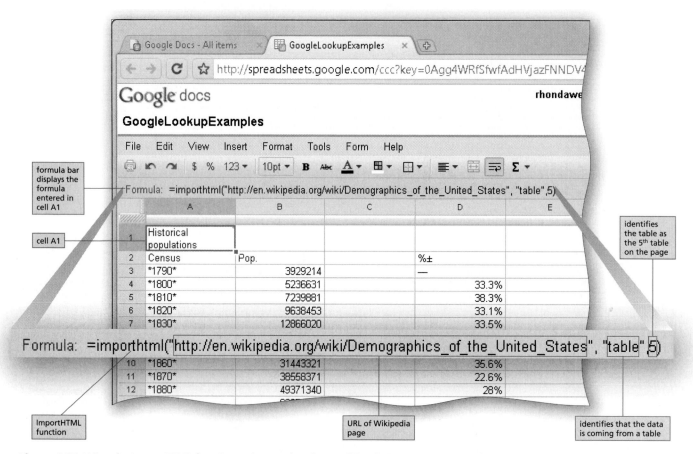

Figure 6-37 Using the ImportHTML function to import data from Wikipedia into Google Spreadsheets.

Selecting the Show formula bar from the View menu will display the formula associated with the active cell in a formula bar above the column headings at the top of the spreadsheet.

USING IMPORTXML   The ImportXML function displays XML data within a Google spreadsheet. The function requires a URL of the XML feed and the XPath for the requested data. Google Spreadsheets can use the ImportXML function to obtain the list of Twitter user rhowebber's friends by specifying the URL for the statuses/friends method of the Twitter API with the XPath `/users/user/screen_name`. As shown in Figure 6-38(a), the formula `=ImportXML("http://twitter.com/statuses/friends.xml?screen_name=rhowebber", "/users/user/screen_name")` in cell A3 collects all of the screen names of rhowebber's friends into a list and displays them in a column below the cell. A similar formula using the statuses/followers method of the Twitter API displays all of rhowebber's followers).

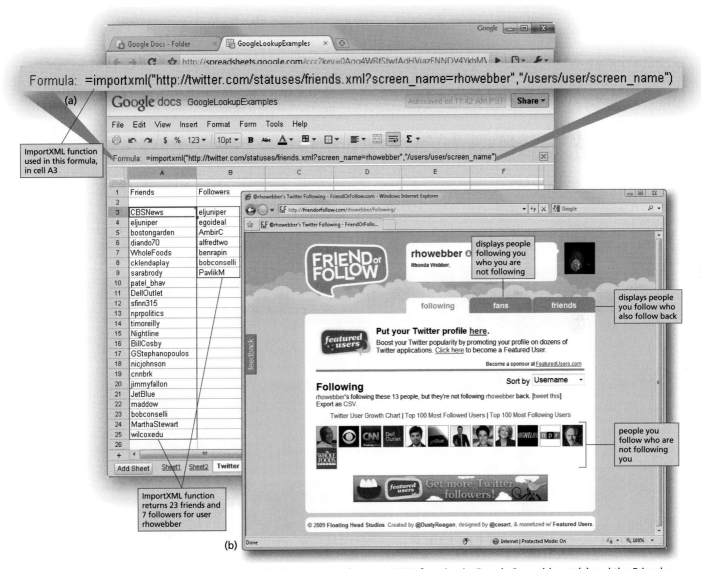

Figure 6-38 Displaying a Twitter user's friends and followers using the ImportXML function in Google Spreadsheets (a) and the Friend or Follow application (b).

Friend or Follow, shown in Figure 6-38 (b), is a Twitter application that calls on the same Twitter API methods to display a user's friends and followers in the browser. The spreadsheet application displays the screen names of your friends and followers in two adjacent columns of a Google spreadsheet. Friend or Follow adds application logic to determine your following (people you follow who are not following you), your fans (people who follow you that you are not following), and your friends (people you follow who also follow you). Though Friend or Follow has a much more visually appealing display, including the profile images for each friend or follower, both the Google Spreadsheet version and Friend or Follow use the same methods from the Twitter API.

Linking Data between Web Applications

Data can be linked between applications in a variety of ways. Web sites such as iGoogle and Web 2.0 tools such as Facebook Connect and OpenID gather data from different online sources to display without modification as part of an existing Web page or application. Web sites such as MSN, iGoogle, and myYahoo are examples of portal pages. **Portal pages** display customized online content from different sources on the same page. iGoogle, shown in Figure 6-39, displays live data from different sources.

Figure 6-39 iGoogle is an example of a portal Web page.

Data on a portal page can include text, such as the weather forecast or news headlines from CNET or Wired; audio content, such as broadcasts from National Public Radio; or video content, such as uploaded videos on YouTube. In a portal Web page, the content from one source does not interact with content from another. The portal page simply serves as a container for data coming from all of the different sources. You can rearrange content on a portal page by clicking and dragging the title bar of any content item to another content region on the page.

Linking Activities between Web Applications

Facebook Connect is a set of APIs that enable applications to allow users to share their identities and activities across many different Web sites. Your Facebook identity becomes your single sign-on, a common username and password that you can use to access sites, such as those shown in Figure 6-40, that use Facebook Connect. Your activity on those sites may appear in your Facebook status updates.

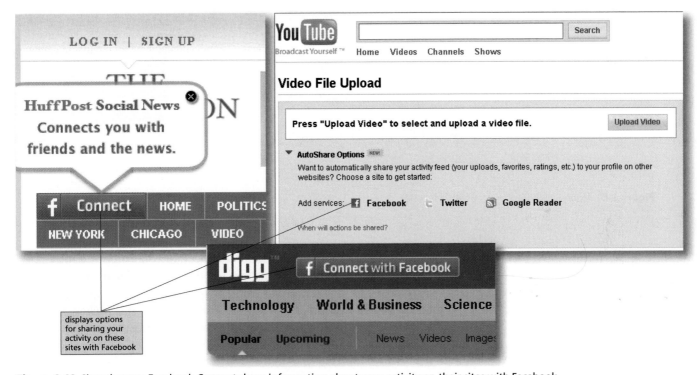

Figure 6-40 Sites that use Facebook Connect share information about your activity on their sites with Facebook.

Huffington Post, Digg, and YouTube are examples of three Web sites that support Facebook Connect. When you sign in to a site that supports Facebook Connect, your activities on that site will appear as part of your Facebook Wall or News Feed in your profile. In this way, your friends can learn about your activities on other sites from one central place, your Facebook profile. Figure 6-41 on the next page describes the process of using Facebook Connect with YouTube.

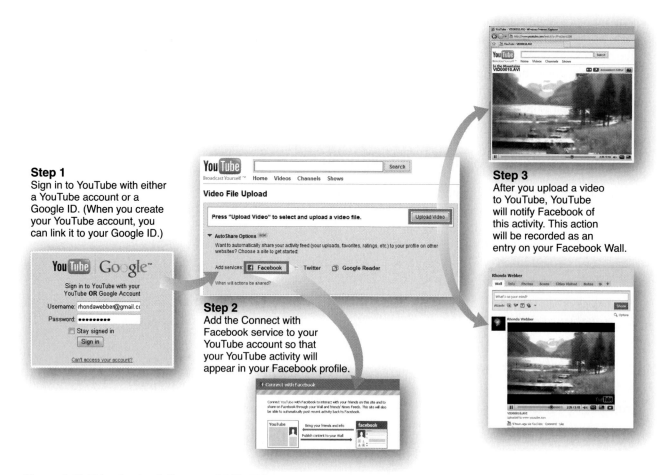

Step 1
Sign in to YouTube with either a YouTube account or a Google ID. (When you create your YouTube account, you can link it to your Google ID.)

Step 2
Add the Connect with Facebook service to your YouTube account so that your YouTube activity will appear in your Facebook profile.

Step 3
After you upload a video to YouTube, YouTube will notify Facebook of this activity. This action will be recorded as an entry on your Facebook Wall.

Figure 6-41 Using Facebook Connect with YouTube.

Facebook Connect is similar to Google's Friend Connect, introduced in Chapter 5, in that it provides a single sign-on to applications that use the service. The main difference between Facebook Connect and Google Friend Connect is that Facebook requires users to sign in using their Facebook credentials and links activity on those sites back to their Facebook accounts. Google Friend Connect allows users to join sites using their Google, AOL, or Yahoo! IDs but does not offer a centralized site that collects and displays all of a user's activities.

Authenticating with OpenID

OpenID is an authentication service. An **authentication service** allows users to sign on to many different Web sites using a single, common digital identity. OpenID allows individuals to register their identities with certified OpenID identity providers such as Google, Yahoo!, Blogger, and AOL. If you have an account on one of these services, you already have an OpenID, as shown in Figure 6-42.

Figure 6-42 Your account on several Web sites serves as your OpenID.

You can log in to a site that supports OpenID using the information shown in Figure 6-42. You can also use a third-party identity provider site such as claimID to create an OpenID that is not associated with other identities that you may already have.

Figure 6-43 claimID is a third-party site that provides OpenIDs that are not associated with an existing account.

An OpenID often takes the form of a URL that contains both the domain name of an identity provider and a username. For example, the OpenID `http://www.flickr.com/rhondawebber` identifies rhondawebber as a user and Flickr as an identity provider. Your OpenID URL usually links to a profile page on the identity provider's site.

MapQuest is an online mapping service. Rather than having to create a new username and password especially for MapQuest, users may sign in with an OpenID. Once logged in, users can save maps of favorite locations in the MyPlaces section of MapQuest so that the maps will be available the next time that they sign in. Figure 6-44 shows the process of logging in to MapQuest using OpenID.

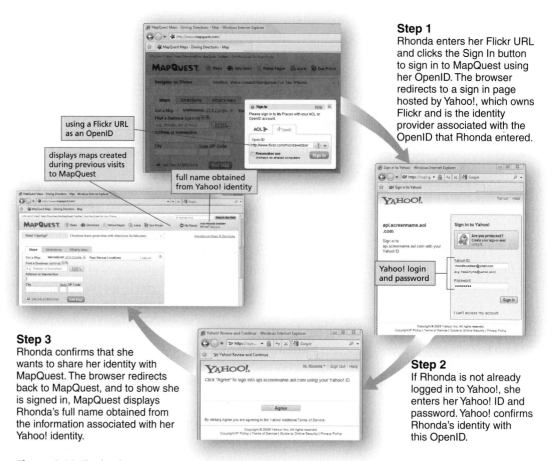

Step 1
Rhonda enters her Flickr URL and clicks the Sign In button to sign in to MapQuest using her OpenID. The browser redirects to a sign in page hosted by Yahoo!, which owns Flickr and is the identity provider associated with the OpenID that Rhonda entered.

using a Flickr URL as an OpenID

displays maps created during previous visits to MapQuest

full name obtained from Yahoo! identity

Yahoo! login and password

Step 3
Rhonda confirms that she wants to share her identity with MapQuest. The browser redirects back to MapQuest, and to show she is signed in, MapQuest displays Rhonda's full name obtained from the information associated with her Yahoo! identity.

Step 2
If Rhonda is not already logged in to Yahoo!, she enters her Yahoo! ID and password. Yahoo! confirms Rhonda's identity with this OpenID.

Figure 6-44 Signing in to MapQuest using OpenID.

OpenID provides a secure way to share information between Web sites. In Figure 6-44, after entering an OpenID associated with her Flickr account, MapQuest redirects the browser to a sign-in page hosted by Yahoo!, which owns Flickr. There Rhonda enters her Yahoo! username and password for authentication. MapQuest, the consumer of the identity provider's service, never has access to Rhonda's username or password. After she is authenticated, Yahoo! returns information from Rhonda's Yahoo! profile, including her full name, to MapQuest.

By using OpenID, users need only remember a single URL to access many different Web sites. Sites that use OpenID may attract users because they do not have to create a special account for each site that they visit. Despite its benefits for users and owners of Web sites, the OpenID is not without risk. Because the same sign-on is shared by many sites, an unauthorized individual who learns a user's OpenID and associated login credentials will be able to access all of the sites to which the user signed on using that OpenID.

Creating New Applications from Data in the Cloud

Data can be linked between applications by simply collecting and displaying the data without modification as part of an existing Web page or application, as used by portal pages or Facebook Connect. Web applications such as Friend or Follow access data from a Web site through its API and apply processing rules in order to create a new application that enables users to interact with that data in new ways.

Mashups are Web applications that combine content or data from multiple online sources into new Web applications. Mashups have become a popular type of Web 2.0 application because many Web sites that host applications for social networking, photo and video sharing, searching, and mapping also provide APIs to access their data. Because mashups interact with live data on the Web, their contents are continually updated. Software developers can use these APIs not only to access the data, but also to make use of it in new applications. The ProgrammableWeb, shown in Figure 6-45, is a blog about mashups. It reports that mapping mashups are the most popular type of mashup, and photo mashups are the second-most popular.

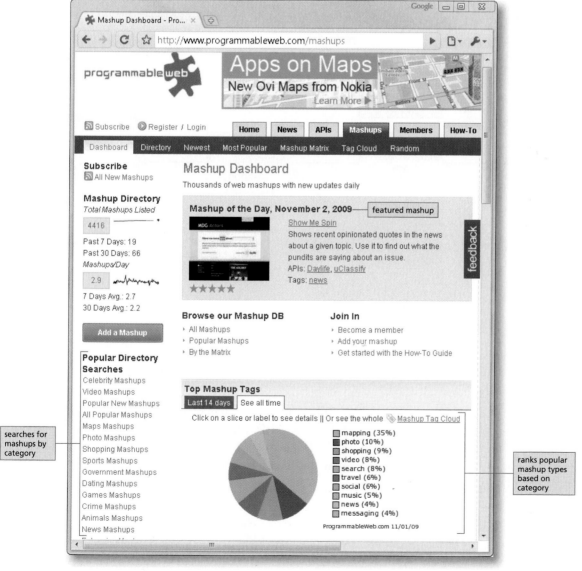

Figure 6-45 The ProgrammableWeb is a blog about mashups.

Content for mashups often comes from Web feeds and Web services, both of which structure their data in XML format. Many organizations provide APIs for developers to access their data at no or little cost. The data being mashed—photos, items from RSS feeds, or other items—are often provided as the result of Web feeds or Web services that run on remote servers maintained by the respective providers.

Creating mashups usually requires significant Web development experience. The source code to access APIs and Web services is written in a programming language such as Java or C#. The data from the chosen APIs is then "mashed up," or obtained and combined, using mashup application logic. A mashup may access data from several Web servers and multiple content providers before being displayed in a browser so that the user can view or interact with it.

For example, SongLyricsBook is a mashup that finds the lyrics for a song and a YouTube video of an artist performing it. Figure 6-46 suggests the flow of data between different components of the SongLyricsBook mashup in order to accomplish this task.

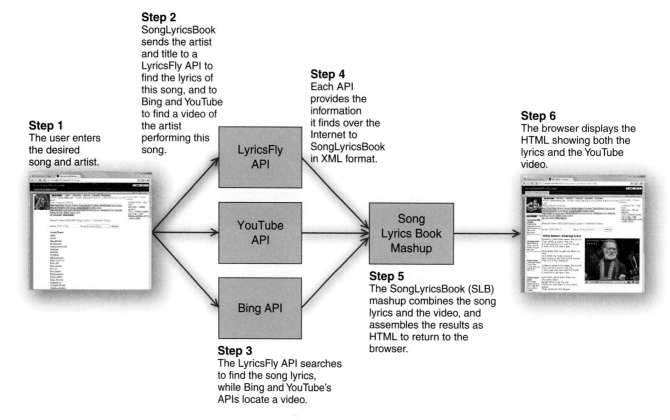

Step 2
SongLyricsBook sends the artist and title to a LyricsFly API to find the lyrics of this song, and to Bing and YouTube to find a video of the artist performing this song.

Step 1
The user enters the desired song and artist.

Step 4
Each API provides the information it finds over the Internet to SongLyricsBook in XML format.

Step 6
The browser displays the HTML showing both the lyrics and the YouTube video.

LyricsFly API

YouTube API

Song Lyrics Book Mashup

Bing API

Step 5
The SongLyricsBook (SLB) mashup combines the song lyrics and the video, and assembles the results as HTML to return to the browser.

Step 3
The LyricsFly API searches to find the song lyrics, while Bing and YouTube's APIs locate a video.

Figure 6-46 SongLyricsBook is a mashup that combines data from LyricsFly, YouTube, and Bing APIs.

This mashup makes use of APIs from Bing, Microsoft's search engine; LyricsFly, a database of song lyrics; and YouTube, the online video service. The user's input (a song and an artist) is sent to each of the three APIs, which then search for matching Web content. Each API produces the XML-formatted data that SongLyricsBook mashup logic processes and combines to display the song lyrics next to a video of the artist performing the song.

Another mashup, SpotCrime, displays the locations of criminal incident reports on a Google Map to illustrate where crime takes place in a neighborhood, as shown in Figure 6-47.

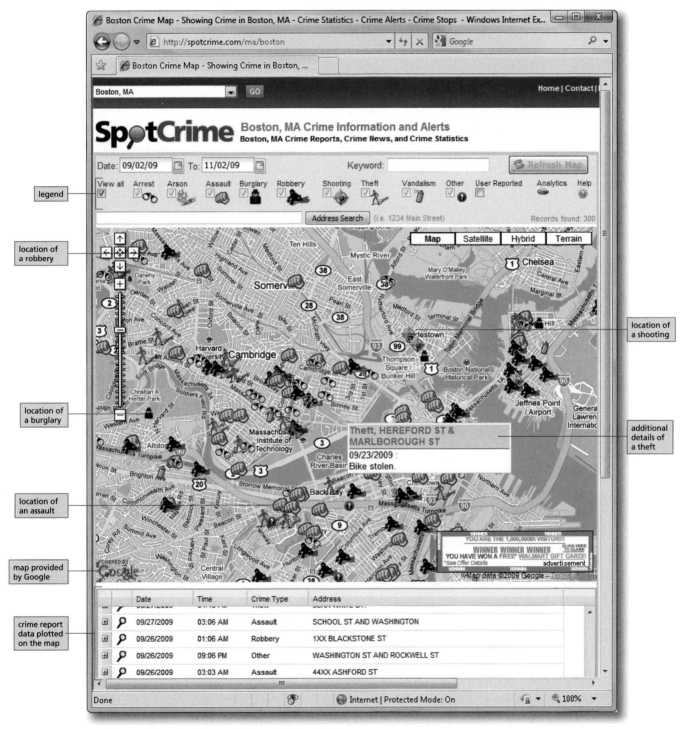

Figure 6-47 SpotCrime combines incidents of crime with Google Maps.

SpotCrime uses various icons to identify the type of crime. Hovering over a crime displays additional details about the crime. Because the crime data is pulled in from live databases on the Web, each time you visit the site the map will be updated to show the latest information about local crime incidents.

Wordle is a mashup application that creates a word cloud based on the frequency of words in a specified text. In a word cloud, the more times that a word appears, the larger it will appear in the diagram. Figure 6-48 displays a Wordle based on the text of all six chapters of this book.

Figure 6-48 A Wordle visualization of this book.

Wordle also can create a word cloud using blog posts, content from Web feeds, or Delicious tags. If you specify a Delicious user name, Wordle will create a word cloud based on that user's tags. Wordle uses the Delicious API to access a user's Delicious tags with which to create the word cloud. The word cloud has become a way to visually represent content, because terms or tags used more frequently appear in larger font sizes.

Schmap, shown in Figure 6-49, is a travel mashup that combines photos from Flickr users with user-generated content for attractions and destinations around the world, as well as Google maps that display the locations of those photos.

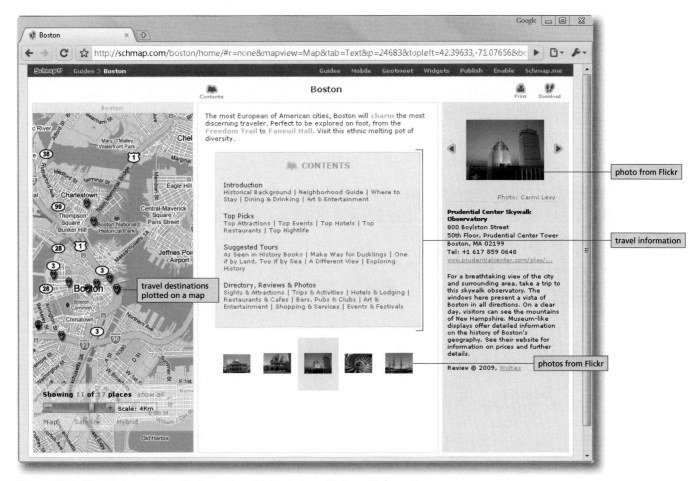

Figure 6-49 Schmap is a mashup that combines Flickr photos with travel information.

Schmap relies on the fact that Flickr has a large number of users who both regularly post, tag, and geotag photos from around the world and set Creative Commons licenses that give permission for their photos to be reused. Schmap uses the Flickr API to search for photos to include in their virtual travel guide. Schmap also provides a mobile application so that users may easily access the site on their cell phones.

Linking Data in Context:
A Prelude to Web 3.0 and Beyond

The World Wide Web provides a means for people to post documents and information online for others to view and download. Web 2.0 introduced browser-based collaboration and publishing tools that simplified the process of creating, sharing, and finding content on the Web, allowing anyone to contribute. Content expanded from text and image to include voice and video, as bandwidth increased to support these forms of multimedia. Web 2.0 created a culture of participation, allowing people to share their ideas and stories online and to come together in online communities. Web 2.0 is a database-backed Web where information is exchanged through RSS feeds, Web services, APIs, and XML technologies. Finally, Web 2.0 casts the Web as a platform for applications, with data and applications stored in the Cloud and accessed from laptops, netbooks, cell phones, and gaming consoles.

Just as Web 2.0 is the name given to an evolving Web that linked people in new ways, Web 3.0 is the name that is being used to describe emerging trends that allow people and machines to link information in new ways. Web 3.0 proposes a Web where both people and ideas are connected with each other and where personal Web assistants, called **agents**, can make decisions and take actions based on a user's preferences and past behaviors. Web 3.0 suggests that meaning can be added to information and relationships. Figure 6-50 displays the evolution of the Web, from the simple consumption of content in the early Web, to the person-to-person connections of Web 2.0, to the possibility of a decision-making Web with Web 3.0.

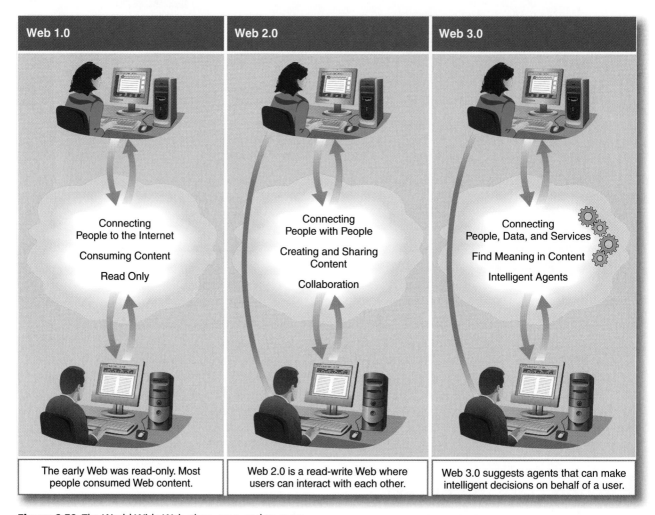

Figure 6-50 The World Wide Web, then, now, and to come.

There is a lot of speculation about just what is possible in a Web 3.0 world. Figure 6-51 shows a sampling of results of several Twitter searches for tweets about Web 3.0.

nicjohnson Where **Web** 2.0 was participatory, **web 3.0** will be anticipatory. You heard it here first. More detail soon. :)
21 minutes ago from Tweetie

BCwonders: How **Web 3.0** Will Work - The Future Will Allow Us to Search Using Complex Sentences Rather than Keywords Alone: http://bit.ly/5nXOjz (expand)
3 days ago from web · Reply · View Tweet

Qrobo› qrobo: What is **Web 3.0**?: **Web** 3. 0 is a collection of technologies that consist of the semantic **web**, linked data, natural I... http://bit.ly/7GlZUg (expand)
3 days ago from twitterfeed · Reply · View Tweet

ahoova: @hakerem according to who's defining **3.0** ? **Web** 1.0 was only only labeled after 2.0 was coined?
about 5 hours ago from m.slandr.net · Reply · View Tweet · Show Conversation

prudnikov: **Web 3.0** = Realtime **Web**?
1 day ago from Tweetie

adambeas: @josh_sternberg Are we still only on 2.0? Will **3.0** be when my mind is hardwired into the **web**? #cantwait #twitterthought #litterally
26 minutes ago from UberTwitter · Reply · View Tweet · Show Conversation

Figure 6-51 A variety of expectations for Web 3.0 are voiced by Twitter users.

Whereas Web 2.0 was about participation, as one tweet suggests, Web 3.0 is about anticipation. Many describe Web 3.0 as the rise of the **Semantic Web**, where intelligent software tools can read Web pages and discern useful information from them, much as people do, in order to anticipate a user's needs and to perform tasks on a user's behalf. Semantics, or the study of meaning, involves developing ways to represent knowledge and information. Semantic-based software applications analyze meaning to create new knowledge and draw useful conclusions from it. Tim Berners-Lee, who is credited with inventing the World Wide Web, coined the term Semantic Web.

"The Semantic Web is not a separate Web but an extension of the current one, in which information is given well-defined meaning, better enabling computers and people to work in cooperation."

Tim Berners-Lee, inventor of the World Wide Web

Berners-Lee envisions a Web where software agents will follow content in order to find useful information for us. Imagine a personal Web agent that can help you make travel arrangements for a business trip to Washington, DC, as shown in Figure 6-52.

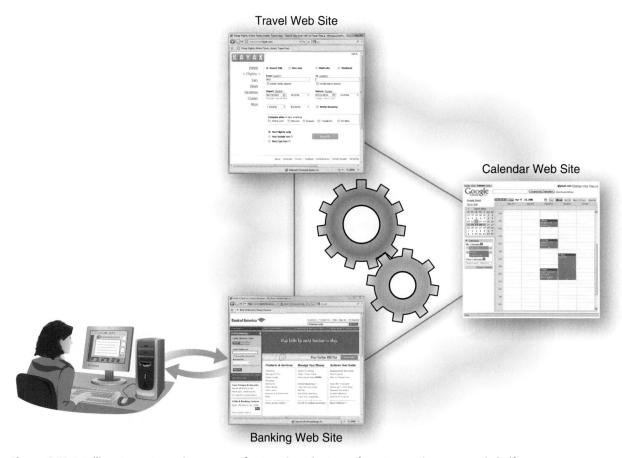

Figure 6-52 Intelligent agents monitor your preferences in order to perform transactions on your behalf.

You might ask your personal Web agent to find the least expensive airline ticket available between Boston and Washington that departs on October 3 in the morning and returns on October 10 in the afternoon, book the trip, and add it to your calendar. The flight information, your bank information, and your calendar are already stored in the Cloud. All that is necessary to make this a reality is intelligent software that can determine which Web services to access to book travel, charge your credit card, update your calendar, and put these pieces together.

As you continue to use the Web, your personal Web agent would learn more about your behaviors, preferences, and activities. As Web 3.0 develops, your personal Web agent may already know that you live in Boston, and based on your pattern of previous flights, may know that you like morning flights and aisle seats. For example, when you receive notification of the business trip, your personal Web agent could begin to search for flights so that when a low fare is offered or a cut-off date approaches, it can make the necessary arrangements on your behalf. All of this may be possible in a Web 3.0 world.

Text-based search engines, such as Google, use a set of algorithms to find relevant pages on the Web that match the terms that you enter. When you search for "Washington," Google does not understand that you are looking for information about Washington, DC, and not the state, the president, or the university, all of whose entries may show up in the search results. The results from a text-based search engine will match your terms, but not discern your meaning. The next wave of search engines will try to add meaning to your search requests and then present the results in ways that go beyond a simple list of hyperlinks to other Web pages. Microsoft Bing, Wolfram|Alpha, and Google Squared are three examples of the next wave of search tools: a semantic search engine, a computation knowledge engine, and structured search. Each of these applications brings closer the Web 3.0 ideal of a system that anticipates and provides results for user queries, and is able to make connections between information from different sources, media types, or Web sites.

A Semantic Search Engine: Bing

Microsoft's Bing search engine attempts to understand a search query in order to provide meaningful results. Unlike search engines whose search results are based on keyword matching and incoming hyperlinks to a Web page, semantic search engines have the ability to discern meaning from a search query in order to provide related relevant information. The results of a Bing search for information about Mount Rushmore are shown in Figure 6-53.

Figure 6-53 Bing takes a semantic approach to search.

Bing infers meaning from a user's search query. For example, Bing recognizes that "Mt Rushmore" is an abbreviation for Mount Rushmore, and provides search results for both terms. Bing also organizes search results by category and suggests queries for users to obtain specific information, such as the names of the presidents who appear on Mount Rushmore or related information, such as information about other national parks. To improve the user's experience, Bing provides a preview of each search results page and adds meaning by displaying a summary and hyperlinks to sections of search results pages. Bing partners with other information providers such as Wikipedia, Twitter, Wolfram|Alpha, a computational engine, and Freebase, an open online database of the world's information, in addition to performing a keyword pattern search, to provide meaningful search results.

A Computational Knowledge Engine: Wolfram|Alpha

Wolfram|Alpha is a computational knowledge engine that tries to understand user questions and calculate their answers. User questions may be in the form of keywords, mathematical expressions, or categories. Wolfram|Alpha's knowledge base is composed of verified data from public Web sites, such as the United States Census Bureau for population and demographics information. Computations are derived from Mathematica, a software platform for performing mathematical modeling, and upon which Wolfram|Alpha is built. Results are generated by analyzing data, performing mathematical computations, and analyzing how search terms are used in context. Rather than presenting results as hyperlinks to existing Web pages, Wolfram|Alpha presents its results as statistics, tables, facts, mathematical formulas, charts, graphs, or other visualizations. Figure 6-54 shows sample computations from Wolfram|Alpha.

"What we're trying to do is take all the things that can be computed about the world . . . and try and package it to the point where we can just walk up to a Web site and have it deliver the knowledge we'd like to have. Like interacting with an expert, it will understand what you are talking about, do the computation and present to you results."

Stephen Wolfram, creator of Wolfram|Alpha

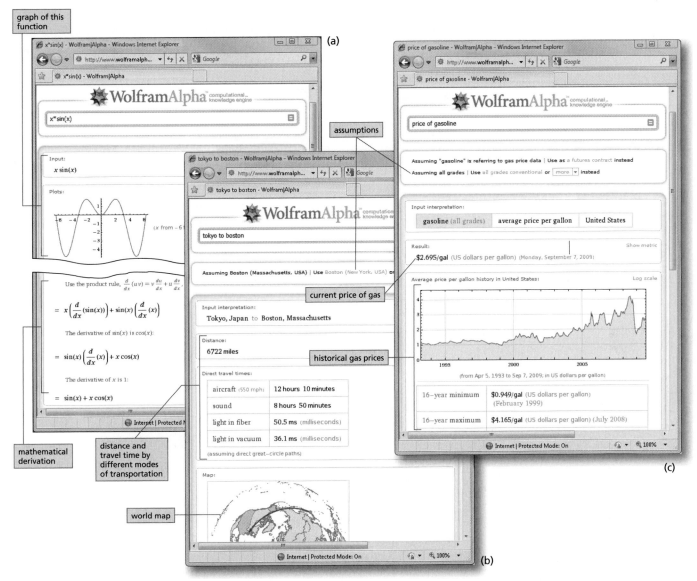

Figure 6-54 Examples of Wolfram|Alpha computational results: mathematical calculations (a), travel distances (b), and historical gas prices (c).

When given a mathematical expression, Wolfram|Alpha plots a graph on x and y axes and performs additional computations, including showing the steps for calculating the mathematical derivative. When given a travel query about the distance from Tokyo to Boston, Wolfram|Alpha assumes that Boston is located in the United States but provides New York as a nearby alternative. It calculates the distance if travelling by air, sound, or light and includes the travel path between both locations on a world map. When the "price of gasoline" is entered as a search term, Wolfram|Alpha returns the current price per gallon of gasoline in the United States, along with a chart showing historical prices, and statistics about high and low gas prices during the past 16 years.

Structured Search: Google Squared

Google Squared adds structure to search results by providing the results in a table, or square, instead of as a list of Web sites. The first column of the table contains a list of items identified in the search that share a common category. Google Squared adds meaning to the search results by displaying the attributes for each of the items in the columns to the right. Users can search for and display additional attributes by adding a new column and can add additional items to the category by adding a new row. A Google Squared search for "New England colleges" is displayed in Figure 6-55.

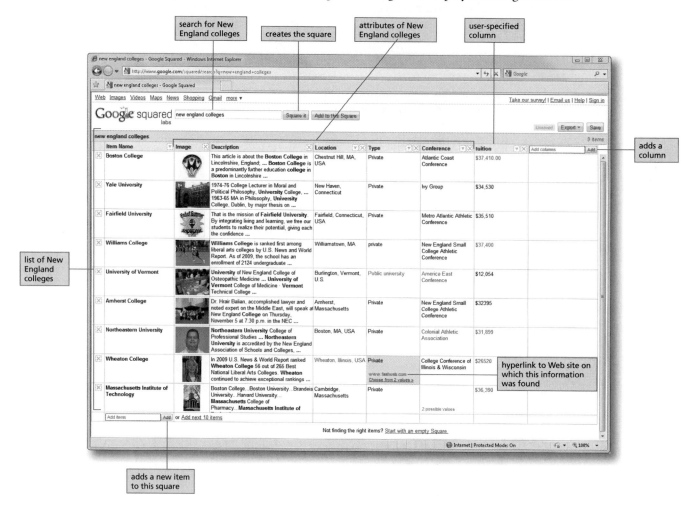

Figure 6-55 Searching using Google Squared.

Google determines the items and the attributes that appear in the columns, including, in this example, Image, Description, Location, Type, and Conference. A hyperlink to the Web site from which the information was obtained is included in each square. You can add additional attribute columns, such as tuition, to the square by entering the attribute name in the Add columns text box and clicking Add. You can also add a new item at the bottom row of the square by entering its value in the Add items text box and clicking Add. In both instances, Google Squared will also offer suggestions for new items or attributes. Google Squared will update the entire square to display the values for the new row or column.

Summary

Cloud computing combines the convenience of Web hosting with the flexibility of Infrastructure, Platform, and Software as a Service so that developers can focus on creating applications rather than maintaining the necessary hardware and software. Cloud computing offers an unlimited amount of computing resources available on an as-needed basis. Providers often use a pay-as-you-go format when charging customers to use those resources. Cloud computing also holds the promise to reduce costs for both application providers and consumers. Companies need not manage their own data centers or hardware to host their applications, saving money on equipment, storage, and bandwidth. Virtual servers provide the infrastructure for managing scalability, performance, and deployment remotely. Both consumers and businesses benefit from the Cloud as a platform for providing applications and sharing data, as the most up-to-date software is available within a browser. Users can access their data and applications from many Internet-connected devices.

Web 2.0 companies provide APIs and Web services so that others can access their data to create new applications and mashups that run in the Cloud. These return XML-formatted data to facilitate data exchange between applications.

As the Web continues to mature, applications will rely not only on data but also semantics, or the meaning of data to make intelligent decisions on behalf of their users. Web 3.0 will mark the shift from a Web where users participate to one where intelligent agents anticipate the needs and actions of users.

Think

Submit responses to these questions as directed by your instructor.

1. What is an API? Why do you think that companies would allow other applications to access internal data for free by means of an API?

2. Distinguish between IaaS, PaaS, and SaaS. Name a core feature and an application of each.

3. How is interacting with a virtual server different from interacting with a physical server that might be located on-site?

4. Describe a question whose answer you might be able to find by writing a formula containing the GoogleLookup function in Google Spreadsheets. What formula would provide the answer to your question?

5. How is a mashup different from a portal?

6. Draw a distributed architecture diagram showing the different components of the Schmap Web site and how they relate to each other.

7. What role do Web services and APIs play in sharing information between applications?

8. Name one feature found in each of Google Documents, Spreadsheets, and Presentations that takes advantage of the fact that the application and its data both live in the Cloud.

9. What is the purpose of an XPath when analyzing XML data?

10. Has Web 3.0 arrived yet? What are some examples that you may have seen?

Watch

Watch the video for Chapter 6 on the Online Companion at scsite.com/web2. Be prepared to answer or discuss the questions posted on the Online Companion as directed by your instructor.

Try

Visit the Online Companion at scsite.com/web2 and follow the steps as you complete the tutorials for this chapter.

Tutorial 6-1 Creating a Mashup
In this tutorial, you will create a mashup using Google Spreadsheets and Google Maps.

Tutorial 6-2 Creating a Weather Forecaster using Google Spreadsheets
In this tutorial, you will create a weather forecaster in Google Spreadsheets that makes use of XML data provided by calling Weather Underground's APIs.

Complete these exercises on the blog that you created for this class.

1. Visit the Wordle Web site and create a word cloud based on your online content from Twitter, your blog's RSS feed, your Delicious tags, or the text of a document that you wrote. Use screen capture software, such as the Snipping Tool in Windows or Grab in Mac OS X, to save the image and then post it to your blog. Be sure to provide proper attribution in your post, as Wordle images are shared under a Creative Commons license.

2. Consider how your use of the Web has changed since you began your study of Web 2.0 earlier this semester. Which tools and technologies did you find the most useful that will become part of your Web 2.0 toolbox? What trends have you seen in terms of new applications or ways that applications interact with each other on the Web?

These activities encourage you to explore Web 2.0 sites and applications on your own. Submit your responses as directed by your instructor.

1. Try two of the Cloud storage providers described in Table 6-1 or search the Web to find other Cloud storage providers. After using both for a few days, write a report or blog post summarizing your experience using each service.

2. Create a new document or presentation using Google Docs. Share it with a friend and edit it at the same time. Based on what you know about using Microsoft Word and PowerPoint, can you identify any features of those applications that are not available in Google Documents or Presentations? Do the Web-based applications have any features that are not in their desktop equivalents?

3. If you have a Facebook account and a YouTube account, follow the steps described in Figure 6-41 to use Facebook Connect with your YouTube account so that when you upload or comment on a video, the result of that activity will appear in your Facebook status updates.

4. If you have a Facebook account and a Twitter account, add the Twitter application to your Facebook profile and configure it so that your Facebook Wall will automatically display all of your Twitter tweets.

5. Figure 6-44 outlines steps to sign in to MapQuest with OpenID. Follow these steps to sign in to MapQuest or another site that relies on OpenID for authentication. Select an account that you already have with an identity provider as your OpenID.

6. Visit the Web site for Meebo, a Web-based instant messaging application. Compare its features with those of client IM applications such as Google Talk, AOL Instant Messenger, Yahoo! Instant Messenger, or MSN Messenger that you might install on your computer. Do you find any advantages in a Web-based instant messaging application over its client counterparts?

7. Create the Google Spreadsheet example shown in Figure 6-35 to look up states and their governors. Add formulas in adjacent columns to determine the population, nickname, and flower of each state.

8. Create a Google Spreadsheet similar to that in Figure 6-35 to generate translations. First use Google Sets to generate a list of several items in a particular category, such as sports, food, or colors. Write a formula that translates each item into another language. You will need to know the appropriate two-letter code for each language. Some common languages and their codes are English ("en"), French ("fr"), Spanish ("es"), and Italian ("it"). To find the two-letter codes for other languages of interest, use a search engine.

9. Compare Bing, Wolfram|Alpha, and Google Squared. Are there search queries for which you think one works better than another?

10. Compare the results of a Bing search with a Google search on a topic of interest to you. Are the results similar? What semantic information does each search engine use, if any, in order to provide meaningful search results?

Collaborate

If your instructor set up a class wiki, complete these exercises.

1. Perform a search on ProgrammableWeb or Mashable for interesting mashups. Contribute links for interesting mashups to the class wiki.

2. Perform your own Twitter search for Web 3.0 or Semantic Web. Create a Wikipedia-style article about Web 3.0 based on resources that you find from your search.

Index

Credits

Chapter 1: 1-4 Photo by Ragib Hasan, Licensed under the Creative Commons Attribution ShareAlike 2.5; Photo of Tim O'Reilly, Courtesy of O'Reilly Media Inc; 1-14a PRNewsFoto/Verizon Wireless; 1-14b PRNewsFoto/RadioShack Corporation; 1-14c Courtesy of Microsoft Corporation; 1-14d Courtesy of Apple Inc. **Chapter 2:** Photo of Jimmy Wales, Manuel Archain, Buenos Aires, www.manuelarchain.com **Chapter 3:** Photo of Dave Winer, Photo by Joio Ito, Licensed under the Creative Commons Attribution ShareAlike 2.0; 3-21 & 3-22 Courtesy of Christopher S. Penn, www.ChristopherSPenn.com; 3-43a Image © Goran Kuzmanovski, 2009. Used under license from Shutterstock.com; 3-43b Courtesy of Olympus; 3-43c Courtesy of Sony Electronics Inc.; 3-43d Image © Petar Tasevski, 2009. Used under license from Shutterstock.com **Chapter 4:** 4-14 Image 2 © Henrik Winther Andersen, 2009. Used under license from Shutterstock.com; 4-14 Image 3 © Mike Brake, 2009. Used under license from Shutterstock.com; Photo of Joshua Schachter by James Duncan Davidson. Licensed under the Creative Commons Attribution ShareAlike 2.0 **Chapter 5:** 5-2a Used with permission of Brandon Schug; 5-2b Used with permission of David Lanphear; 5-3 Courtesy of Eric Olson; Photo of Mark Zuckerberg Courtesy of Facebook; Photo of Gina Bianchini Courtesy of Ning, Inc.; Photo of Chris Anderson Courtesy of Chris Anderson; Photo of Evan Williams James Duncan Davidson/O'Reilly Media, Inc.; 5-50 Courtesy of Brian Solis, www.briansolis.com and Jess3, www.jess3.com; 5-53 Courtesy of IBM Corporation; 5-56 Courtesy of Salesforce.com **Chapter 6:** 6-2 Gmail logo Courtesy of Google; 6-15 Courtesy of Salesforce.com; 6-48 Images created by the Wordle.net web application are licensed under a Creative Commons Attribution 3.0 United States License; Photo of Tim Berners-Lee, Donna Coveny; Photo of Stephen Wolfram Courtesy of Wolfram Research, Inc.

Sources of Quotes

Anderson, Chris. You may be on Facebook, but the money's in the long tail. The Long Tail—Chris Anderson's blog. May 8, 2008. http://www.longtail.com/the_long_tail/2008/05/you-may-be-on-f.html
Berners-Lee, Tim, James Hendler, and Ora Lassila. 2001. The Semantic Web. *Scientific American Magazine*, May.
Bianchini, Gina. Ning – The viral expansion loop at work by Mark Stelzner. Examiner.com, May 26 2009. http://www.examiner.com/x-10924-Networking-Examiner~y2009m5d26-Ning—The-viral-expansion-loop-at-work
O'Reilly, Tim. O'Reilly Radar blog. http://radar.oreilly.com/2006/12/web-20-compact-definition-tryi.html
Schachter, Joshua. Joho the Blog, October 25, 2005. http://www.hyperorg.com/blogger/mtarchive/berkman_joshua_schachter.html
Wales, Jimmy. Wikipedia: The rules are principles. Wikipedia, 2005. http://en.wikipedia.org/wiki/Wikipedia:The_rules_are_principles
Williams, Evan. The Curious Genius of Twitter by Kermit Pattison. Fastcompany.com, March 7, 2008. http://www.fastcompany.com/articles/2008/03/interview-williams.html
Winer, Dave. Dave Winer interviewed by Andrew Keen. Politicscentral.com, August 17, 2006. http://politicscentral.com/2006/08/17/dave_winer.php
Wolfram. Stephen. Wolfram/Alpha's demo: Search results meet analytics by Larry Dignan. Zdnet.com, April 28, 2009. http://blogs.zdnet.com/BTL/?p=17129
Zuckerberg, Mark. The Wired Interview: Facebook's Mark Zuckerberg by Fred Vogelstein. Wired.com, June 29, 2009. http://www.wired.com/epicenter/2009/06/mark-zuckerberg-speaks/

Selected Bibliography/For Further Reading

Anderson, Chris. 2006. *The Long Tail: Why the Future of Business Is Selling Less of More*. New York: Hyperion.
Friedman, Thomas L. *The World Is Flat: a Brief History of the Twenty-First Century*. New York: Farrar, Straus and Giroux.
O'Reilly, Tim. What is Web 2.0 Design Patterns and Business Models for the Next Generation of Software. O'Reilly Media, Inc. http://oreilly.com/web2/archive/what-is-web-20.html.
O'Reilly, Tim and John Batelle. Web Squared: Web 2.0 Five Years On. O'Reilly Media, Inc. and TechWeb. http://www.web2summit.com/web2009/public/schedule/detail/10194.
Weinberger, David. 2007. *Everything Is Miscellaneous: the Power of the New Digital Disorder*. New York: Times Books.